TRADITIONAL BAKING RECIPES OF SPAIN

Malcolm Coxall

"With bread, all sorrows are less",
Sancho Panza, Miguel de Cervantes

Cornelio Books

Published by M.Coxall - Cornelio Books
Copyright 2018 Malcolm Coxall
First Published in United Kingdom, Spain, 2018
ISBN: 978-84-945305-5-5 - Printed

Table of Contents

Preface

Why a book about Spanish baking?

As an organic farmer in Spain, I am interested in good food and especially Spanish food. However, I am also fascinated by history and sociology and especially in how our history and social development affects our contemporary day-to-day lives.

The positive and negative impacts of industrial food on Western society are well known and I will not labour the point. But, I had a nagging feeling that the whole subject of traditional food was being neglected. Surely, this should be the natural counter-balance to the pre-prepared, fast food invasion that is taking place? Yes, there is much talk about localism, slow food, and real food. But, where are the practical guides to understanding and preparing such food, I wondered?

Food, like many other subjects, has become a fashion statement. Chefs spend lifetimes trying to create new dishes, sometimes with outrageous recipes, in a quest to become the "next big thing". They come and they go. They serve a useful purpose in experimenting with food as chefs have done for centuries. However, who, I wondered, is writing about traditional food and how it is actually made? Who is documenting the wealth of local cuisine that passes by word of mouth and from generation to generation? For me there seemed an urgent need to document this "real food" along with the practicalities of making it. Many a Spanish cook takes such knowledge for granted but increasingly this knowledge is in danger of being lost.

Therefore, with this in mind, in 2013, I started to research traditional Spanish cuisine with the objective of documenting the methods, materials, background and recipes used in the Spanish traditional kitchen. For me it was logical and important to combine my interest in food with my interest in social history in describing what I see around me. But, I soon realised that this was no small task! Spanish food is one of the most diverse and complex food scenes anywhere in the world. It combines influences from the Far and Middle East, North Africa, the Americas and its Mediterranean neighbours together with an extremely long and very complicated history.

Another motivation for writing these volumes was the huge knowledge gap between cultures. This is especially true and important when it comes to food. I am firmly of the belief that when we understand how and what other people cook and eat, we get a little closer to understanding those people and their culture.

Yet, despite the ever-increasing interest in "foreign food", there is still very little practical writing on the subject. Certainly, much has been written about Spanish food, but mostly it is written for a Hispanic audience that already understand their own food fairly well. It seemed sad to me that the Anglo world lacked any real exposure to the wealth of the Spanish culinary experience. This, of course, is apart from a very limited contact with a handful of famous dishes, a few star products promoted in Spanish tourist destinations and the uptick in interest in tapas in the Western world. There is so much more!

The challenge of attempting to document "traditional" Spanish cuisine quickly led me to realise that the subject needed to be divided over several volumes. This is the fourth book in my series "Traditional Recipes of Spain". It is certainly the largest, most localised and diverse. Spanish bakery is quite unlike any other branch of Spanish cuisine and is unique within Europe. The following pages are going to explain why this is.

This book was a long time coming. The subject matter is as vast and complex as Spain's landscape, incredible history and the imagination of its people and, as any baker will tell you, "it cannot be rushed".

To attempt a complete collection of Spanish traditional bakery in a single lifetime is impossible, so I am sure that we have probably missed some recipes. Nevertheless, at the same time, I believe that we have unlocked a wealth of delicious and often ancient recipes and I hope we have helped to bring these to life not only to you but also into the kitchens and bakeries of future generations. Enjoy!

Acknowledgements:

Grateful thanks to Mohamed Abdel-Hady, the food photographer who provided the wonderful cover photograph. Contact him via his website: http://www.mohamedabdulhady.com/

---o0o---

1. Introduction

What is this book about and not about?

This book is essentially about *traditional Spanish* bakery. For this reason, we have excluded all those baked products that have arrived in Spain in recent years from other countries as food has become more internationalised. As a rule, we have confined ourselves to bakery goods that are at least 100 years old and are or have become typical of Spain. In fact most of our recipes are centuries old. For this reason, you will not find chocolate chip cookies, croissants or Swiss rolls here. Nevertheless, you may well discover the originals of many modern recipes that are in daily use throughout the rest of the world.

Why is Spanish bakery different from bakery in the rest of Europe?

Spanish bakery is unique in many ways and there are several reasons for this:

Firstly, Spain has a very diverse and ancient tradition in baking, which began several thousand years ago. A veritable flood of different cultures arriving in the country then influenced the original traditional bakery. The degree and duration of cultural interaction is unprecedented in any other European country's cuisine. History thus plays an enormous role in the development of Spanish baking.

Secondly, Spain was the first country in Europe to experience the use of sugar in confectionary baking. By the early Middle Ages, the availability of sugar as a low-cost sweetener had revolutionised sweet bakery in Spain.

Thirdly, Spanish sweet bakery traditions are very well preserved. A lucky twist of history meant that the latest conquest of Spain was by northern Christians with a sweet tooth! They enthusiastically adopted and preserved many of the recipes of their predecessors.

Fourthly, one of the most extraordinary facts concerning the Spanish kitchen and bakery is the level of regional diversity that exists. The geographical isolation of the country, the differences in climate between North and South, taken together with a very rich supply of regional ingredients, created a diverse patchwork of traditional bakery. Many of Spain's baked products are considered so extraordinary that they have been granted special protection under European law to guarantee their integrity and quality.

Finally, Spain is exceptional within Europe, sitting, as it does, between Northern Europe and Africa. This meant that many of the recipes that we take for granted in the countries north of the Pyrenees actually originated in Spain or passed through Spain into Northern European kitchens and bakeries.

The social history of baking

Bakery in Spain is unlike any other branches of its culinary tradition. Of course, every traditional recipe has a history - sometimes a very ancient one - but, importantly, baking in Spain is intimately connected with celebration, religious and cultural observance. This is often the result of the tangled political and social history of the country. Thus, there is a wealth of traditional sweet dishes associated with every conceivable religious festival. Many a pastry has a religious name, made only on a particular saint's day, as a celebratory treat. The convents of Spain still do a roaring trade in sweet bakery and confectionary.

The economic history of the country also played a part. There are scores of delicious rural bakery recipes using leftovers like stale bread, or plentiful and cheap young wines - a testament to the country's frequent famines, past poverty and imaginative bakers.

And coming to the present day, one may walk along any shopping street in any town in Spain and find a wealth of independent bakers, their windows and shelves brimming with local breads and traditional pastries. The invasion of industrial food has not yet defeated the Spaniards' love of their bakery. Baking in modern Spain is alive and well.

Every recipe has a story

With each recipe that follows, I have spent some time trying to provide the reader with a reasonable history. There are many recurrent themes in the recipes and I have tried to explain the background of the recipes as accurately as possible without too much repetition. However, many recipes do share a common origin. Some traditional recipes however, have stories attached to them that have become seriously embroidered with the passage of time - sometimes quite hilariously! Other recipes are easy enough to trace because they were well documented. The history of yet more recipes has been completely rewritten in the past for political or religious reasons. In any case, I have tried to filter out the fantasy and propaganda and provide the reader with the most likely history of each recipe, if any is to be found.

Modernising recipes

Apart from the history of a recipe, I have also tried to provide the reader with an insight into how a particular recipe was used in the past and how it fits into modern Spanish life. This includes details of when it is usually eaten and with what accompaniment.

For instance, several types of rural bread were "designed" in the past to last a long time. This reduced the work of the woman of the house to a single weekly bake, but it also provided the long-distance shepherds with bread that could last them for several days on their epic travels with their flocks. This type of bread is still used for this purpose but it also works a treat for tapas. Many bars use long-life traditional crusty bread for tapas because they then do not need to buy fresh bread every day. Modern fresh bread lasts for a day at most before it is too hard to eat.

One minor complication in modernising a recipe is that much traditional bakery used baking methods that no longer exist, such as baking under hot wood ash. In the interests of keeping these recipes alive, I have tried to use versions adapted to modern methods. For instance, it may be a delight to use a wood-burning oven to bake your "cateto" bread but it is not practical in today's urban society. However, you can get the same result (minus the flakes of wood ash) using a modern fan oven.

The same principle applies to raw materials and methods. In previous times, the types and quality of flour was inferior to our modern products. Using yeast was much more a matter of luck than baking with today's standardised products. In the past, raw materials varied widely in terms of quality and consistency. Bakers worked with what they could get. Nowadays there is a wealth of highly specialised raw materials available to the baker. These help enormously in producing exactly the result that the baker wants and there are flours for every type of dough. Modern yeasts and raising agents have radically altered the work of the baker for the better and it is now much easier to get consistent results than in the past.

The same can be said of modern kitchen equipment such as blenders and mixers. Grinding aniseed in a mortar and pestle is no problem but making a kilo of almond flour from raw almonds by hand is unnecessary now we have the convenience of the modern electric blender. Thus, in the recipes, we have not been purist about using some modern conveniences to make an old recipe work.

On the other hand, the resurgence of traditional sourdough bakery ("masa madre") in Spain is a reminder that some traditional methods, though less convenient, produce a superior and more authentic result than some pre-packed, dehydrated yeast ever can.

And so, in modernising these recipes, we have sought to guarantee the integrity of the recipe whilst being pragmatic about the use of modern resources and equipment.

What is it called?

Finally, one of the most difficult concepts in Spanish bakery is how bakery products are named and classified. Indeed, there is often a question of whether some products should be included in a baking book at all! Here I am thinking about the many fried sweet doughs, the pancakes, the cheesecakes and nougats that you may find in any reposteria.

In Spain the definitions are somewhat fuzzy (that's a big understatement) and there is a fine line between the definition of biscuits, cakes, pastries and those sweet dishes served as desserts with a meal ("postres"). Added to this, the naming rules for bakery can vary enormously, even from village to village. It is testimony to the slightly anarchic attitude in Spain that the Spanish find substance more important than labels!

Therefore, so as not to miss some wonderful recipes, we have added a chapter on baked desserts and another on sweets and confectionary but indeed, many baked products could reasonably be found under several categories. We have also extended the definition of bakery to include some traditional bakery products that are fried, not baked. Every bakery in Spain will sell some of these fritters and they are both old and traditional. It seemed wrong to ignore them.

To try to make some sense out of the naming conventions we have included a section dedicated to the nomenclature of Spanish baking.

---o0o---

1.1 A History of Baking in Spain

Spain has a very diverse and ancient tradition in baking, which began several thousand years ago, with its own ancient Celtiberian civilisation. This was enriched by Phoenician, Roman, Arabic, Jewish and, later, Northern European influences. The final important influence that came to Europe via Spain came from Spain's colonisation of the "New World" with its wealth of new ingredients and techniques.

Of course, all traditional Spanish food has a story, but bakery is somewhat different. Much traditional bakery in Spain comes from outside the country. It arrived in Spain because of dramatic political, military or cultural events. For instance, the arrival of the Moors in Spain brought the introduction of spiced bakery, whilst the populations of Sephardic Jews brought many sweet fried dough recipes. The arrival of the Christians ushered in the use of alcohol and lard into bakery. Add to these the dramatic impact of the discovery and colonisation of the New World that began in the 15th century and the consequent arrival of a host of new grains, fruits, and vegetables.

We are now going to explore the history of Spanish baking in a little more detail.

Spain's position in the world

Spain sits at the crossroads between Europe and Africa and this geographical fact has been both a blessing and a curse. Spain has a generous range of climates from snow-covered mountains to arid deserts. Gladly, much of Spain is highly fertile land and the country has the capacity to grow almost anything successfully. In the past, this made Spain a highly desirable target for invasion and colonisation stretching back many thousands of years. Spain is truly an ancient country with layer upon layer of history. This history has radically affected food culture in Spain.

Spain's geographical location, with its huge coastline, makes it very much a Mediterranean country in the South and East and very much an Atlantic-facing nation in the North and West. This contrast between Mediterranean and Atlantic influences not only affects the climate but also had an important effect on the country's history and its culinary development.

These differences in climate between North and South taken together with a very rich supply of regional raw materials has created an immensely diverse patchwork of traditional breads and pastries. One can find a great diversity of baked products within the borders of Spain to this day - ancient flat bread recipes which originated in the Celtic seaboard of Galicia or sweet honey-flavoured delicacies straight from medieval Baghdad or Sephardic fritters that have been made in the same way for 2000 years.

Another factor that influenced the traditional Spanish bakery was the sheer size of the country and its remoteness. Spain is a mountainous country (the second most mountainous in Europe) and this fact alone means that there are many parts of the country that are quite inaccessible and isolated - to this day. In the 19th century, a traveller in Barcelona could reach Havana in Cuba more quickly than he could get to Sevilla in Andalucía. This regional "disconnection" encouraged a lot of regional culinary experimentation. There are thus many thousands of local recipes for all manner of dishes. Baking is no exception to this great diversity.

Spain's proximity to North Africa and the entrance to the Mediterranean was probably the single most important aspect of Spain's history in terms of its eating habits. Almost every one of the old world's imperial powers has invaded or colonised Spain at some time in its history, including the Carthaginians, Greeks, Romans, Visigoths, Moors and finally the European Christians. This has given rise to an immensely chequered history and these influences are to be found everywhere in Spanish cooking. Added to the millennia of Spanish inward colonisation, Spain was itself a hugely important imperial power for several centuries. In addition, of course, Spain discovered and colonised the "New World" whilst being the heirs of the vast Habsburg Empire. The new foods and cooking practices coming from the Americas brought yet another layer of influence to Spanish food as returning colonials brought back native recipes and exotic ingredients to their homeland. Just one such ingredient - chocolate - has had an unmistakeable effect on bakery everywhere. But there were many more.

Practical influences

Apart from these important historical and cultural influences, the evolution of Spanish baking traditions was also based on several very basic practical considerations:

Firstly, Spain has a generally warm climate and historically food adulteration was a problem. Baking food provided a means of sterilising ingredients. Hygiene standards were poor in pre-industrial

Europe. Baking offered a method of taking adulterated ingredients and "heat-treating" them (by baking) with very tasty results! This principle was fully understood by the Arabs and they re-introduced the communal ovens that the Romans brought to their imperial outposts. Many rural villages in Spain and urban barrios had communal ovens until very recently.

Secondly, baking provided a means of preserving ingredients. Baking biscuits began as a means of providing a high protein, long-life food for the epic voyages of the Galician Atlantic sailors. Whereas bread would last at most a week, biscuits with salt and / or sugar could last for many months and still be edible, nutritious and tasty. The Arabs of the Moorish period baked sweet or savoury dishes in pastry wraps for their armies on the march. These early precursors of the Cornish pasty and the Apfelstrudel were a way of providing "portable food" which was both safely sterilised and would last for a week or more. The arrival of sugar not only fed the Moorish love of all things sweet but it also gave them a way of preserving food for months on end. What a fortunate coincidence that sugar is also a great preserving agent!

The background of Spanish food is well documented. Cookbooks have existed for a very long time fortunately and there are sources of information from the Romans and Arabs right through to the present day. However, for the uninitiated, the following is a short explanation of how these many historical epochs have shaped traditional baking in Spain. We give a few examples of important influences here, but there are many, many more, which we will explore in the main body of the book.

The Celtic Connection

Before the arrival of the Roman Empire and the colonisation of Spain, a group of Celtic and Iberian tribes occupied the peninsula. Their origins are still the subject of some speculation but these tribal civilisations were well established by the 6th century BC. The various groups were well-organised pastoralists and protected their land with stone forts and local militia.

There is evidence that these early inhabitants encountered the sea-faring Phoenicians who traded into the Western Mediterranean and the Atlantic. It is likely that this early contact with the Phoenicians and their successors (the Carthaginians) introduced the use of ground grain and the baking of bread to Celtiberia. They also brought wine and grape vines to Iberia. At any rate, by the time the Romans arrived the baking of bread was well established in the peninsula.

The modern descendents of the Celts are still famous for their bakery. Galicia, on the Atlantic coast, is one such example; credited with the invention of the biscuit and various types of pancake Galicia is now the home to a wealth of traditional breads, crêpes, biscuits and pies.

Roman Rule

The production of bread from ground cereals dates back to ancient Egypt and Mesopotamia. In reality, it probably began in Neolithic times in a primitive form. One of the earliest bread ovens was discovered in Babylon, modern Iraq, dating from 4000 BC. The Egyptians were blessed with fertile flood plains and were large cereal and bread producers. They went further and developed the use of yeast in the baking of bread (and the making of beer) around 2000 BC.

Trade between Egypt and ancient Greece soon saw bread becoming a staple in the Greek empire and the Greeks expanded the range of possibilities using different cereals, nuts and fruit to produce breads that began to resemble those of the modern bakery. At first, bread was seen as something religious and "heaven sent" but it soon permeated Greek society and became a staple food for the masses.

The Romans were slow to adopt bread. They considered bread to be an alien food - a Greek invention! In the early years, the richest members of the Roman aristocracy were the only consumers of bread. They considered it a novelty food. The rest of the population ate various forms of porridge. However, gradually, bread became widespread in the Roman world and by 30 BC Rome had 300 bakeries operated by qualified Greek bakers. By the year 100 AD, the Roman government had regulated bread production and controlled its price. Bread became a mainstream staple in the Roman Empire and the Romans applied themselves to improving production methods.

Thus, while the Romans did not invent bread, they did develop and industrialise the techniques of milling flour and designed new, more effective ovens for the baking of bread. The Romans also developed "long-life" breads that they could issue to their armies and established well-organised military bakeries throughout the empire. The staple cuisine for the Roman soldier soon became bread and wine. Thus, bread making spread throughout the Roman world. The Romans, however, were surprised to discover that in Spain, the native Celtiberians had been baking bread for many generations, having discovered the process of grinding grain and making dough long before the Roman conquerors arrived.

Moorish and Jewish History

The impact of Arab food culture during the Moorish period was probably the most intense of all in Spain's history and eventually these Arab and Jewish influences spread to all of Europe. The proximity of Spain to the Semitic world and centuries of Arab influence on European culinary practice have certainly left an unmistakable mark on the food of Spain and Western Europe, as we shall see.

For instance, Spain was the first country in Europe to experience the use of sugar in confectionary baking. The introduction of sugar cane from India was made by the Moors in the early Middle Ages. Sugar rapidly became a relatively low-cost substitute for honey in sweet baking. To this day, Spain is the only European producer of sugar cane. The effect of this innovation was revolutionary not only in bakery but in society in general.

Few modern Europeans realise that Spain was actually a collection of Moorish kingdoms between the 7th century and the end of the 15th century. This Moorish period only ended when the Christians of Northern Europe finally conquered the entire peninsula following centuries of slow-burning war and numerous crusades. Indeed, Spain was an Arab, largely Muslim country for much longer than it has been a Christian country. In fact, Spain as a country did not legally exist until the early 18th century. The way food is prepared today in Spain is very much a reflection of this long-standing Moorish influence.

The Arab occupation of Spain came on the heels of the collapse of the Roman Empire as the power vacuum left by the Romans drew traders and eventually their rulers to take control of the peninsula. However, the Arabs were keen to learn from their Roman predecessors and they adopted much of the infrastructure built by the Romans, including their sophisticated agricultural techniques, protective forts and irrigation systems. Food production flourished.

Gladly, during much of the Arab epoch, Spain was also quite open to other religions and cultures. Sephardic Jews and Christians generally thrived under the various caliphates, despite being taxed as non-Muslims. Indeed, many Jews and Christians held trusted senior positions in many of the Arab Spanish caliphates. This open society brought a lot of cross-pollination in many aspects of daily life, including in the spheres of cooking and baking.

After the arrival of the Catholic Monarchs, things changed. In the end, most of the Muslims and Sephardic Jews were expelled from Spain or forced to convert to Christianity. Fortunately, these "conversos" did not forget their baking traditions! During the overlapping years of Christian rule and Moorish occupation, the Spanish Christians and Jews (known as Mozarabs) adopted many Arab and Jewish recipes and cooking methods. Many of these are still in use today and, strangely enough, especially noticeable during Christian religious festivals such as Christmas and Easter. Indeed, many minor religious festivities for a local patron saint still include the making of particular sweet pastries, many of which have their roots in the Moorish or Sephardic baking customs.

The Moors loved to bake using fruit, nuts, sugar and spices. This practise eventually spread throughout the Spanish-controlled Habsburg Empire into Europe, North of the Pyrenees. It still exists in modern Spanish and European festive bakery. Spicy Christmas puddings in Britain and marzipan-filled "Stollen" in Germany are all derivatives of these Moorish recipes. They are laden with sugar, raisins and other dried fruits, nuts and spices - all ingredients alien to the agriculture of these Northern countries, but imported, like their recipes, from the South of Europe or North Africa to be a special treat for an important religious festival.

However, the influences worked in all directions. Arabs learned much about the use of yeast in the baking of bread from the Jews and Christians. The use of sugar and honey in the baking of sweet confectionary united all traditions with a sweet tooth and was very much an Arab speciality. Whilst there was much that separated these groups in a cultural and religious sense - much united them when it came to bakery.

One of the important developments of the Moorish period was the organisation of communal ovens. A village or barrio would have one or more ovens that everyone would use to bake their bread. Each would make their own dough at home and form their loaves with their own distinguishing mark to recognise it when baked. These communal bakeries were great sources of recipe swapping and experimentation.

The influence of the Arab world at this time cannot be underestimated. Their merchants ranged from China to the Atlantic coast of Africa and Spain and operated a sophisticated network of trading routes that passed through North and West Africa, the Levant, Persia, Central Asia, Indonesia and into China and India. Herbs and spices and other exotic ingredients traded from India and Africa reached Spain via these Arab traders across the so-called "spice routes".

These trade routes were also great conduits of knowledge and a way of bringing new plant species from the Far and Near East into Europe. Oranges, bananas and sugarcane are just a couple of obvious examples that came from China, India and what is now Indonesia. These plants and fruits came to Europe courtesy of Moorish traders and quickly caught on. These long-distance traders also brought new cookery methods and exotic recipes such as samosas - the ancestor of the modern pie that originated in India. Indeed, the Arabs were even responsible for the introduction of ice cream and sorbet into Spain and eventually all of Europe. Where would the Christmas bakery of Europe be without the almonds, lemon, dried fruit and cinnamon, all of which the Arabs introduced into Europe a thousand years ago?

The Middle Ages and the Christian Conquest of Spain

After the fall of the Roman Empire, much of Europe suffered from the collapse of Roman security and infrastructure. Grain production fell dramatically. The period up to the 10th century became known as the "dark ages" as famine and conflict stalked large tracts of the continent. Fortunately, for Spain, the Moorish colonists had taken up the reins of the Roman Empire and Spanish agriculture flourished under Moorish control. In Northern Europe, the beginnings of the feudal system and the spread of Christian monastic settlements meant that agriculture began to come under some kind of control again. These monasteries became the main producers of bread in large parts of Europe. By the 12th century, guilds of bakers began to be organised and the production and price of bread again came under the control of these new feudal powers.

At this time, the Christian alliance and their armies began to slowly advance south into Spain in constant crusades to expel the Muslims. Following military advances, the production of bread and the beloved sweet breads and pastries of the Arabs was gradually taken over by the Christian monastic orders. Clearly, the Christian Monarchs saw the advantage of controlling production and distribution of bread and the fantastic marketing opportunities in producing, selling and distributing the popular sweets.

Hence, we arrive at the reasons for the intriguing link between Christian festivals and sweet Arab and Jewish bakery traditions. Nothing was more enticing than the promise of bread and sweet pastries and when linked with Christian dogma and religious events, the temptation for the remaining Jews and Muslims to convert represented probably the first use of sugar in marketing!

The monasteries of Spain became sophisticated producers of sweet pastries. To this day, many monasteries and convents produce a huge range of sweet bakery based on traditional Moorish recipes, which they have rebranded under a plethora of religious labels.

One of the changes the Christians made to the many Moorish recipes that they plagiarised were the inclusion of wine or spirits in festive baking. They also started to use pig lard instead of butter or olive oil as a source of fat in baking. These recipe changes served the secondary purpose of excluding any die-hard Muslims or Jews, hiding in the conquered areas, from the consumption of highly treasured sweet bakery. To say that bakery production became a political tool in the hands of the invading Christians would be an understatement.

The Spanish Empire -The New World

Added to this already impressive culinary background, Spain, during its imperial period, discovered and colonised the Americas - thus opening a Pandora's Box of new raw materials.

Simultaneously, Spain rose to become the most important political influence in 16th and 17th century Europe, as it took control of the Habsburg Empire. This gave the Spanish monarchs control of the Lowlands, parts of Germany and France, the East Indies, parts of Italy and for a time the Portuguese Empire. Spain's influence spread far and wide.

One important and often forgotten fact is that the Kingdom of Naples (which included Sicily) was a Spanish possession on and off for several centuries. Having a similar climate to central and Southern Spain brought together many developments in their mutual culinary traditions. Both countries had experienced the influence of the Moors and many new dishes that came from Spain were popularised in Italy - such as pizza (cocas) or sponge cake (aka "pan di Spagna"). On the other hand, the Southern Italians had developed new forms of light pastry such as choux pastry and they are even said to be responsible for the development of the meringue, both great favourites in traditional Spanish baking. In any case, the bakeries of both nations benefited from their connections and mutual love of all things sweet.

Similar transfers of culinary knowledge extended across the entire Spanish empire. For instance, the humble empanada spread to all the Spanish colonies to such an extent that empanadas are now considered by many to have come from Latin America! But the empanada is also found in the Philippines and Sicily. Few realise that the empanada originated in the Moorish tradition of baking unused food in a pastry envelope and came to Spain sometime around the 10th century AD. The "samosa" is the modern descendent of this and, to this day, is a much-loved snack in the Middle East, Levant and North Africa.

In the opposite direction, the discovery of potatoes, maize and a host of new vegetables in the New World somewhat revolutionised culinary practice in Spain. Potatoes were (and are) often used as a filling in sweet pastries and several bread recipes use potatoes as part of the dough mix. Mexican maize has similarly worked its way into the baking of bread in some parts of Spain.

Modern Times

From the 18th century onwards, the techniques of milling flour and baking improved markedly in Spain and bread became more universally available. Thus, ordinary workers could afford even white bread as prices dropped. Other technological advances included the development of more effective yeasts and the use of mechanical devices to knead dough.

Despite these advances in raw material quality and baking techniques, it is intriguing to see that most traditional bakery favourites still use ingredients and recipes that are many centuries old.

The Monastic and Religious History of Baking in Spain - a Special Mention

No history of the Spanish bakery would be complete without a special mention of the role of baked products in the Christian religious life of the country.

Of course, bread has held a special religious significance for thousands of years in many different cultures and religions, but Christian Spain took the link between baking and religious fervour to a new high point. It is for this reason Spanish sweet bakery traditions are very well preserved.

The monastic orders of the Christian conquerors of Spain quickly recognised the great attraction of sweetened dishes. By the 16th century, the religious orders had cornered the market on rich sweet bakery and become important producers (many still are). The Church cleverly linked many sweet dishes to both Christian religious allegiance and adherence to their feast days. Thus, sweet bakery became an ideological and political tool in 16th century Spain. This was a society fractured by war and religious differences. The Iberian Peninsula, at the time, still had a large population of Muslims and Jews. The fundamentalist "Catholic Monarchs" were determined to Christianise the country by any means possible. Thus, the use of sugar in sweet bakery spread quickly across Spain and thence into all parts of Europe. Meanwhile, Spanish baking traditions and recipes were preserved inside the cloistered walls of many a convent and monastery.

A walk through any Spanish town will soon bring you to a convent or monastery. Very often, these institutions sell their own particular baked products to the public. These are almost exclusively sweet baked products and they are very often quite delicious.

The names of these sweets are evocative and often medieval. The "Bones of Saint Expeditus", "Tarts of the Alcázar of Saint John of La Mancha" are just a couple of examples. There are literally thousands of such products with antique religious names.

Almost all religious festivities in Spain have a sweet baked dish to accompany the celebrations. These are often very local recipes - each village could well have its own delicacy dedicated to its own patron saint. Often these sweets are made communally and blessed in the local church before being given or sold to the public. The wealth of religious fervour and tradition surrounding sweet baking in Spain is quite phenomenal.

How did this link between religion and sweet bakery come about? The answers to that question lies in the way that the Christians conquered Spain. Firstly, we have to remember that the Christian conquest of Spain was considered a "Holy Crusade" by the Northern invaders. It was (theoretically) a religious war sanctioned by the church in Rome and not just a "land-grab". Secondly, the process of conquest was extremely slow. It lasted for well over 300 years. During this time, the influence of the Christian kingdoms of the north was cemented by the founding of monasteries. These acted as a social service to the community, providing some very basic services, but also as the propaganda wing of the crusading aristocracy to promote their "holy war" (and acquire more land). Generally, the monasteries were financed by wealthy patrons and these refuges were often used in troubled times or when their patrons were travelling. The monasteries were a pillar of the Christian feudal administration as it advanced south into Arab-held territories. Thus, the first wave of conquest was military and the second religious.

One of the many tasks of the monastic orders was to convert the reluctant Muslims and Jews that they encountered. This was no easy task. The invading Christian rulers realised that killing or expulsion of the local Muslim and Jewish populations would bring economic catastrophe to an already sparsely populated country. In fact, this is precisely what eventually happened when the Christians later decided to expel or murder the Moors and Jews. This later ethnic cleansing of Spain left the invaders with an empty countryside and deserted villages. Finally, they had to bring in Christians from the North of Spain to take over the land and economic activities of the expelled Muslims and Jews.

However, during the period before the expulsions, the Christians tried persuasion rather than violence to convert the recalcitrant "Moro" and they went to extreme lengths to do this. In Córdoba, unable to persuade the Muslims to abandon the grand Mosque of the city in favour of converting and attending a Christian church, the Catholic Monarchs built a Cathedral *inside* the Grand Mosque and it is there to this day - a bizarre reminder of the fanaticism of the Catholic Monarchs Isabel and Ferdinand. Nonetheless, more subtle means of persuasion were also at hand.

Clearly, the Christian religious leaders of the time recognised the power of food as a persuasive marketing tool and they had one of humanity's most potently addictive ingredients at their disposal: sugar! The monasteries had already become skilled bakers of bread, often supplying their aristocratic patrons. Now they expanded their product range to sweet bakery - almost exclusively based on Moorish and Sephardic traditional recipes. It was a marketing strategy pure and simple: rebrand traditional Arab and Jewish sweets with Christian names and make and sell (or give) them to the local population during Christian religious festivals. Bearing in mind that such treats were far from common in those days, the strategy was a great success. Offering conversion to Christianity and a diet of weekly Latin masses held little interest to the average Muslim or Jew, but when linked to their favourite sweet pastry, the temptation to conform and convert was, for many, just too great.

Thus, what started as a cheap trick to buy off the local Muslim and Jewish population became a means by which the church acquired and held on to its congregations. Festivals like Christmas and Easter became synonymous with rich, sweet, aromatic baking - and what is not to like about that? The golden glow of good food and plenty at Christmas and Easter was a masterstroke of salesmanship!

In addition to this religious marketing exercise, the monasteries were also great innovators in their own right. Their rich patrons would often bring their own chefs and ingredients during their "retreats" and these contacts brought new ideas into the monastic bakery, such as the use of chocolate. Nevertheless, the religious orders were also very adept at using the materials they had. For instance, the wine industry used a huge amount of egg whites to clear their wines. This left a large quantity of egg yolks. These ended up in the convents where the nuns created rich fillings and the basis for many an irresistible monastic sweet dessert.

Whatever about the motives or behaviour of the monastic communities in Christian Spain, two things are certain: the religious orders participated in the first documented case of the powerful marketing potential of sugar in food. Nonetheless, the monasteries of Spain also preserved many delicious Moorish-Sephardic-Spanish recipes that survive until the present day - almost without change and we should be grateful for this quirk of history.

---o0o---

1.2 The Role of Baking in Spanish Society

Baking is important in Spain. In 2016, El País reported that every year the Spanish spend €40 million on baking at home. Whilst many Northern European countries and the USA have just rediscovered home baking, the Spanish never actually forgot it. Baking at home is as natural and routine in Spain as cooking a proper meal from real raw materials.

Baking is very close to the heart of every Spanish household. No meal would be complete without bread. Sweet baking is everywhere: starting with sweet pastries at breakfast, a dessert after lunch and "something sweet" with coffee or tea during merienda. Even quite small villages will have a local, independent bakery and their repertoire will not just consist of some basic bread, but will also include a range of sweet pastries. The Spanish have quite a sweet tooth!

Unlike many industrialised countries, Spain's regime for dining is quite rigid. People do not skip meals in general. However busy they are, food comes first. Eating is a civilised and important priority and meals are always taken at a relaxed pace. They are often very communal, social events.

To get some idea how important baking is to modern Spanish society just look at a typical day's menu.

Breakfast - Desayuno

Most Spanish people start the day with just a coffee and nothing more. This is NOT breakfast!

Breakfast is eaten at around 10 to 11 am after a couple of hours of work. It usually lasts for about 30 minutes. Entire offices are deserted during this time, building sites halt all work and agricultural workers will congregate under a tree to enjoy breakfast together.

A normal urban breakfast typically consists of a cup of coffee - and there are many combinations - which will often be accompanied by a tostada. A tostada is a slice of fresh bread, toasted and covered with jam, or tomato, olive oil and garlic purée, or ham and cheese. Breakfast is often accompanied by a sweet pastry. Another traditional breakfast in many parts of Spain consists of the ever-popular churros served dunked in a thick hot chocolate. In rural districts, breakfast will be a bread roll with something like a slice of ham or chorizo and tomato.

Lunch - Comida

Spaniards work a long day in most parts of the country and take a long lunch. It is the main meal of the day and more important than dinner. Generally, lunch is eaten between 2:00 and 4:00 in the afternoon and it is a time to sit quietly with family, friends or colleagues and enjoy a leisurely meal together. Lunch in Spain is the antithesis of "grabbing a quick snack" which has become the norm for lunch in modern, industrial Northern Europe.

Because it is the day's main meal, lunch is traditionally quite a bit larger than dinner ("cena"). In urban areas, most Spanish workers will eat lunch in a café or restaurant. In rural areas, workers will bring their own elaborate cool boxes with pre-prepared dishes and fresh bread.

A typical lunch in a restaurant will have several courses. The first course is the lighter part of the meal, usually consisting of a salad or soup, while the second course is normally a fish or meat dish. A dessert may be a simple piece of fruit, but more usually is a sweet pastry, cake, or flan. Meals are always served with fresh bread.

Afternoon Tea / Coffee - Merienda

Merienda is a short, late afternoon break that people take some time between 6 pm and 7 pm. For some this is a post-siesta tea or coffee. For the workers, it generally consists of tea or coffee taken with a sweet pastry and it lasts for maybe 30 minutes. For the more leisurely, it may consist of churros and chocolate or coffee. A walk around the famous square of Bib Rambla in Granada at this time of day will reveal large numbers of people eating churros or cake with tea, coffee or chocolate. The workers may just snatch a few minutes but the elderly of the city make a daily occasion of merienda to meet their friends and sit to gossip, socialise and enjoy a sweet delight.

Tapas

Tapas are served at any time, but traditionally they are taken after work when having a drink in a bar. In Spain, drinking without eating is considered unwise and so tapas are served (often free) with drinks. The most basic tapas are a piece of bread with a piece of cheese or ham. Bread is the basis for many Spanish tapas.

Dinner - Cena

This final meal of the day is eaten late in Spain - even later at weekends and during the summer. It is quite usual to start dinner after 9 pm and continue until midnight or later. While there are, of course, many people who eat a full dinner in the evening, the Spanish dinner is traditionally much smaller than lunch. It often consists of something light like a bread based dish or a selection of tapas. Nonetheless, dinner is often finished with a sweet dessert of some kind.

Special Occasions

Baking is a hugely important part of celebrating special events in Spain. Festivities such as Christmas, Easter, and many other religious festivals, saints' days and personal moments such as birthdays are all accompanied by some special sweet baking.

The Spanish love to celebrate and as you will see, there is a baking recipe for every possible occasion. When it comes to religious celebrations - big and small - there are literally hundreds of traditional festive recipes. You do not need to be religious to enjoy them. For most Spanish people, enjoying a fiesta and all the trappings that go with it is more important than any religious motive!

---oOo---

1.3 Categories of Bakery and Confectionary in Spain

Introduction - When is a cake not a cake?

There is a confusing overlap of bakery categories in Spain. This makes it difficult to define exactly into which category a particular baked product falls since it might easily fall into several.

Adding to the confusion, the time at which a sweet is eaten also alters how it is classified. Sweet cakes and pies are often eaten with coffee during "merienda", but are also eaten as a sweet ("postre") after lunch or dinner. They may also appear at the breakfast table. Typical Spanish breakfasts include a sizable array of sticky buns, churros and sweet cakes, and these are often referred to as "bollería". Finding sponge cake or cream pastries at breakfast raises many a visitor's eyebrow!

To add to the confusion in names it also depends where a term is being used. Even within Spain the same word can have quite different meanings. A "coca" in Valencia refers to an open tart, either sweet or savoury which is made like a pizza. It has a very specific meaning in that area. However, the word coca in Huelva is given to a famous local sweet sponge cake served as a dessert.

The word "bizcocho" should be straightforward enough. It generally refers to a sponge cake, except when it refers to an unbaked milk pudding from Castilla-La Mancha! The word "tarta" or "torta" can used to define anything from a pancake to an apple pie.

There are many biscuits ("galletas") that are small and crispy, as you would expect. However, there is a whole range of galletas that are really small cakes. During Christmas, most shops offer their clients these traditional Christmas "biscuits" called "mantecados" and "polvorones". These little cakes are crumbly (not crunchy) and are often taken with a shot of anís liquor or brandy. However, these same galletas are also eaten for breakfast and found with the other "bollería" or taken with coffee at merienda. They are also served as a Christmas "postre" with lunch. The word galleta is also used for savoury biscuits served as an appetizer. "Pastas" can also be hard or soft biscuits but they may also be small cakes.

Many small pastries and fried dishes such as crêpes and various fritters are often served as a formal dessert with lunch but may also be taken with breakfast or afternoon coffee. Churros are a case in point. In principle, they are just pieces of fried dough - a snack, but when served on heaped plates with large cups of thick dark chocolate, churros become a meal in themselves, at either breakfast or merienda. To call churros a "sweet snack" trivialises their serious filling power. This is no snack - this is the ultimate comfort food!

The apparent confusion of categories is not confined to sweet bakery. Empanadas can be small bite-sized triangular pasties or huge family-sized filled pies. They can be sweet or savoury.

Naming is just as unclear with bread. Sometimes, it is almost impossible to know what kind of bread you are getting based simply on the name. Naming a bread is not as rational as a description such as "rye bread with 6 cereals" where you have a fair idea of what you will get. Most traditional Spanish breads have a unique local name. Fortunately, everyone knows what that these local names mean in terms of the type of bread to expect and so the system of naming works fine ..... as long as you know!

If you are now confused about Spanish baking names, then read on for a description of the common traditional Spanish bakery categories.

Bizcocho: Bizcocho generally refers to a sponge cake of some kind. Of course, there is a vast range of different formats and added ingredients and the word is used to describe everything with a sponge base from cup cakes ("magdalenas") to huge multi-layered and decorated sponge cakes.

Sponge cake is thought to have come from Spain and many countries still refer to it with some reference to the country. For instance, in Italy sponge cake is called "pan di Spagna" meaning "Spanish bread". In Japan, sponge cake is still called "Castella", having been introduced by the Portuguese; "Castella" refers to Spain's largest mediaeval kingdom Castile.

The term bizcocho comes from the Latin "bis coctus", which means cooked twice, and describes the traditional custom of baking cakes first in a mould and then removing the mould and baking them again in order to better preserve the cake. The Latin phrase also gave rise to the English word "biscuit". The modern usage of the word "bizcochos" also refers to finger-shaped sponge biscuits that are specially designed to be dunked into a hot drink.

Bollería: This word (officially) refers to a range of sweet bread buns ("bollos"), generally created in individual pieces. They are often rounded but can also be elongated. However, it is not that simple, of course. The word "bollería" also refers to the bakery itself where these and other sweet baked products are made and sold and the word is interchangeable with the terms "repostería" or "pastelería". However, there are subtle differences (see repostería and pastelería).

According to ASEMAC (Spanish Industry Association for Bakery, Pastries and Cakes), "bollería" are made with a dough with yeast - sweet breads in fact. Nowadays, this distinction is less strong and other products using non-yeast doughs, such as puff pastry, are loosely called "bollería". The word bollería is often used colloquially to refer to all sweet baked products eaten at breakfast and merienda.

Traditionally, bollería consists of two types of pastry: those that are unfilled and uncoated and a second that have either a filling or coating or both.

Buñuelos: These may be fritters or can be similar to doughnuts. They may be round with a hole in the middle like a doughnut, or shaped like a ball. They may be bite-sized or quite large, thick or thin and often flattened. Generally, buñuelos are fried and sugared and sometimes served coated with hot honey or molasses, or sprinkled with cinnamon sugar. They are often made with delicious fillings, such as sweet chestnut cream, or with a dough made with almond or orange.

There are many types of buñuelo, both sweet and savoury. Buñuelos have a long history, going back to the Romans via the Moors and Jews occupying Spain, and they are still widely eaten in the Levant and in Latin America. There are documented references to honey fritters in Granada, where the last Arab kingdom held out against the Christian invasion until 1492. These fritters were made with dough fried in oil and then bathed in boiling honey. After the Christian invasion of Spain ended, buñuelos continued to be made. The Christians made them during Lent, the Sephardic Jews made them for Hanukkah and the Muslims continued to make them for the daily breaking of the fast during Ramadan. They are still very popular indeed.

Churros: Churros (and their longer, thicker cousins the "porras") are such an institution in Spain that they deserve their own classification. A churro is a fried-dough pastry eaten as a snack - often quite a big snack! They are eaten for breakfast or merienda, dipped in sweet, thick, hot chocolate or with café con leche (coffee with milk). Churros are widely available in cafés and from street vendors called churrerías. They are always made fresh and the dough is a mixture of flour, water and salt. Some versions are made with potato dough. The dough is extruded through a nozzle and deep-fried. Churros are thin and sometimes knotted. Porras are similar to churros that are long and thick. Both may be coated in sugar. Both are popular throughout the Hispanic world in various forms.

There are two theories about the background of churros: first that they were brought back by Portuguese sailors trading with China, where a similar dish exists. Another theory is that nomadic shepherds in Spain developed them as a simple bread. This could be easily fried on an open fire during the shepherds' long sojourns in the remote mountains with their flocks. Perhaps both theories are correct.

Cocas: Cocas are a typical dish of Eastern Spain, including the regions of Valencia and Cataluña. The word "coca" in Spain is a bit confusing because it can refer to anything from a flatbread to a pizza (even in some cases a sponge cake). They can be salty and made with meat and/or vegetables, or sweet, prepared as a dessert or eaten at merienda. Generally speaking, they are a piece of flat bread dough coated with a topping and baked.

The word "coca" comes from the Latin verb "cocere" and is related to the English word "cake" and the German word "Kuchen", to mention but two examples. Cocas have been made in Spain since the early Middle Ages and are probably the inspiration for the modern Italian pizza - after all, Naples was a Spanish colony for many years.

Confectionary and Sweets: In this category, we include sweet products that are not normally served as a course in a formal meal - although some are served in this way. They range from sweets such as sugared almonds to quite elaborate baked and sugared almond balls and include several fritters sold as street food. Many of these sweets are eaten during ferias or in street cafes as a fast snack. However, some are also to be found in more elaborate forms in a restaurant as a post meal treat. Generally, these products are not to be found in bakeries in Spain.

Dulces: This is a very generic term used in Spain to describe all kinds of sweet baked products and desserts from simple sweet biscuits to complex filled pastries.

Empanadas: Empanadas are anything baked with a surrounding pastry. The word "empanada" derives from Galician and Portuguese and means "to wrap in bread" ("pan").

The origin of the empanada was the need to preserve food by baking (or frying) it into a strong pastry "envelope". This process had the dual benefit of sterilising the food and giving it several days of extra life. This was particularly important in the hot climates of the Arab world, including Spain and Portugal, where travellers, soldiers and farm workers were often obliged to eat on the road or out in the field.

The fillings of empanadas were often made with leftovers from previous meals. The baking technique came from the Middle East around the 10th Century AD. Empanadas also made their way to India and Pakistan with Arab traders. They arrived in Spain during the Moorish period.

The so-called "samosa" is to be found across the Middle East, Asia and North Africa to this day, has a wide range of fillings and many local names and variants. In Morocco and several other Arab countries, one of the most well-like dishes is the "Fatay" which is just a type of empanada, with a variety of fillings.

Empanadas spread throughout to Latin America, where there is a vast variety, brought there by the Spanish and Portuguese "conquistadores". Of course, Northern Europe has its own versions of empanada. Some even claim that dishes such as apple strudel originated in Spain's Arab past as a way of preserving apples and raisins in a pastry envelope. The idea was then brought to Germany and Austria during Spain's control of the Habsburg Empire.

Nowadays, empanadas are also pies and pasties of various sizes made with a variety of fillings, both sweet, with fresh or dried fruit and nuts, and savoury, with meats, vegetables, fish, cheese or eggs.

Even within Spain, there are many types of empanada. The shape and size vary considerably: from a semi-circular pasty, round pies, small triangular folded pastry "envelopes", all generally known as empanadillas, to family-sized savoury pies, called empanadas. These are served in slices as a main course.

Empanadillas and empanadas make excellent tapas because they are either small or easily cut into small portions. They are quite easy to make. They are served either alone or with a variety of accompanying sauces.

Several new variations on the empanada use modern baking techniques. These bring many new possibilities to this old dish. These modernisations include making open tarts with pre-made pastry of various kinds and focussing on the fillings, and the use of puff pastry, for example. Ultimately, though, they are all forms of empanada.

Ensaimada is a spiral-shaped soft cake from the Mediterranean island of Mallorca, typically eaten with coffee for breakfast or in the afternoon. The name "ensaimada" comes from the word "saïm", the local name for a kind of reduced pork fat used in the Christianised recipe.

Flans: These are much loved in Spain as a dessert. Whilst, strictly speaking, they do not always involve any baking (some do have a pastry base), we have included a few here since many Spanish bakers make and sell them.

Flans have quite a history. The Romans developed flans as both sweet and savoury dishes to use up excess egg production. They then introduced flans into parts of the empire, including Spain. The sweet flan became especially widespread in Spain during the early Middle Ages, when a new recipe evolved using eggs, milk and honey. When the Moors introduced sugar into Spain, cooks began to make flans with sugar instead of the more expensive honey. During Lent, Christians ate these egg-rich flans as a substitute for meat.

Galletas: This is the Spanish word for biscuits but includes a vast variety of small cakes as well as simple sweet biscuits. Biscuits can be hard or soft, sweet or savoury. They range from dried salt biscuits designed for sea voyages to rich, sweet shortcakes such as the Christmas mantecados.

Hogaza: The word derives from the Latin and means "bread baked under the ashes". Hogaza refers to a type of round bread (between 500g and a kilo in weight) made with wheat flour. It usually comes from the Northern part of the region of Castilla y León but you can also find hogaza-style breads in other parts of Spain and indeed in many other Hispanic countries.

This is a group of typical rural breads. Traditionally, these breads are baked in a wood-fired oven and have a thick, dark crust that allows the bread to be kept for a long time. The bread and its crumbs are widely used in a variety of other dishes such as the thick porridge-like savoury dishes called "porra" and the famous "migas".

Hornazos: The Spanish word for oven is "horno", and the word hornazo simply means "something from the oven". Thus the word covers a large range of baked products. In some parts of Spain, "hornazo" is a meat or other savoury pie. In other parts of the country, the word is used to describe various breads, sweet cakes or pies.

The most famous festive hornazo is a sweet bread eaten at Easter and made with a hard-boiled egg embedded in the dough. Eggs were considered to be like meat in some localities and could not be eaten during the Lenten fast. This gave rise to a large surplus of uneaten eggs. The problem was partly solved by hard-boiling the eggs and then eating them after Lent as part of an hornazo. Some food historians even consider this custom to be the source of the modern Easter egg.

Magdalenas: These come from Northern France, where they are called "Madeleine". Over the years, they have become so popular in Spain that no bakery or supermarket would be without several varieties of magdalena. They are small sponge cakes similar to "cup cakes" or "fairy cakes" but usually a bit drier. There is a wide range of different flavours and added ingredients. In Spain, magdalenas have a distinctive flavour because Spanish bakers use olive oil instead of butter to make them.

They are rarely eaten by themselves as they do not have a filling or topping, but are made more interesting when dunked in coffee, hot chocolate or milk!

Mantecados: This is a class of soft biscuit. There are many types of mantecado. The common factor is the use of pig fat (lard - "manteca"). One of the most famous mantecados is the "polvorone". These are a quintessimally Spanish Christmas treat.

Despite their Christmas connection and the fact that mantecados are now considered a Christian invention they are in fact Moorish as demonstrated by the existence of written recipes for an identical sweet being made by the Moors in Andalucía long before the arrival of the Christians. Indeed, they are still being baked (minus the lard) a few kilometres away across the straits of Gibraltar in Morocco!

However, since the Christian conquest of Spain, mantecados have been made with pig lard. In fact, the Spanish Inquisition decreed that polvorones must be produced using only pork fat. This seemingly petty religious insult was apparently an attempt to detect Jews and Muslims hiding within Spanish society. The eating of these sweets at religious festivals such as Christmas was seen as a way of proving that one was a "real" Christian and not a Jew or Muslim hiding from expulsion, persecution or worse; pork fat being forbidden to Jews and Muslims.

Mantecados are mostly produced in Andalucía (most famously in Estepa, Antequera and in Córdoba province) but also in Toledo and Valladolid. After the Christian conquest, the cultivation of pigs increased dramatically in some areas, especially in forested areas such as Estepa. The combination of large surpluses of pig lard and cereal production gave rise to the mantecado industry that flourishes in Estepa to this day. Several convents also produce and sell traditionally produced mantecados.

Mantecados are made with various flavours including cinnamon, almond, lemon, anís or chocolate. In earlier times, Muslim and Jewish bakers produced them with olive oil. Today they are again made with olive oil for the same groups and for the growing vegetarian market.

Pan de Molde: Most traditional bread in Spain is moulded into shape by hand. "Pan de molde" refers to breads that are baked in tins. There are actually not many traditional Spanish breads baked in this way.

Panadería: The word refers to bread in general but also to a bread bakery. In a panaderia they traditionally bake and sell just bread and no pastries, but in small villages, the local panaderia will also bake some sweet pastries to sell.

Panecillos: This is a generic terms for a small bread roll, often made with a sweet or savoury flavour. Thus, you may find "panecillos de cebolla" which are rolls baked with onion.

Pastas: These are nothing to do with pasta! Pastas are biscuits (or small cakes). Pastas de té (tea biscuits) are very common and come in a large variety of flavours, shapes and sizes.

Pastelería and Repostería: This class of baked products also refers to the bakeries where they are made and sold. These baked products may or may not use yeast and they may be sweet or savoury. (Note that "bollería" refers to sweet buns made with yeast).

According to the ASEMAC definitions (Spanish Association for the bakery, pastries and cakes industry), "pastelería" and "repostería" are made with 5 basic dough types. These are:

> Puff pastry dough ("Masa de hojaldre")
>
> Short crust pastry dough ("Masa azucarada")
>
> Choux pastry dough ("Masa escaldada")
>
> Sponge cake mixture ("Masa batida")
>
> Batter mixes

Pasteles: This is another generic term referring to the products made in a pastelería. The classification excludes confectionary. In Spain, generally speaking, the implication is that a pastel is an individual sweet pastry. In other Spanish-speaking countries, a pastel may be savoury.

Postre: This is the word used to describe the dessert course of a meal. It literally means "after", and is a bit like the English colloquial word "afters" used to describe a sweet course after the main course. A "postre" in Spain include can be any sweet dish ranging from a fritter to a slice of cake.

Pudin: Obviously, the word is similar to the English word "pudding" and has the same modern meaning in Spain: a generic term used for a sweet dessert course at lunch or dinner. Both words descended from the French "boudin" from a Latin root and originally were applied to sweet and savoury dishes.

Polvorones: Polvorones are soft biscuits, similar to small crumbly cakes, made of flour, sugar, and pig fat, seasoned with cinnamon and often using ground almonds. They are a type of mantecado. Polvorones are very crumbly ("polvo" means powder or dust in Spanish).

Polverones are a typical Christmas treat and most of the country's huge production comes from the town of Estepa in the province of Sevilla. During Christmas time in the countryside, every village shop and bar will have a tray with bottles of anís liquor and brandy and a plateful of polvorones or other mantecados for customers to help themselves. It is a delightful festive act of generosity.

The Moors brought polvorones to Spain. There is still a strong similarity with a well-known Levantine sweet known as "ghurayba".

When you buy commercially made polvorones, each small biscuit is individually wrapped in thin paper often with a very traditional and/or religious motif. Polvorones have spread throughout the Hispanic world and are found as far apart as Cuba and the Philippines.

Quesada: This word is used to describe cheesecake, especially the traditional variety coming from Cantabria known as "Quesada pasiega".

Roscos and rosquillas: These terms are used for any bakerd product shaped in a ring. It may be a small plain bread ring, one of a huge range of filled doughnuts or a large elaborately decorated, sweet, ringed Christmas cake.

Spain has many types of "rosco" in all shapes, sizes and flavours. In some parts of the country, a sandwich may be made using a bread rosco. Roscos seem to have their history in the Roman culinary world. During the feast of Saturnalia, which marked the beginning of a new year, round, sweet cakes were made with figs, honey and dates and served to the slaves and peasants by their masters. Festivities lasted for several days with a "King" being crowned from amongst the temporarily-freed peasants. A good time was had by all!

These round Roman sweet cakes contained a single bean and the finder of the bean became the temporary "king" of the feast. To this day, the Spanish Roscos de Reyes (Ring of the Kings), now Christianised, are still baked with little gifts in them such as small statues of the three kings. These are traditionally eaten at Epiphany to celebrate the adoration of the three kings.

From a more Moorish - Jewish tradition there is also the fried rosco, which is basically a deep-fried, flavoured dough. This tradition of deep-fried dough continues in hundreds of modern recipes in the Levant and Middle East and many similar recipes have survived in Spain.

Tartas: The term seems to derive from the French word "tarte" and describes a large pie filled with various sweet or savoury ingredients. It may be open or closed with pastry but it is always baked. However, it may be finished using cold ingredients such as fresh fruit or cream. A "tarta" may be served as part of the merienda or as a sweet ("postre") after lunch or dinner.

The nearest English word to describe a "tarta" is, of course, a "tart". In recent years, the word "tarta" has been inaccurately used for birthday and wedding cakes.

Tarta de Queso: This is the most commonly used word for cheesecake. These are found in all of Spain and eaten as a dessert or with coffee. There are many different varieties.

Tortas or Tortitas: In the past, the word "torta" in Spain referred to a round flatbread made without yeast and it is still used to refer to flat soft sweet biscuits such as the sweet "tortas de aceite". These are basically large flat, soft, sweet biscuits made with olive oil and spices.

In recent years, the word "torta" has also started to be used to describe all kinds of cake such as birthday cake. In other parts of the Hispanic world the word is used to describe a variety of both sweet and savoury baked dishes. The word tortita is sometimes used to refer to various sweet or savoury pancakes or small fritters such as the "tortitas de plátano" from Las Islas Canarias (the Canary Islands).

Turrón: Turrón is thought to have developed as an emergency ration to feed Moorish soldiers on their long marches in Arab Spain. Ironically, it is now proudly produced in many Christian monasteries such as the ancient Monasterio de Santa Clara in the province of Palencia.

Turrón (or nougat) is another example of how almonds dominate Spanish and other European confectionary at Christmas time. Turrón appears to have originated in the Andalucian Arab kingdoms. Arab culinary tradition at the time included a similar dessert named "turun", so it seems that nougat or turrón production was introduced into the Arab Kingdoms of Al-Ándalus sometime after they started cultivating almonds in the Caliphate of Córdoba after the 10th century AD.

There is also evidence of a similar confection, named cupedia or cupeto, produced in Ancient Rome and probably adopted by the Arabs as they colonised the abandoned remnants of the Roman Empire in the Levant. At any rate, Turrón or Torró has been known at least since the 15th century in the city of Jijona / Xixona in Alicante.

Spanish turrónes are classified as follows:

> - Hard (the Alicante variety): A compact block of whole almonds in a brittle mass of eggs, honey and sugar; 60% almonds.

> - Soft (the Jijona variety): Similar, but the almonds are reduced to a paste. The addition of oil makes the mix more chewy and sticky; 64% almonds.

In the past, these turrones were exclusively Christmas sweets, though they are now available all year round.

---oOo---

1.4 Traditional Ingredients, Flours, and Doughs

Courtesy of its climate, geography and colourful history, Spain has a unique range of raw materials in the bakery. Apart from a vast range of ingredients, the country has developed and adopted many methods of baking from the constant influences of invaders and occupiers. To give the reader an understanding of these materials and methods we have made a guide to the most common raw materials and later explain the different types of dough used in traditional Spanish bakery.

1.4.1 Traditional Ingredients

There are many ingredients in Spanish bakery that you would rarely find in more Northern countries and here we give you an alphabetical list of the most common ingredients that you will encounter in this book.

Almonds: Almonds are ubiquitous in Spanish sweet baking. The country is a large producer of almonds. They come in various forms, apart from in the shell. They can be whole, raw and in the skin (brown). Almonds are also blanched to remove their skin. They are then sold whole, in slices / flakes, chopped or finely ground. The latter is also known as almond flour.

Anís Liquor: Anís is a traditional flavour in Spain, especially in seasonal sweet bakery. The use of alcohol in sweet bakery is also quite common. Put the two together and anís liquor becomes a natural ingredient in quite a few seasonal sweets and cakes. There are many brands of anís liquor available in any Spanish supermarket and it comes in sweet ("dulce") and dry ("seco") versions.

Angel Hair - "Cabello de Ángel": Angel hair (cabello de ángel) is a well-liked pastry filling as you will see from the many recipes in this book that use it.

It is a transparent preserve made by caramelising the fibrous flesh of pumpkins together with white sugar syrup. It comes from Mallorca but it is widespread throughout Spain and the rest of the Hispanic world. In South America, it is also made with mangos. It is usually flavoured with cinnamon or lemon skin or juice.

Angel hair has roughly the consistency of jam and is a golden colour. Indeed, it can be simply spread on bread like a jam. It is made by boiling the pulp of a pumpkin in strong syrup, consisting of sugar in equal amounts to the quantity of pumpkin used. The pulp of the pumpkin becomes soft, but remain a little fibrous; hence the name.

Angel hair seems to have been a sweet preserve made in mediaeval times in the Middle East and brought to Europe either by the Arabs or by returning crusaders. The use of "New World" fruits or vegetables such as squash was apparently an adaptation of a much older preserve.

In Spain, every supermarket sells jars of angel hair, so most people do not bother to make their own.

Baker's Cream - "Crema Pastelera": Also called "pastry cream" in English, crema pastelera is widely used in Spanish pastry baking. Its basic components are milk, eggs, sugar and white flour. Some people replace the flour with corn starch. It is sometimes flavoured with vanilla, cinnamon, and lemon or orange essence or grated citrus peel.

Baker's Yeast: In times gone by, bakers would create and maintain a colony of yeast that they would use to bake. The colony would be based on naturally occurring wild yeasts. Often, these yeasts were taken from the skin of grapes or raisins. They were then "fed" using potato water (water in which potatoes have been boiled). These colonies were often passed from one generation to the next. Later, yeasts became more standardised and the advent of dehydrated yeast made the keeping of a yeast colony unnecessary and baking with yeast much more convenient.

Baker's Yeast Types: These days, there are two basic types of yeast for baking: active dry yeast and compressed fresh yeast. Active dry yeast comes in two varieties: normal and quick rising. All three can be used successfully in any recipe that requires yeast.

Dry yeast is dehydrated yeast, usually in the form of granules. Sometimes recipes require that dried yeast be mixed with warm water before use and sometimes a little sugar is added. Quick-rising yeast is also active dry yeast, but it is formulated to raise the dough in between one-third to one-half of the time. Dried yeasts should be stored in a cool, dry place. If you buy sachets, store opened sachets in the fridge.

Fresh yeast is the moist type of yeast that is sold in compressed cakes. It is quite perishable, so it needs to be stored in the fridge and used within two to three weeks. Generally it is wise to bring it to room temperature before using. Sometimes a recipe requires that fresh yeast is mixed with a little tepid water (but no sugar). Avoid contact with salt. Fresh yeast is a good choice for breads that need a long, cool fermentation.

Dried or fresh yeast can be used interchangeably but what varies is the quantity used. With dry active yeast you generally need to use only 50% of the quantity of fresh yeast stated in the recipe. If you are using the so-called "instant yeast" you only need to use 25% of the quantity of fresh yeast. There are no hard rules about how much yeast should be used in baking. It depends on the type of flour, the desired result and other ingredients. However, when baking bread with dried yeast, the amount used varies between 0.5% and 1.5%. Using too much yeast can cause dough to rise too quickly and cause the possible collapse of the risen dough.

Baking Soda and Baking Powder - the difference: Baking soda is a simple mineral chemical called Sodium Bicarbonate. It is a harmless substance that reacts with any acid to produce carbon dioxide gas. It is therefore used in some recipes to "raise" a dough by reacting with any acidic ingredients to cause a dough to become full of carbon dioxide and rise.

Baking powder is similar to baking soda, except that baking powder also contains an acid with which the baking soda can react. The baking soda in the mixture does not react with the acid until it becomes moist - the two components in baking powder are kept apart using a neutral component such as corn starch. Thus, baking powder is useful when a recipe has no acidic component and an (artificial) raising agent other than yeast is needed. Baking powder needs to be kept dry or it will lose its raising power.

Chestnut Cream - "Crema de Castañas": This is a traditional sweet bakery cream found in many parts of Spain. It is made with chestnuts, sugar, butter and milk. It was previously more widely used than it is now. Chestnuts were an important source of carbohydrates in rough mountainous regions of Spain where cereals where less available.

Cinnamon: One of the great culinary legacies of the Moorish period in Spain is the use of certain spices in bakery. Cinnamon is certainly one of the most widely used spices in Spanish bakery. It is also a very powerful spice and can be overwhelming. Thus, when a recipe calls for cinnamon "to taste", it is important that you have a feeling about how much you like cinnamon and how much you want it to dominate the taste of what you are baking. Less is often more.

Corn starch: Depending on where you live this may be called cornstarch, corn starch or maize starch. It is a thickening agent manufactured by extracting starch from maize in a simple industrial process. It is not to be confused with maize flour or corn flour, which is just the flour made from maize.

Honey: Before the introduction of sugar into Spain by the Arabs, all sweetened dishes used honey as the main sweetener. The Romans had a wealth of sweet dishes using honey, as did the Arabs. The tradition of producing and using honey has continued in Spain and every household will have a jar or two of honey in the kitchen. It is used in many recipes as a sugar substitute but is also used as a sauce after a little gentle heating. There are many types of honey. These are usually sold according to the flavour and aroma of the dominant flowers frequented by the bees. Some are strongly scented such as thyme, citrus or eucalyptus honey and it is worth making sure that the type of honey works well with what you are preparing.

Lard - "Manteca": There is no doubt that many traditional bakery recipes use pigs' lard. In traditional Spanish sweet bakery, lard is ubiquitous. A mixture of religion, politics, and agriculture complicates the reasons for this use of lard as already mentioned.

Gladly, for those amongst us that prefer not to use lard, it can be substituted by either full-fat margarine or butter without altering the result of a recipe. (With a little experimentation, you can also use olive oil as a substitute.)

Olive Oil: Many Spanish bakery recipes call for the use of olive oil. Rather than constantly referring to "Extra Virgin Olive Oil" in every single recipe, we assume that the reader understands that they should always use this grade of olive oil.

Generally, all oil used in cooking and baking in Spain is of this quality. Lower quality oils, if they are used at all, may occasionally be used for deep-frying but even these oils will be Virgin Olive Oil.

There are many types of olive and the oils made from them have quite different flavours. If you are baking with olive oil its worth checking to see if an oil is fruity or more bitter and which taste is best suited for what you are baking.

Orange or Lemon Peel: Orange and lemon peel (also referred to as "zest" in English) are often used grated in sweet Spanish pastry baking. Be careful not to include the white pith under the skin when grating orange and lemon peel. This is quite bitter and may spoil the taste.

Wash fruits thoroughly. With non-organic, supermarket oranges and lemons, this may mean washing with soap and water to remove the protective waxes that shippers use to protect against insect attack. Rinse very thoroughly and then use a fine grater that only takes the skin and not the pith.

Orange and lemon peel is also used in slices to infuse hot oil with their flavours before adding the oil in a recipe. In this case, the peel can be fried directly without any grating but try to minimise the amount of pith attached.

Sugars: There are three basic types of sugar found in the bakery: Granulated sugar, icing sugar and caster sugar. Granulated sugar in its refined white form is the most common sugar in baking. However, several types of brown sugar are also sometimes called for. Brown sugar is brown due to the presence of molasses.

Icing sugar is finely ground white sugar, often with a little corn starch added to stop it becoming lumpy. It is also known as confectioners' sugar or powdered sugar (USA). It is frequently used to create icing or to decorate pastries, biscuits etc.

Caster sugar is rarely used and can be hard to find in Spain anyway. It is simply super-fine white sugar.

Wines in Baking: The wines most required in baking in Spain are the traditional sweet wines, such as Muscatel or Málaga Dulce but sometimes a recipe will simply call for a quantity of red or white wine, in which case this can be any reasonable Spanish wine.

Some recipes call for "mosto", which is very young wine. Mosto comes in lots of varieties and the geographical source of the recipe will indicate the most authentic local mosto. However, mostos are local wines with a very limited shelf life and will be hard to find outside Spain. If it gets too complicated just use a similar quantity of slightly sweet white wine.

1.4.2 Types of Flour

As a generic term, flour can mean any fine, dry powder ground from some form of vegetable matter but, unless a recipe says otherwise, what is meant is white wheat flour. Obviously, flour from different cereals has quite different properties and the grade of flour also affects how it behaves. Here we will take a look at some different types of commonly-used flour and how they affect your baking.

A note of caution: flours vary a great deal from country to country in terms of standards, moisture content, protein etc. It is best to first check locally which flours are best for your particular purpose.

White Flour: White flour is flour with the bran removed. Since the earliest times, there has been a quest to produce white flour. Even the ancient Greeks tried to produce white flour and upper class Greeks preferred white flour, if they could afford it! In Rome, dark flours were used to make bread for the poor. Roman white flour would still have been much darker than modern white flour. It was not until the 19th century that technology made it possible to remove all the bran during the milling process and produce a really white flour.

Now, however, class preferences have reversed. With a better understanding of the nutritional value of wholegrain flours, there is an increasing tendency for the wealthy to prefer darker flours for bread, whilst white industrial bread has, sadly, become the bread of the poor in urban society.

Because of this traditional preference for white flour (however misguided), almost all bread and pastry recipes here call for white wheat flour.

Gluten: Despite the recent upsurge in the fashion of perfectly healthy consumers buying "gluten-free" foods, there is absolutely no reason to do so. Apart from a relatively small, unfortunate group of people that is intolerant to gluten, or those specifically prescribed a low-gluten diet by a doctor, there is no reason whatsoever to avoid gluten in your diet. Gluten is a natural part of many cereals.

Wheat contains proteins. From a baking point of view, when mixed with water, these proteins form gluten. This is an elastic framework of protein within dough. Gluten traps gases released by yeast in fermenting bread dough. This gives bread its light texture, and allows it to rise. The more protein a flour has, the stronger the gluten framework to trap the gases during rising. Thus, good flour for bread baking has a high protein content.

Flour also contains "proteases" which like to digest gluten, making bread dough sticky, inelastic, and flat. Almost all bread recipes call for the addition of salt for this reason. This is because salt keeps these proteases from being active and reducing the gluten in your dough.

Baking with flour is all about how much gluten you need. For bread, you need a lot of gluten, otherwise you will get very flat, lifeless loaves. On the other hand, you do not want a lot of gluten in cakes or pastries or they will develop tough crusts and a coarse, unappealing texture. Thus, there is a wide range of flours available for baking. The level of protein in flour is usually expressed as a percentage.

Flour Comparisons: Each country has its own classification for types of flour. In spite of the differences that may exist between the various definitions, all are based on common parameters that give us a lot of information about the characteristics of each flour.

Protein Content: The amount of protein is expressed as a percentage. Here is a guide to the uses of flour according to protein content:

> Pastry flour: 8% - 9% (USA 7% - 10%)
>
> General purpose: 10% (USA 11% - 12%)
>
> Medium strength bread flour: 11% (USA 13%)
>
> Strong bread flour: 12% - 14% (USA 14%)

To confuse matters a little bit, flour producers in Spain use an alternative measure of protein content which measures the strength of the dough but which actually just relates to the amount of protein. The "strength" (W) is marked on the flour packaging and has the following meaning:

> W less than 130 - flour for pastry
>
> W between 130 and 200 - flour for general bakery
>
> W 220 - 350 - medium strength flour, used for most breads
>
> W360 - strong flour, used for breads and buns that contain a lot of butter, fat, oil or eggs and also for bread with a long fermentation period

White Flour versus Whole Wheat: For white flours only one part of the wheat grain is used - the endosperm. Whole-wheat (wholemeal) flour includes the bran; whole grain flour uses all of the wheat grain - the endosperm, the bran, and the germ. The extra fibre in wholegrain flours is good for digestive health.

However, the germ and bran (found in whole grain flours) impede the development of a good, elastic gluten which promotes rising, so using wholemeal flour is not just a question of substituting it for white flour. You will need to experiment. Sometimes a mixture of the two types of flour should be tried.

1.4.3 Types of Dough:

There are many types of dough in Spanish bakery but what follows is a description of the main types.

There is nothing especially unique in the composition of most Spanish doughs but it is interesting to revisit the subject of traditional doughs in terms of their history and development and it does help to get a feeling for how these doughs arrived where they are today.

On the other hand, Spanish doughs have one distinguishing feature and that is the frequent use of flavourings (such as anís or wine) in dough mixes and the liberal addition of fruits, spices and nuts.

Choux Pastry Dough - "Masa Escaldada": The Spanish name for choux pastry ("Masa escaldada") means blanched (scalded) dough, which gives us some idea of the recipe of this dough. The word "choux" in French means cabbage, and choux pastry gets its name from the fact that the little balls of choux pastry used to make cream puffs resemble little cabbages.

The "blanched" part of the name in Spanish refers to the fact that the dough is traditionally made by adding flour to very hot water together with salt and some form of fat and finally (in some recipes) egg.

Choux dough relies on high moisture content and the internal production of steam within the dough to make the dough rise into a light pastry. There is no raising agent or yeast used.

Choux pastry dough is used in both fried and baked pastries. Churros, for instance use a simple form of choux dough to produce a physically light pastry that is then deep-fried, making for a rather 'heavy' experience! There are many choux pastry recipes and they are generally characterised by producing a light pastry such as that for éclairs and "puffs" of various kinds. Of course, deep-frying choux dough will alter that result.

The common view of choux pastry is that it was developed in Italy. It was later introduced into France where it quickly became fashionable amongst the aristocracy.

One story states that choux was invented in 1540 by a chef of Catherine de Medici. Given the turbulent times, it's hard to say when the pastry arrived on the table and exactly how, but by the 19th century French pastry chefs were using choux pastry in many light, sweet pastries. It was similarly adopted in Spain and used in pastries such as the famous "profiteroles".

Choux dough is not very rigid like other bread or pastry doughs and it is therefore often piped or spooned onto a tray before baking.

Filo Pastry - "Pasta Filo": According to mediaeval Arab literature, filo pastry is one of the most delicate, soft, crunchy, thin, elegant, versatile doughs that exist. The use and history of filo pastry ranges from Greece through Armenia, the Balkans, modern Turkey to the Levant and Morocco, and the whole Middle East. The word "filo" derives from the Greek word "phyllo" meaning a thin sheet such as a sheet of paper.

Some food historians believe that the first filo pastry was made in the kitchens of the Topkapı Palace during the time of the Ottoman Empire, based on earlier Central Asian and Romano-Byzantine techniques. Baklava is probably the earliest recorded dish using filo, documented in the 13th century and still made today.

Filo pastry is an unleavened pastry and uses no raising agents. Filo-based pastries are often made by layering many sheets of filo brushed with olive oil or butter and then baked but there are other uses.

Filo pastry lends itself to wrap any stuffing, sweet or savoury, and dried fruit mixtures, etc. In many Near and Middle Eastern countries there are numerous examples of filo pastry in traditional bakery. For instance, in Turkey, "baklava" is a honey and nut pastry held together with layers of filo pastry. The acceptance of filo pastry spread rapidly and entered Northern European cuisine. There are many examples of its use, such as some versions of Apfelstrudel.

Most people buy ready-made filo dough but it can be made at home. Many bakeries still make their own. Filo dough is made with flour, water, and a small amount of oil or white vinegar, though some dessert recipes also call for egg yolks.

Filo takes time and skill to make, requiring progressive rolling and stretching to a single, thin and very large sheet. A very large table and a long rolling pin are used, with continual flouring between layers to prevent tearing. Machines for producing filo pastry were perfected in the 1970s, and machine made filo has now come to dominate the market.

These days, ready-made filo pastry is widely available and sold chilled and prepared for immediate use. It is generally unpacked at the very last moment when all fillings are prepared. This is because the dough sheets dry up very quickly when in contact with air. Unused sheets should be quickly wrapped up again to exclude the air and should be kept cool.

Before using the filo pastry sheets, they are usually thinly spread using a basting brush with melted butter, in the case of a sweet pastry, or with olive oil in the case of savoury fillings. There is no hard rule about when to use butter or olive oil. This use of a fat between layers of pastry dough makes it crisp and golden and slightly blistered when it is baked. Baking is always done at a high temperature.

Puff Pastry - "Hojaldre": Puff pastry, known, as "hojaldre" in Spanish, is a very light pastry made in layers that expand when cooked, leaving large air pockets inside. It is used for sweet or savoury dishes and is extremely widespread in Spanish bakery.

There are several versions of the history of puff pastry. The Spanish cook Hernández Macias in his work "The Art of Cooking" ("Libro del arte de cozina") published in 1607, gives a recipe for puff pastry that is very similar to the one we know today.

Sweet or savoury puff pastries were certainly made in Spain prior to the seventeenth century. In these versions, each layer of pastry was made separately and, coated with oil or some other fat and then merged together as is still the case with many Moroccan pastries using filo. The same principle applies with modern puff pastry. The fat layer has the effect of retaining steam from the dough and separating the layers somewhat like the leaves of a book.

However, the standard French version of the dough's history states that puff pastry was first created by the painter and master pastry chef, Claude Gelée. This does not quite fit in with the Spanish version of events. Gelée, was born in 1600 and when Hernandez Maceras published his recipe for puff pastry in Spain, Gelée was only seven years old!

However, Gelée did indeed spend time perfecting his version of puff pastry and promoting his pastry in France and Rome. Another well-known French baker, Marie Antoine Carême, went further with the development of French puff pastry. He is famous for the creation of the vol-au-vent.

The reality is that puff pastry is to be found in the medieval pastries in many areas under Arab influence. Nonetheless, there is also plenty of evidence to suggest that puff pastry even predates the Arab era. There are references to a type of puff pastry in both classical Greek and Roman culinary writings.

Shortcrust Pastry Dough - "Masa Quebrada" (sweet: "Masa Azucarada"): The Spanish name "masa quebrada" means "broken dough" and this gives some inkling of the texture of shortcrust pastry. When baked, it is very crumbly and light and it breaks easily.

Shortcrust pastry in Europe seems to have come from Venice around the year 1000 when cane sugar was first imported. It later became synonymous with French baking and the advent of the quiche.

Whereas many types of dough are made to be flexible, shortcrust pastry is quite the opposite. It is made to be quite stable and rigid, not contracting before baking and not expanding much during baking. For this reason, it makes a good base for tarts, pies, quiches etc. The pastry is used for both sweet and savoury baking.

Shortcrust pastry recipes usually use about twice as much flour as fat by weight, although there are many variants of shortcrust pastry doughs. The fats used include full fat margarine, lard, or butter and sometimes these are combined.

In preparation, the fat is rubbed into plain flour to create a loose mixture that is then bound using a small amount of cold water at the last moment. The ingredients must be kept cold. This is to avoid the fats melting into the flour before baking. The dough is then rolled out, shaped and placed in a baking tin to create the top or bottom of a flan or pie.

When the dough is baking the fats melt and there is a release of steam which helps create the crumbly texture. Overworking shortcrust dough can be a problem because it encourages the formation of gluten strands that makes for a pastry that is tough, rather than light and crumbly.

Sourdough - Mother Dough - "Masa Madre": In Spanish this is known as "masa madre". It is known in English as sourdough. A simple sourdough is made by mixing flour and water together and allowing the mix to ferment for a day or two. The process takes advantage of naturally occurring wild yeasts that brewers and winemakers use in the fermentation of beer and wine production. Traditionally, sourdough was used before baker's yeast was readily available to bring about fermentation of bread. It is a form of yeast, in fact.

Sourdough can be made fresh every time you want to bake but, because it takes a couple of days to start to ferment, it is more convenient to store a little of the sourdough for daily use either as a liquid or as a piece of dough (separated from the bread just before baking). These natural yeasts are quite resistant to cooling and can be refrigerated (but must be kept above zero degrees) and may be "fed" on flour and water.

There are various recipes for sourdough and later in the book we provide a classic recipe to make your own. It is quite simple.

Sponge Cake Mix - "Masa Batidas": The sponge cake was first "officially invented" by the Italian pastry chef Giovan Battista Cabona at the Spanish court when his master, the Genoese marquis Domenico Pallavicini, visited around the middle of the 16th century. Whether he actually invented it or simply adapted what was there already, we do not know. However, we do know that sponge cakes existed long before this date. They are considered the first cakes made without any yeast.

The dough and resultant sponge has many Spanish connections. It is called "pan di Spagna" (Spanish bread) in Italy and, introduced to Japan by Portuguese explorers, still referred to in Japan as "castella"; from the old kingdom of Castile in Spain.

There are many forms of dough using the same basic technique. Generally, the ingredients are flour, sugar, butter and eggs, and (in its more modern form) it is sometimes leavened with baking powder. In its unleavened form, the rising of the sponge actually occurs because of air trapped in the dough that raises the sponge as it bakes.

In Jewish tradition, the dough is used in an unleavened form and does not use wheat flour when eaten for the Passover festival. This is because of Jewish religious customs to avoid wheat flour and leavened bread during Passover.

Sponge cakes in Spain are mostly referred to simply as "bizcocho".

Starter Dough - Pre-ferment: This term refers to a fermenting mixture prepared in advance to help with the process of bread fermentation. Sourdough is one such "pre-ferment" mixture but there are many variants around the world.

Another pre-ferment mixture seen in Spain is similar to the Italian "biga", which is a mixture of water, flour and baker's yeast. Sometimes it contains a small amount of sugar. It is known as a "prefermento". These pre-ferment mixtures were once very common in domestic bakery but now are largely confined to commercial artisan bakery.

---oOo---

2. The Recipes

We have confined ourselves to recipes that have been traditionally made in Spain for at least one hundred years, though many recipes are much older. We have excluded modern international recipes that may be popular now but are not intrinsically Spanish.

The recipes follow the same format, firstly with a brief background to the history and importance, local versions, when and with what the dish is eaten, etc. We explain any variants of the basic recipe. This is then followed by a list of ingredients, expressed, where possible, in standard metric measures. Finally, we give a detailed description of the preparation of the product.

We have taken special care to try to explain the history and sociological context of each recipe where this is known. For some readers this may seem irrelevant. However, we find that understanding how a dish evolved to become what we know today is important in understanding how people lived and ate in the past. It says much about how we perceive food now and how our ancestors considered food in previous generations and in other cultures. This knowledge can tell us a lot about the way we prepare food today.

One of the more difficult tasks in documenting traditional recipes is to provide a useful but descriptive translation of the original name. We have done our best to do this but in some cases, it is impossible to translate into English words that actually do not officially exist in Spanish. They are just colloquial names. For instance, one of the continuous problems in discussing bread recipes in Spain is name confusion. The same name for a bread may be used in several different provinces but refer to an entirely different type of bread. This makes creating an accurate index of baked products quite a feat! The converse is also true. There are many types of bread which have very different names in different towns or villages but which are essentially the same. In cases like these, we have tried to use the most popular name and recipe as being the most representative. Sometimes we have provided alternative names as a reference.

In such cases, we have tried to give translations that describe the baked product so that, at least, the reader can find it. In other cases, the Spanish names, whilst known to everyone in Spain, have little meaning to an outsider. A "nun's kiss" or "virgin tart" are not going to evoke any culinary images at all for most foreign readers so again we have tried to provide a useful description in English. Sometimes we use the original name *and* a description in English!

When it comes to ingredients, we have tried to be as specific as possible. However, flour varies quite a lot from country to country in terms of protein content and moisture content. When a recipe requires a particular type of flour, we have specified this. When a recipe uses white general purpose or plain white wheat flour, we simply refer to it as "flour".

---o0o---

2.1 Breads

As in the rest of Europe, bread is an important and integral part of the diet. In Spain, bread is eaten in some form with every meal of the day and no lunch or dinner table would be complete without fresh bread. Bread is the basis for much of the popular traditional tapas "culture" and many a Spanish recipe calls for the use of bread crumbs in sauces, soups and "porra" (a thick sweet or savoury porridge).

The history of bread in Spain is a complex one. Bread was being baked in Spain in a primitive form before the Roman invasion but the recipes were greatly influenced by the Romans and later by the Muslims and Jews who lived in much of the country for many hundreds of years. The Christians also brought some Northern European baking influences with them in the Middle Ages, especially to Northern Spain. Indeed, there have been guilds of bakers in parts of Spain for over 800 years. The baker's guild in Barcelona, for instance, was founded in 1200 AD. Many types of bread developed to adapt to prevailing circumstances. Thick-crusted breads were developed in rural areas to provide long-lasting bread that shepherds could bring on the long treks with their flocks across the plains. Sailors in Galicia developed biscuits that could last for months at sea, as they journeyed to distant North Atlantic fishing grounds and to the New World.

This cultural and social mix of influences has given rise to a wealth of bread types ranging from simple unleavened flat breads to huge crusty breads made with sourdough and multiple fermentations. Many of these traditional recipes continue to be baked to this day.

Thus, Spain has developed a diverse range of breads. There are a bewildering number of regional bread varieties in Spain and, indeed, there are bread varieties that are only found in certain towns or villages or only in a particular province. Some bread types are only baked for special events such as a particular religious feast. Obviously, many types of bread are quite similar but there is also an amazing range of variations in terms of size, shape, ingredients and preparation. Bread that is baked in a baking tin, with which most Northern Europeans are best acquainted, is simply referred to as "pan de molde" and is only one of hundreds of bread types in Spain. It is a relatively new arrival in Spain. Many traditional recipes called for breads to be kneaded and shaped by hand, giving them a uniquely artisanal appearance.

Translating traditional Spanish bread names can be a bit of a challenge. This is because breads are often named according to how they look, such as "bola", meaning ball. Another sweet bread is called "caracol", meaning snail! The bread in question has no connection with snails at all but this rustic name is used because this small sweet bread looks like the shell of a snail. Despite this difficulty in translating bread names, we have tried to give English translations that accurately describe the bread - but it is also fun to understand some of the original names.

Several Spanish breads are considered so unique that they have been designated to have a specific geographical significance, known in the European Union as "Indicación Geográfica Protegida (IGP)" - meaning "Geographical Indication (GI)". This designation provides for the legal protection of the name and production of a food product that is specific to a particular area and, in the case of bread, is made using particular traditional baking recipes and methods.

Aside from the historical and cultural importance of bread, it is a delightful staple food in its own right and we hope that the reader enjoys the following recipes.

ALBARDILLA DE MÁLAGA

Albardilla Bread of Malága

This dense, white, rather hard loaf is typical of Málaga. It is known for its fine crumb and the fact that it keeps very well (for several days). It is baked either as a long wide roll or in smaller loaves of up to one kilo. It is very easy to make.

Ingredients:

>   1000 g bread flour
>   500 ml water
>   18 g salt
>   200 g sourdough (see recipe)
>   20 g dried yeast

Preparation:

1. The dough is prepared in two stages. First mix all the ingredients together by hand or using a mixer, and then manually knead the dough until it is smooth and consistent.

2. Divide the dough into pieces of about 500 g.

3. Mould each piece of dough into an oval-shaped loaf and make a deep cut across the centre of the dough.

4. Allow the dough to rise until it has doubled in size and make two cuts in the sides of the loaf.

5. Bake at 210°C for 35 minutes.

BOLLO PREÑAO DE ASTURIAS

Chorizo Buns of Asturias

The word "preñao" means pregnant, so named because this roll is baked with a filling, usually chorizo. It is a typical and popular bread from Asturias and is often served as a snack with a glass of Asturian cider. It can be made, as described here, with fresh chorizo or with chorizo cooked in cider.

Ingredients:

> 500 g bread flour
> 300 ml water
> 10 g salt
> 20 g fresh yeast
> A little milk to coat
> 300 g fresh Asturian chorizo

Preparation:

1. Put the flour in a bowl, add the crumbled yeast, and mix.

2. Add the water and the salt and mix the ingredients by hand for around 3 minutes into a dough.

3. Knead and aerate the dough on a work surface.

4. When the dough is firm, form it into a ball and place it in a bowl greased with olive oil, cover the bowl with cling film coated with olive and place it in a warm place for an hour or so.

5. After this time, knead the dough to expel any built-up gases.

6. Cut the dough into 50 g portions, roll them into small balls and let these stand for 5 minutes covered with a cloth.

7. Roll out the small balls into rectanles, put a piece of skinned chorizo in each of them, then fold the sides over the chorizo, and form into a bun. Place these on an oven tray with enough space to expand and allow them to rise for another hour.

8. Preheat the oven to 220°C.

9. Paint the buns with a little milk and salt.

10. Bake for 20 minutes without fan until they are golden brown.

11. Remove from the oven and allow them to cool on a mesh.

BORREGOS DE CARDEDEU, CATALUÑA
Toasted Anís Breads of Cardedeu, Cataluña

This sweet, anís-spiced toast is famous in the small Catalan town of Cardedeu where its production was first documented in 1770. There are many variations and several "secret" recipes in the town's bakeries. They became famous when the bakery of Pere Sabatés in the town sent some to King Alfonso XII, after which the bakery was appointed as a "Provider of the Royal Household" in the year 1878.

The word "borrego" actually means "lamb". Despite the fact that this is a kind of sweet bread, it is eaten with both savoury and sweet toppings (generally for breakfast) with either jam or sausage. It is also eaten with pâté and used as a base for savoury canapés.

Ingredients:

First dough mix:

> 100 g flour
> 60 ml water
> 10 g fresh yeast

Second dough mix:

> Grated peel of 2 oranges
> 500 g flour
> 150 g brown sugar
> 10 g butter or oil
> 20 g aniseed
> 300 ml water
> 20 g fresh yeast
> Oil and water mix to baste rolls

Preparation:

1. Prepare the "first dough" by thoroughly mixing all of the ingredients. Place this dough aside and let it rise for 1.5 hours.

2. To this mix, add in the ingredients of the "second dough". Knead together thoroughly. Allow this to rise for another 30 minutes.

3. Cut and roll the dough into rectangular bars. Place on a greased oven tray and baste with a mixture of oil and water.

4. Preheat the oven to 170°C

5. Bake the borregos for 20-30 minutes until golden.

6. Remove from the oven and allow to cool. When the borregos have cooled, cut them into 2 cm slices. Place the slices on a baking tray and bake in the oven again until lightly browned and crispy.

7. Serve with a savoury or sweet topping for breakfast or as a base for a tapa or canapé.

BRONA (BORONA) DE GALICIA

Maiz and Rye Bread of Galicia

This traditional Galician maize and rye bread has many different names, such as boro, borona, boroña, brona or boroa. Similar bread is also made in other parts of Northern Spain, including Cantabria, Asturias, El País Vasco (Basque Country) and northern Castilla y Leon.

The name of the bread comes from the Celtic word "bron", meaning bread. Traditionally it was made to be quite dense and round with a dark hard crust but quite moist inside. Modern recipes make the bread lighter. It can also be made in a baking tin.

Brona is often eaten with fish or meat dishes but is just enjoyed by itself with a glass of wine. The dough of this bread is also used to make some traditional regional empanadas and other pies.

Traditionally, the brona is baked on a bed of kale leaves, which adds to the distinctive flavour. This is quite an ancient bread variety peculiar to Northern Spain and before the arrival of maize from the new world, similar bread was made with a mixture of barley and rye flour.

Several simple variants of this bread incorporate small pieces of chorizo into the dough.

Ingredients:

> 450 g maize flour, unprocessed
> 150 g rye flour
> 50 g wheat flour (optional)
> 30 g fresh yeast
> 15 g salt
> 500 ml boiling water
> Kale leaves

Preparation:

1. Form a pile of the maize flour in a bowl and add two-thirds of the water (this needs to be very hot) together with the salt. Mix whilst adding the water gradually.

2. When the water is incorporated, leave the mix to cool a little and then add the other flours. Finally, gradually add in the remaining - lukewarm - water mixed with the fresh yeast. Mix the dough by hand -

it should be very sticky and moist. You can adjust the amount of water, if necessary.

3. Wet your hands and form the dough into a high, round loaf. Smooth the surface.

4. Cover a baking tray with baking paper. Traditionally, the bread is baked on a bed of kale leaves and these can be use instead of, or as well as, baking paper.

5. Leave the dough to rise for an hour or until it has doubled in size and the top has cracked.

6. Preheat the oven to 200°C.

7. Lightly sprinkle the dough with maize flour.

8. Bake in an over at 180-200°C for about 60 minutes until golden brown and the crust is hard. Remove the loaf and allow to cool.

CABEZÓN DE NAVARRA

Rustic Bread of Navarra

The literal translation for this traditional bread is "big head". This is an obvious description since the loaf is often made in an almost spherical shape. This is a typical, very simple, rustic bread type and is popular in Navarra where it is also used to make the famous local breadcrumb dish known as "migas de pastor".

The following recipe is sufficient to make two small loaves though this type of rustic bread is often made up to one kilo. If you wish, one half of the dough can be frozen to be used later.

Ingredients:

> 200 ml water
> 50 ml olive oil
> 25 g fresh yeast
> 400 g bread flour
> A teaspoon of salt
> Water to spray the loaf during baking

Preparation:

1. Mix all the ingredients together into a consistent dough. Cut the dough in half to make two small loaves.

2. Shape the dough into a ball and place it on a non-stick oven tray coated with a little flour.

3. Make some cuts in the top of the dough and sprinkle with a little flour. Let the dough rise for an hour or until doubled in size.

4. Bake at 200°C for 20-30 minutes, spraying the loaves with some water a couple of times. The first time not till after about 15 minutes of baking.

5. Remove the loaves and let them cool on a rack.

CAÑADA DE BAJO ARAGÓN

Shepherds' Bread of Lower Aragón

This sweet bread is typical of the towns in "Bajo Aragón" (Lower Aragón) but is also found in other Aragonese provinces. The bread is usually oval and quite flat. The dough is perforated and then coated in olive oil with a sprinkling of sugar before baking.

This is a long-lasting bread and its name derives from the word used to describe the natural riverbeds (cañada) used by shepherds to transport their flocks to new grazing areas. Sometimes the distances involved were huge and these shepherds needed supplies for many days.

Ingredients:

500 g bread flour
300 ml water
150 ml olive oil
70 g sourdough
10 g salt
Handful of sugar
10 g fresh yeast

Preparation:

1. Put the water, 25 ml of olive oil and sourdough in a bowl.

2. Add the flour and salt and mix well.

3. Crumble the fresh yeast into the mixture and mix again. Then knead the dough thoroughly. Finally form the dough into a ball.

4. Put the dough in the bowl, cover it with a damp cloth and leave it to rise at 20-25°C until the dough has doubled in volume.

5. Knead the dough again to release the gases and then cut it into 2 or 3 pieces.

6. Roll out the dough into rectangular pieces with rounded corners.

7. Cover the pieces again and allow them to rise until about doubled in volume.

8. Preheat the oven to 220°C and place an ovenproof bowl with water in the bottom of the oven to provide steam during baking.

9. When the pieces of dough have risen again, place on a lined baking tray, score the dough horizontally and vertically or you can perforate the top of the dough to make little holes.

10. Brush the dough liberally with olive oil and shake a handful of sugar over the top of the pieces.

11. Place the baking tray in the oven and bake for 15 to 20 minutes. When golden brown, remove and allow to cool.

CARQUINYOLIS

Almond Bread of Cataluña

Carquinyolis is typically Catalan sweet bread made with whole almonds. It is traditionally eaten accompanied by a glass of sweet wine, but also often taken for breakfast or merienda with tea, coffee or ice cream.

Ingredients:

    300 g flour
    2 large eggs
    150 g whole almonds (with skin)
    50 g ground almonds (with skin)
    190 g sugar
    9 g baking powder
    4 g cinnamon powder
    5 g grated lemon peel (or to taste)
    1 g salt
    1 large egg to coat

Preparation:

1. Soak the whole, raw almonds in water for a maximum of 30 minutes. Drain well and put aside until dry.

2. Finely grind 50g of almonds into the consistency of flour.

3. Put the eggs, sugar, cinnamon and lemon peel into a large bowl and whisk until you have a smooth cream.

4. Sift the flour into another bowl together with the baking powder and salt. Add the almond flour and mix thoroughly.

5. Add the flour to the egg mix stirring constantly. When thoroughly mixed, knead the dough and form a ball with it.

6. Place the dough on a lightly floured work surface and spread it out by hand.

7. Distribute the almonds evenly across the dough and push them into the dough.

8. Divide the dough into four pieces then put the pieces one on top of the other and knead the dough until the almonds are evenly distributed throughout.

9. The dough should have the consistency of marzipan, so you can add small amounts of flour or milk, as necessary, to make the dough drier or softer.

10. Moisten your hands lightly with water and divide the dough into 4 portions of about 200g each. Mould each piece of dough into a bar or cylinder shape with a thickness of about 4 cm.

11. Wrap the 4 pieces in kitchen film and leave them in the refrigerator for about 30 minutes.

12. Preheat the oven to 200°C.

13. Remove the bars of dough from the fridge, take the kitchen film off and place the 4 pieces on a baking tray lined with baking paper.

14. Flatten the bars to about 1.5 cm and then coat each one with well-beaten egg.

15. Reduce the oven temperature to 180°C and bake them for about 20 minutes, until they are a light golden brown.

16. Remove the loaves from the oven and, immediately, cut them into slices diagonally, of about 1 to 2 centimetres thick. (Hold the hot bread with a cloth).

17. Place the slices on a baking tray lined with baking paper and put them back in the oven at the same temperature for 5 more minutes, until they are well browned.

18. Remove the Carquinyolis from the oven and allow them to cool completely on a rack before serving.

CORONA DE QUESOS Y NUECES

Crown of Cheese and Walnut Bread

This is particularly rich, cheesy bread. The origin is not quite clear, but variations of this recipe seem to be related to the traditional sweet "Rosco del Reyes", which is eaten on the "Día de los Reyes", the Feast of Epiphany on January 6th, but in this case, the Rosco is savoury rather than sweet. You can use some discretion in the type and amount of cheese you use. A strong cheese that bakes well may be the best to choose.

Ingredients:

        100 ml milk
        1 egg
        1 teaspoon of sugar
        0.5 teaspoon of salt
        300 g bread flour
        40 g butter
        12 g fresh yeast
        200 g cream cheese
        2 tablespoons of milk
        50 g ground walnuts
        75 g blue cheese or similar strong cheese
        100 g chopped walnuts

Preparation:

1. Dissolve the yeast in 50 ml of lukewarm milk. Mix in 50 g of flour and let it stand until it starts to ferment.

2. Mix the egg with the remainder of the milk and add the salt and sugar. Add the flour and knead into a dough. Add the butter and knead again before adding the yeast mix to the dough. Knead the dough thoroughly, place it in a bowl, and allow to rise until it has doubled in volume.

3. In the meantime, prepare the cheese mixture. Thoroughly mix the ground walnuts with the cream cheese and the 2 tablespoons of milk. Put aside.

4. Crumble the chopped walnuts and the blue cheese together and put aside.

5. When the dough has risen, roll it out on a smooth, floured surface into a rectangle of about 30 x 35cm.

6. Spread the cream cheese mix almost to the edges of the dough and scatter the crumbled walnut and cheese mix on top of this.

7. Roll the cheese into the dough and extend the dough into a roll that should be about 50 cm long.

8. Now, we need to plat the dough to make the "crown". Use a knife to cut all the way along the length of the dough roll, leaving one end uncut.

9. Turn the parts in which the filling is visible upwards. Plat the two parts of the dough until you reach the end.

10. When it is all platted, join the two ends and form a ring. Line a baking tray with oven paper and place the dough ring on it. Leave the dough to rise again. Preheat the oven to 200°C.

11. When the dough has risen, place the "crown" in the oven and bake for 25 minutes at 200°C.

12. When the crown is baked, remove it from the oven and allow it to cool on a rack.

HOGAZA DE LEÓN

Country Bread of León

The city of León, in Northern Spain, is famous for this particular bread but similar breads can in fact be found in many parts of Spain. The hogaza is a round loaf (between half a kilo and a kilo) and is originally a typical country bread of the campesinos and the herdsmen. It has a thick crust and this keeps the crumb fresh for a long time - an important characteristic if you were herding sheep over long distances and thus away from home for a long time. A hogaza will stay fairly fresh for about 7 days. It was famously mentioned in Cervantes' Don Quixote and has been baked in much the same way for centuries.

Traditionally, the bread was baked with rough rye flour in the upland areas of the region and with wheat flour in the plains. The modern version is generally baked with ordinary wheat flour. The traditional version was often made with flour with a high bran content as this was cheaper in those days. Generally, slices of hogaza are eaten as an accompaniment to other, cooked dishes and slices of the bread were often toasted and used as a base for meat, fish or stews.

When the bread has dried out too much it is also often used as a basis for a variety of other dishes, such as garlic soup, and even as the base for a wine soaked dessert. There are quite a lot of variants of hogaza and indeed the bread recipe also travelled to Latin America where versions of the hogaza are still popular to this day. This traditional recipe uses a sourdough made with fresh yeast, which should be prepared a day in advance.

Ingredients:

Yeast Sourdough:

> 90 g bread flour
> 75 ml water
> 1 g fresh yeast

Main Dough:

> 500 g bread flour
> 370 ml water
> 8 g fresh yeast
> 10 g salt
> 3 g sugar

Preparation:

Yeast Sourdough:

1. Prepare the yeast sourdough the day before you plan to make the bread.

2. Warm 15 ml of water and dissolve the yeast.

3. Warm the rest of the water to about 55°C and pour into a small glass bowl. Mix the flour with the water and add the yeast mix. Stir with a spatula for 1 minute and lightly knead for 1 - 2 minutes.

4. Pour a little olive oil on the surface of the dough, cover the bowl with kitchen film and leave it to ferment for 12 to 16 hours at between 18°C and 21°C or 24 to 72 hours at between 0°C and 4°C in the fridge. If the sourdough is allowed to ferment in the fridge, then let it warm up at room temperature for at least 1 hour before you use it.

Main Dough:

5. Warm 15 ml of water to 25°C - 30°C and dissolve the yeast and sugar in it. Allow it to rest for a few minutes until the yeast starts to ferment.

6. Mix the flour with salt in a large bowl. Gradually add 300 ml of water to the flour whilst mixing with a spatula.

7. When the mixture is consistent, add the sourdough, broken up into pieces, and mix well. Cover the bowl with a dry cloth and let it stand for about 10 minutes.

8. Next, add the remaining water little by little and then the yeast, sugar and water mixture. Mix well into the dough. Repeatedly knead the dough in the bowl for a minute at a time, allowing it to rest for 5 minutes in between, until the mixture is consistent. The dough is ready when it no longer sticks to the sides of the bowl and is completely smooth.

9. Lightly flour a work surface and put the dough onto it. Flatten the dough and fold it together again.

10. Place the dough in a greased bowl and cover it. Put it in a warm place and let it rise for about one hour, or until it doubles in volume.

11. To get rid of some of the fermentation gases, place the dough again on a well-floured work surface and lightly knead for a short while. Then form into a ball. Place the dough on a floured cloth and cover with another floured cloth. Let it stand for 10 minutes.

12. With the dough still on the floured cloth, flatten it by hand into a disk of about 2-3 cm thickness.

13. Prepare a greased baking tray and place the dough top down onto the tray using the cloth to help. Cover with the cloth and allow the dough to rise in a warm place until it has doubled in size (around 2 hours).

14. Preheat the oven to 220°C.

15. Use a sharp knife to make 4 cuts, each about 1cm deep, in the top of the risen dough to form a square shape close to the edge of the dough.

16. Reduce the oven temperature to 200°C, and bake the loaf for between 45 and 60 minutes until it has turned a golden dark brown. During the first 10 minutes you should put an oven proof bowl containing water in the bottom of the oven to create some steam to help the baking.

17. Remove the bread from the oven and let it cool on a rack before serving.

JALLULLA DE ALFACAR

Sugar Bread of Alfacar, Granada

Jallulla is sweet, flat bread that is somewhat similar to "Cañadas", but this particular version comes from the old Arab town of Alfacar close to Granada and is a sweet bread.

Jallulla is a type of primitive flat bread that had its origins in many rural parts of Spain where communal village ovens were not available and remote farms baked their own bread "under the ashes". There are various local names for this type of baking such as "jayulla", "jallulla" or "hallulla". This original primitive bread leant its name to this sweet version.

This is a simple bread to make and must have been a very special sweet treat in the days when remote farms could be difficult places to survive and were spartan at the best of times. Nowadays it is taken with breakfast or merienda.

Ingredients:

> 500 g flour
> 10 g salt
> 300 ml water
> 200 g sourdough (see recipe)
> Granulated sugar to coat
> 15 g fresh yeast

Preparation:

1. Mix and then knead all the ingredients together into a consistent dough.

2. Divide the dough into 2 equal pieces and roll these into balls. Allow the dough to rise until it doubles in volume.

3. When the dough has risen, roll out each dough ball until they are about 0.5 cm. thick.

4. Allow the dough to stand at room temperature to rise again for about 30 minutes.

5. Prick the surface of the dough every centimetre approximately.

6. Preheat the oven to 230°C.

7. Coat the tops of the loaves with olive oil and sprinkle with granulated sugar.

8. Bake at 230ºC for about 20 minutes.

9. Remove from the oven and allow to cool on a rack.

MEDIAS NOCHES

Midnight Rolls

These slightly sweet, soft bread rolls are every child's favourite treat in Spain. They can be eaten with a sweet filling such as a jam or a savoury filling such as ham or cheese. They acquired their name because they make a very easy late night snack - being quite soft and easy to cut and eat. They are best eaten the same day as they are baked as they become a little dry if left. There are a couple of variants including a recipe using honey instead of sugar.

Medias noches come in various sizes ranging from small bite-sized buns to full-sized sandwich buns. Despite their name, medias noches are eaten at all hours of the day, including for breakfast and even with lunch. No bakery in Spain is without them!

Ingredients (18 media noches):

> 500 g flour
> 200 ml milk
> 120 g butter
> 50 g sugar
> 25 g fresh yeast or 10 g dry yeast
> 1 teaspoon of salt
> Beaten egg to coat

Preparation:

1. Warm the milk a little and add the yeast. Mix thoroughly, adding the rest of the ingredients and knead until you have a smooth and consistent dough.

2. Let the dough stand in a warm place for an hour until the volume doubles.

3. Form the dough into balls (about 18) and place them on a greased baking tray. Remember they will double in size so don't make them too large and leave enough space between them.

4. Cover the tray lightly with kitchen film to avoid draughts and allow the rolls to ferment for about an hour or until they double in size. (You can accelerate this process by putting the tray in the oven at 40°C for about half an hour).

5. Preheat the oven to 190°C.

6. When the dough balls are fully risen, coat the tops of the buns with beaten egg.

7. Bake for only a few minutes (8 - 12 minutes, depending on size). They should be golden brown. Take care not to let them burn.

8. Remove from the oven and allow to cool before serving. They are best eaten within a day.

MOLLETES DE ANTEQUERA

Flat Baps of Antequera

The mollete is a perennial favourite in Andalucía. These flat breads are generally oval or round in shape. They are soft and crumbly, slightly under-baked. The softness of the bread makes them very popular with young and old alike.

Molletes are usually eaten for breakfast, cut in half horizontally, with a variety of toppings, such as olive oil and grated tomato, but any topping, sweet or savoury, works well. They are lightly toasted (to make up for the under- baking) and controversy still rages whether they should be toasted and then cut in half or cut in half and then toasted!

This flat bread has its origins in Jewish and Arabic bread baking traditions in the time of Al-Andalus and may even have come from India, according to some food historians. The word "mollete" originates from a word meaning "soft" according to 15th century dictionaries of Spanish.

Today, the epicentre of mollete production is the ancient city of Antequera but other famous bakeries are to be found in the little towns of Ecija and Algodonales. Many of the best molletes in fact come from bakeries in small villages well off the beaten track.

Ingredients:

Sourdough:

> 10 g fresh yeast
> 85 g flour
> 50 ml warm milk

Dough mix:

> 600 g flour
> 50 ml olive oil
> 350 ml water
> 1 teaspoon of salt
> 1 teaspoon of sugar

Preparation:

Sourdough mix:

1. Crumble the yeast into the warm milk and stir until the yeast is fully dissolved.

2. Pour this mixture over the flour and knead until the dough is smooth and consistent. Form it into a ball.

3. Put some warm water in a bowl and submerge the ball of sourdough. Cover the bowl with kitchen film. As soon as the ball of dough rises to the surface (5 to 10 minutes) the sourdough can be used.

Main dough mix:

4. Thoroughly mix the sourdough with all the other ingredients in a bowl, adding the water gradually as required (the amount depends on the type of flour) and knead until you have a smooth dough.

5. Form the dough into a ball, rub it with flour and put it in a bowl. Cover the bowl with a cloth and keep it away from drafts. Leave the dough to rise until it doubles its volume, which takes about 1 hour.

6. Preheat the oven to 190°C and put an ovenproof bowl of water in the oven to provide some steam during baking.

7. Remove the dough from the bowl, roll it out to remove the fermentation gases and then divide it into pieces of about 90 g each.

8. Form each piece into a ball and then mould them into a flat oval shape. Dust each mollete with flour and place them on a paper lined baking tray.

9. Bake for the first 10 minutes whilst spraying a little water into the oven and finally bake for a further 5 minutes.

10. Remove the molletes from the oven and leave them to cool on a rack.

OCHÍO DE BAEZA-ÚBEDA

Spicy Bread of Baeza-Úbeda

This is a bread roll made with olive oil, aniseed and sometimes with paprika powder. It is eaten both as a savoury bread (when made with paprika) and as a sweet roll (without the paprika but with a little sugar or honey).

It was traditionally baked in the convents that surround the Guadalquivir river valley in Andalucía. In the past, it was only eaten at Easter but gradually it has come into daily use, in the areas of Baeza, Úbeda and Jaen.

Green beans and salted cod often accompany the savoury version. This is a speciality during the Pilgrimage of the Virgin of Guadalupe, the patron saint of Úbeda or at the Pilgrimage of the Virgin of the Yedra de Baeza.

It is also common to fill these rolls with tuna, tomato, pate, or sausage. In Úbeda, it is usually eaten filled with chorizo and many bars in the region serve it as a generous tapa - the area is famous for its huge - free - tapas!

Here we give the recipe for the savoury version.

Ingredients:

> 500 ml warm water
> 1 kg flour
> 250 ml olive oil
> 1 tablespoon of salt
> 50 g fresh yeast
> 2 eggs
> Juice of half a lemon
> 1 tablespoon of aniseed
> Sweet paprika to taste
> Olive oil for coating
> Coarse salt to coat

Preparation:

1. Mix the warm water with the yeast in a large mixing bowl.

2. Add the salt, eggs, aniseed and lemon juice and mix well.

3. Add the flour and knead until you have a consistent dough.

4. Add the olive oil and continue to mix and knead until the dough is soft and manageable.

5. Divide the dough into pieces of around 80 g each and shape them into flattened balls. Place them on a baking tray lined with baking paper - leaving enough space in between pieces for them to rise.

6. Cover them with a clean cloth and allow the dough to fully rise.

7. Preheat the oven to 180°C.

8. In a separate bowl put some olive oil and mix in some sweet paprika powder - the amount you use is a matter of taste.

9. Gently brush the rolls with the oil and paprika mixture and scatter a little coarse salt over each roll.

10. Bake at 180° C with fan for about 20 minutes.

11. Remove from the oven and allow to cool on a rack before serving.

PAN DE CEA DE GALICIA

Cea Bread of Galicia

This bread is one of the breads in Spain that are protected under EU rules because they unique to a particular geographical zone (known as "Protected Geographical Indication"). Pan de Cea is considered typical of the area around the small town of San Cristovo de Cea in Galicia. This means that breads made using the name Pan de Cea must follow some very strict rules for the traditional preparation of the bread in order to use this name commercially.

San Cristovo de Cea is a town with a very long tradition of baking, with documented records of baking dating from the 13th century. The history of baking in the town centred on the Cistercian monastery of Santa Maria la Real de Oseira. This monastery sits on one of the busy pilgrimage routes to Santiago de Compostela. The village soon established its reputation as the "town of good bread" and the Pan de Cea is now famous and popular throughout Galicia.

In fact, the bread is so important to the area that the town celebrates an annual bread fiesta every July. Traditionally, the bread is baked in wood-fired ovens and most bakers in the area maintain this tradition. The bread is made with wheat flour and has a dense crumb and hard, crispy crust. The original recipe uses a sourdough as a raising agent.

Unfortunately, the recipe for authentic Pan de Cea is quite a closely guarded secret amongst the bakers of the town and there is no very clear and reliable recipe available for the mere mortals! Although many have tried to replicate the bread, the only way to taste the authentic Pan de Cea is to buy it locally.

PAN BENDITO DE SAN BLAS, MURCIA
Sweet Bread of San Blas, Murcia

This sweet bread from Murcia is associated with the feast of San Blas that takes place on the 3rd of February. There are several variants of this decorated bread but this most typical recipe comes from the old Arabic town of Yecla where the feast of San Blas has been celebrated since the 16th century and where giant versions of the bread have become incorporated in the town processions honouring the saint.

Smaller versions of the bread are blessed and distributed from house to house in the area and are very popular with everyone - especially the children of the town who are allowed to eat as much as they like on this special day.

Some say that the giant breads of the processions were designed to feed the poor in earlier times when the church took the responsibility for "good works". On the other hand, the distribution of sweet bread to the poor and to children created a powerful incentive for these groups to follow the Holy processions in the early days of Christian ascendancy after the Moorish defeats. Food is a powerful religious incentive amongst the poor and sweet food even more so!

Local folklore has it that the Pan Benito de San Blas is a protection against winter sore throats. This particular story seems to originate from the legend that San Blas saved a child with a fish bone in his throat. It is a charming story but has no nutritional basis apart from the use of oranges and lemons as ingredients.

The Bendito bread is traditionally prepared a day in advance to allow the dough to rise overnight - February being a cold time of year to ferment bread. Nowadays, it is eaten either by itself or with some hot chocolate.

Ingredients:

        500 g bread flour
        25 g fresh yeast
        125 ml milk
        125 ml olive oil
        125 g sugar
        1 egg
        Juice of 1 orange
        1 grated orange peel

1 grated lemon peel
1 tablespoon orange blossom water (optional)
A little beaten egg
A little syrup (an equal mix of sugar and water)

Preparation:

1. Traditionally, preparation of the dough needs to begin the day before the bread is to be baked.

2. Dissolve the yeast in the warmed milk. When the yeast is fully dissolved, add the rest of the ingredients, except the flour, and mix well.

3. Next, add half of the flour and mix until well blended.

4. Add the remainder of the flour and mix well. Knead the mix thoroughly by hand. Place the dough in a bowl, cover with a clean cloth and allow it to rise overnight.

5. After the dough has risen, put aside 10% for decorating the loaf.

6. Mould the remaining dough into a ball and place it on baking paper.

7. Traditionally, decorating the loaf includes placing balls, leaves, and flowers around the top of the loaf. The previously separated dough is cut and moulded into these shapes and placed on top of the main bread dough. Generally, it is best to add a little extra flour to this dough so that they don't lose their shape in baking.

8. Cut the dough in five or more places around the perimeter so that it opens slightly during baking and forms segments.

9. When the decoration is completed, baste the dough with beaten egg mix.

10. Preheat the oven to 180°C and bake for approximately 30 minutes until just turning golden brown (ideally with oven heat from above and below). Check the progress of baking by inserting a metal skewer. If it comes out clean, the bread is ready.

11. Whilst the bread is still warm coat with a little syrup and let it cool completely on a rack.

12. If you want to give the Bendito an authentic touch you can decorate it with what is locally called "pajaricas". These thin wooden skewers (as used in kebabs) are decorated with strips of white paper. Of course, if you wish you can also have the bread blessed by the local priest as well!

PAN CANDEAL DE VALLADOLID

Candeal Bread of Valladolid

This is a flat bread made with white wheat flour. Valladolid, a city in the region of Castilla y Leon is famous for its Candeal breads, often decorated with rustic images. The bread has a thin crust and a dense crumb. This bread is also known as Lechugino and can be found in Palencia and Salamanca in the same region. The following recipe is very simple. There are many variants. In some areas of Spain, every village has its own version and name for this bread, such as the well-known Pan de Cruz of Castille-LaMancha.

Ingredients:

    250 g bread flour (higher protein)
    250 g plain flour (medium protein)
    250 ml warm water
    10 g salt
    25 g fresh yeast

Preparation:

1. Put the warm water with the yeast in a large bowl and stir until the yeast is dissolved.

2. Slowly add the flour and salt and mix thoroughly until it forms a dough.

3. Knead the dough by hand until it is consistent.

4. Shape the dough into a round ball and place it on a baking tray lined with a sheet of baking paper. Flatten the dough by hand until it is 2-3 cm thick and round or oblog in shape.

5. Cut the dough horizontally and vertically at 2 cm intervals with a sharp knife. Cover with a cloth and allow it to rise for 45 minutes at room temperature.

6. Place the dough and baking paper on an oven tray. Bake the bread in a preheated oven at 220°C for 25 minutes.

7. Remove from the oven and cool on a rack before serving.

PAN DE CANELA, PASAS Y NUECES

Cinnamon Bread with Raisins and Walnuts

This is a classic traditional fruit bread made in various forms throughout Spain. It is an easy bread to make. It is usually made with raisins and walnuts and is naturally sweet. It is often eaten for breakfast and sometimes with a savoury topping such as ham or Idiazabal cheese. The combination of sweet and savoury tastes is common and popular in Spain.

Ingredients:

500 g bread flour
20 g sugar
10 g salt
6 g dried yeast or 18 g fresh yeast
5 g cinnamon powder
1 egg
30 g butter (softened)
120 ml whole milk
180 ml water
250 g raisins
120 g chopped walnuts

Preparation:

1. Mix the flour, sugar, salt, yeast, and cinnamon in a large bowl. When these ingredients are well mixed, add the egg, soft butter, milk and water all at the same time. Use a spoon to mix and if necessary add a little flour. The dough should be moist but not sticky.

2. Knead the dough for about 10 minutes (again adding a little flour, if necessary). Just before finishing the kneading, add the raisins and chopped walnuts and continue kneading the dough thoroughly until the fruit and nuts are evenly distributed throughout.

3. Let the dough rise somewhere warm until it has doubled in size.

4. Knead the dough again to remove the fermentation gases. Take a rectangular bread baking tin and shape the dough so that it fits the tin and is about half way up the sides.

5. Preheat the oven to 180°C.

6. Bake for about 30 minutes.

7. Take the tin out of the oven and remove the loaf from the tin. Let it cool on a rack before serving.

PAN CATETO DE MÁLAGA

Traditional Country Bread of Málaga - Cateto

The word "cateto" in Spanish has several meanings and implications. It can mean "old-fashioned" but it is also used in a derogatory sense to mean backward. Some urbanites in Spain unkindly refer to their country cousins as "cateto". However, cateto bread is the backbone of the Andalucian diet and no meal or tapa would be complete without some of this old-style country bread. There are many, many variants of "cateto" bread and here we have a recipe for one that is popular in the province of Málaga.

Ingredients:

    1 kg bread flour
    580 ml water
    20 g salt
    8 g dry yeast or 25 g fresh yeast

Preparation:

1. Dissolve the yeast in the water.

2. Put the flour in a large bowl, gradually add the water/yeast and mix with the flour until it is fully absorbed. Add the salt and work it into the dough.

3. Knead the dough on a floured surface until smooth and elastic.

4. Take another mixing bowl, rub some olive oil on the inside and put the dough into it. Cover the bowl with a damp cloth and let the dough rise until it has doubled in size.

5. Take out the dough again and knead it a little. Shape the dough into a ball.

6. Line a baking tray with baking paper and place the ball of dough on it. Cover it with a damp cloth and let it rise a second time until the dough has doubled in volume again.

7. Preheat the oven to 240°C. Make cuts on the surface of the bread dough with a sharp knife.

8. Quickly spray the dough with some water and put it into the hot oven. This will make a crispy crust. Bake for 10 minutes at 240°C

9. After 10 minutes, reduce the temperature to 200° and bake for another hour.

10. Remove the bread and let it cool on a rack.

PAN DE LECHE GOMERO (CANARIA)

Milk Bread of La Gomera, Canary Islands

This is slightly sweet milk bread, traditionally baked on the small island of La Gomera in Las Islas Canarias (the Canary Islands). It is sometimes eaten at breakfast but is also taken as a simple dessert after lunch. There are some variants - such as using fresh cheese in the centre of each bun. They can also be made with wholemeal flour.

Ingredients:

> 500 g flour
> 100 g butter
> 250 ml milk
> 2 eggs
> 1 egg beaten with a little sugar to coat the bread
> 15 g dried yeast
> 1 pinch of salt
> Cinnamon powder
> Grated lemon peel
> Aniseed

Preparation:

1. Put the flour into a bowl. Make a hollow in the middle of the flour and add the yeast, salt, milk, two of the three eggs and the butter (at room temperature). Mix until a dough begins to form.

2. Knead the dough on a floured work surface, adding more flour on the surface as needed, and continue kneading until the dough is consistent and does not stick.

3. Leave the dough to rise in a warm place until it doubles in volume (about an hour).

4. When the dough has risen, divide it into 5 or 6 individual portions.

5. Lightly knead each piece of dough and shape it into a bun. (Some bakers put some small pieces of white cheese in the centre of the dough but this is not essential).

6. Once the dough has been shaped into buns, allow them to rise for another hour, and then make small cuts in the top, with a knife.

7. Preheat the oven to 200°C.

8. The remaining egg is beaten with the sugar. The tops of the buns are then coated with this mixture and the buns are placed on a baking tray lined with baking paper.

9. Bake for 20 minutes until well browned.

10. Remove from the oven and allow to cool before serving.

PAN DE PAGÈS DE CATALUÑA

Catalan Rustic Bread

The Pan De Payés ("Pagès" in Catalan) is certainly the most typical and traditional bread of Cataluña. It was first noted in the 14th and 15th century murals of La Pia Almoina (an almshouse) in the city of Lleida in Western Cataluña. This institution was founded in the 12th century to take in and feed the poor. The murals show the typical breads of the area at the time, quite clearly including the Pan de Pagès. At the time this type of dark bread was eaten by the poorer classes.

Pan De Payés is a round, crusty bread, with a tender open crumb. It is not baked in a tin (it is formed by hand), has a long rising time and tends to have an irregular appearance as often the crust splits.

Despite being simple bread, it has an excellent aroma and taste and remains tender for several days at least. It is often said that it was only necessary to bake once per week because of these excellent storage properties. Modern loaves usually weigh 500g or 1000g but in the past loaves often had a weight of up to 5kg. These larger loaves could be eaten many days after baking and this made them useful for feeding large numbers of people - as in the almshouses of Cataluña.

This recipe uses sourdough (masa madre) and some fresh yeast. Sourdough is an old raising agent that is still popular in many baking traditions. We have provided recipes to make sourdough (see the index). A modern version of the bread is made with just yeast but the sourdough version is more authentic. Also, in addition to wheat flour you can add some whole wheat flour or rye flour, so that the crumb is denser and the bread gains in flavour and appears more rustic.

Like many traditional recipes in Cataluña, an almost identical bread with the same name is made in Las Islas Baleares (the Balearic Islands).

Ingredients:

> 1 kg bread flour
> 700 ml water
> 20 g salt
> 200 g solid sourdough
> 10 g fresh yeast

Preparation:

1. Mix the flour and water in a bowl and let it stand for 1 hour.

2. Add the salt, fresh yeast and sourdough and knead until you achieve a smooth, elastic dough.

3. Put the dough in a bowl and cover it to stop it drying out and let it rise.

4. After 15 minutes remove the dough and place it on the work surface. Fold the dough over on itself (as if closing an envelope). Put it back in the bowl and cover again. Allow to rise for 1 hour more and then repeat the folding. Place it in the bowl again, cover, and finally allow the dough to rise for another hour. Note the total rising time at this stage is 2 hours and 15 minutes (depending on the temperature).

5. After the dough has risen, place it on the work surface again. Cut it into either 4 equal pieces or 2 equal pieces (for 4 or 2 loaves).

6. Shape each piece of dough by pulling the edges towards the centre until forming a ball. Place each piece of dough on a floured cloth, cover them and allow to rise for a further 1.5 hours approximately (depending on room temperature).

7. Preheat the oven to 210°C. Cut a cross in the top of the loaves and bake them until they are golden brown (that can be after around 40 minutes, depending on the oven and the size of the loaves).

8. Remove from the oven and allow to cool on a rack before serving.

PAN DE PAPAS DE LAS ISLAS CANARIAS

Potato Bread of the Canary Islands

Potatoes are an important crop in Gran Canaria and potato bread is a typical and traditional local bread, especially in rural areas. It's a slightly sweet, rich bread which is eaten either cold or warm. It is especially delicious spread with butter and is eaten at any time of the day.

Ingredients:

> 500 g bread flour
> 200 g boiled potatoes
> 250 ml water
> 90 g sugar
> 90 g butter
> 1 teaspoon of dry yeast
> 1 teaspoon of salt
> 1 grated lemon peel
> 0.5 teaspoon of cinnamon powder
> 0.5 teaspoon of aniseed
> 1 egg to coat

Preparation:

1. Weigh out 200 g of boiled potatoes. Mash the potatoes and add the cinnamon, aniseed and lemon peel. Mix well.

2. Add the butter (at room temperature) in cubes, and add the salt and sugar.

3. Add the water along with the flour and finally the dried yeast and mix well into a consistent dough. A mixer is helpful but it can be done by hand.

4. When the dough is thoroughly mixed and kneaded, cover it with a cloth and leave it to rise in a warm place.

5. When the dough has risen, shake some flour on the work surface and knead again to remove the fermentation gases from the dough. If it is too sticky, add a little flour.

6. Divide the dough in two with a sharp knife and shape each piece into a round. Make some cuts across the top of the dough with a knife.

Cover again with a cloth and leave the dough to double in size - which will take at least an hour depending on the ambient temperature.

7. Preheat the oven to 250°C. Prepare some oven proof containers with water and place in the oven to generate some steam to help the baking.

8. Coat the dough with a beaten egg and sprinkle with a little sugar and cinnamon.

9. Bake at 190°C for about 20 to 30 minutes until golden brown. Remove from the oven and place on a rack to cool before serving.

PATAQUETA DE L'HORTA, VALENCIA
Rustic Bread Rolls of Valencia

Reputedly, this country bread originated with an Arab recipe from the garrisons of Valencia and is still baked in a Moorish half-moon shape. In Valencia, it was traditionally the bread eaten by farm workers for lunch and was often filled with whatever was to hand such as tomatoes, broad beans, a local black pudding or simply with some olive oil and a pinch of salt. It has a crunchy crust and a spongy crumb. This version uses a starter yeast mix that needs to be prepared the day before baking.

Ingredients:

Starter yeast:

> 100 ml water
> 50 g flour
> 10 g fresh yeast
> 0.5 teaspoon of sugar

For the dough:

> 450 g bread flour
> 200 ml warm water
> 10 g salt
> All the starter yeast mix

Preparation:

Starter yeast:

1. Thoroughly mix the fresh yeast with the water, flour and sugar in a bowl and cover with transparent film. Leave it in the refrigerator overnight or for up to 48 hours.

Main dough:

2. Take the starter yeast out of the fridge and leave it at room temperature until it starts to frement. The time will depend on the ambient temperature.

3. Once the starter yeast is visibly fermenting, add it to the rest of the ingredients (except the salt) in a mixing bowl.

4. Mix and knead for about 10 minutes until you have consistent dough.

5. Add the salt to the dough and knead again for 10 minutes more.

6. Sprinkle the dough with flour. Divide this into 150 g portions and create a ball of dough with each portion. Let them stand for about 20 minutes until they have doubled in size.

7. To create the characteristic crescent shape: When the round portions of dough have risen, flatten each one with the palm of your hand. Use a sharp knife to make a cut from the centre of the dough to the edge. Carefully open this cut to create the crescent shape. Use the knife to make a cut in the top of the dough.

8. Let the loaves rise again until they have doubled in volume and then sprinkle them with flour.

9. Preheat the oven to 200ºC and place an ovenproof container filled with water in the oven to provide steam during baking.

10 Bake for 30 minutes (with steam).

11. Remove from the oven and allow the pataquetas to cool on a rack.

REGAÑÁ DE ANDALUCÍA

Savoury Crackers, Sevilla

The regañá is a type of very thin, crispy bread originating in Alcalá de Guadaíra, a town about 17 km from Sevilla. In former times, the town was known as Alcalá de los Panaderos (Alcalá of the Bakers) because it provided most of Sevilla's bread. Regañás are now popular throughout Andalucía and are served with various dishes or as part of a tapa. They are simple to make.

Regañás have been made for many centuries and their low moisture content made them suitable issue for soldiers and sailors on long journeys including on the long damp sea journeys from Sevilla during the conquest of the Americas.

Regañás are sometimes seasoned with sesame seed and they vary in thickness. There are similar dry breads from other parts of Spain (and elsewhere in Europe) but around Sevilla, there are small towns and villages that are entirely occupied with the production of these types of dried breads and other savoury biscuits and bread sticks.

Ingredients:

200 g flour
35 ml water
25 ml white wine
50 ml olive oil
Half a teaspoon of salt
1 teaspoon of sesame seed

Preparation:

1. Preheat the oven to 180°C.

2. Mix all the ingredients together until you have smooth, uniform dough.

3. Roll out the dough thinly with a rolling pin (the thickness is a matter of personal preference - everything up from the thickness of a cream cracker may be found).

4. Cut the dough into rectangles or squares (a pizza cutter is useful for this).

5. Bake for about 20-25 minutes. If you have made them very thin, they will be baked sooner, so check at around 20 minutes.

6. Remove from the oven and allow to cool before serving.

SALAÍLLAS GRANADINAS

Granada Flat Bread

In Granada city, and in many parts of Spain, the 3rd of May is a very special and colourful day, the "Día de la Cruz" - Day of the Cross. Every barrio in the city creates a cross of flowers and takes enormous pride in their work. Some of the crosses are huge and very beautifully decorated and locals and visitors can easily spend a day visiting the various barrios to admire these creations. It is an old tradition dating from the 6th century and the Emperor Constantine and his mother's search for the "true cross". Granada is famous throughout Spain for the beauty of these decorated crosses.

Of course, this important day is not just a religious event; there are also lots of culinary delights. The eating of salaíllas in Granada is one of them. Traditionally, this flat bread is eaten on this day accompanied by broad beans, ham, boiled dried cod or chorizo. The bread is also eaten on the first Sunday of February during the feast day of St Cecilio. It is a bread that is often used with tapas and combines well with many sweet and savoury toppings from fried garlic to honey.

This is a very simple bread to prepare and the only complication is that you need to prepare the starter yeast the night before you intend to bake the bread.

Ingredients:

Starter Yeast:

> 400 g bread flour
> 350 ml water
> 1 g fresh yeast

Dough:

> 200 g flour
> 10 ml olive oil
> 10 g salt
> 8 g fresh yeast

To coat:

> Olive oil
> Coarse salt

Preparation:

Starter Yeast:

Mix all the ingredients together, cover with plastic wrap, and let it ferment overnight.

Dough:

1. Use a large mixing bowl and mix the starter yeast together with all the other dough ingredients. Knead until you have consistent dough.

2. Cover the dough with a damp cloth and allow it to stand for 15 mins. Then knead it again.

3. Allow the dough to ferment again for 75 minutes.

4. Place the dough on a lightly floured work surface, knead again and divide it into pieces depending on the size and number of salaíllas you want to make. Pieces of dough that, when flattened, have a diameter of around 10-15 cm, are typical.

5. In terms of shape, you can make them oval or round - it does not matter. The most important traditional feature is that the dough is first pressed flat and then given a series of dimples with your knuckles.

6. Preheat the oven to 250°C.

7. The dimples you formed in the dough are now filled with olive oil and coarse salt, the bread placed on an oven tray lined with baking paper and baked for 12 to 15 minutes.

TORTA DE GAZPACHO MANCHEGO

Flat Gazpacho Bread of La Mancha

The gazpacho of La Mancha is famous. It is actually more of a hot stew than the cold soup of the same name found in Andalucía. It is a warming winter dish. Traditionally, it was made and eaten by shepherds. These shepherds crossed the vast plains of this region with their flocks and needed a simple bread to make on their journeys. This crispy bread is the traditional accompaniment of the gazpacho of La Mancha. This very simple, ancient unleavened bread can be found in many parts of the world but especially throughout the Levant.

Torta de Gazpacho is very simple to make and can be eaten with any stew. Generally, the gazpacho is poured on top of the flat bread and eaten with pieces of the bread or, alternatively, the bread is broken into the gazpacho in a bowl.

No quantities are provided here. Simply mix until you have dry dough.

Ingredients:

> Flour
> Water
> Salt to taste

Preparation:

1. Pour water into a bowl. Add flour and salt (to taste). Mix until you have dough that is not sticky.

2. Sprinkle flour on a work surface and roll out the dough, adding flour if necessary, until you have a thin sheet.

3. Preheat the oven to about 200°C.

4. Cut out large circles of dough and place them on a baking tray lined with baking paper and bake until the bread starts to brown.

5. Remove from the oven and allow to cool. As soon as it is cool, serve the bread with gazpacho.

---o0o---

2.2 Sweet Biscuits

Outside Spain, when we think of biscuits (or "cookies" in the USA), we generally think of them as being small, flat, dry and crispy. However, in Spain a biscuit (galleta) may be almost any size, thickness or shape. They may be dry or moist and they are often closer to a small cake than the dry biscuits of Northern Europe or the USA.

Spain has an immense range of traditional sweet biscuits and many are associated with special events such as religious festivals. At Christmas time, for instance, the shops of Spain are full of a huge range of seasonal biscuits, produced by many artisan biscuit manufacturers and often packed in their original old-fashioned cartons and wrappings.

Entire towns are dedicated to biscuit manufacturing and these towns are often based in the areas where raw materials originate. In the old Moorish town of Estepa (Arabic: "Istabba") in the province of Sevilla, dominated by an ancient Arab castle, it seems that almost every second house is a manufacturer of traditional mantecados or polvorones. The hinterland of the town has kilometres of olive and almond groves and pig farms that supply the raw materials for the town's biscuit industries. Production for the huge Christmas biscuit season ramps up as soon as the almond harvest begins in August or September and the scale of production is truly impressive. Estepa alone produces around 18 million kilos per year, employing around 2000 workers from the surrounding villages.

Many of the traditional sweet biscuits of Spain originated during Spain's Moorish period. The Moors brought many sweet products to Spain (including sugar) but they also realised that sweet biscuits provided an ideal way of using up excess production of flour and other ingredients in a way that gave them a longer storage life. The Moors use of sugar in biscuits and the dry texture of biscuits allowed for them to be stored and remain fresh for months at a time.

In a strange twist of history, the most famous and popular Christmas biscuits, mantecados and polvorones, which were originally based on a similar Levantine sweet known as "ghurayba" are now made with pork fat ("manteca" in Spanish). This change in recipe resulted from an official decree from the Spanish Inquisition that had the objective of uncovering Jews and Muslims merging into the local Christian population in order to hide from the inquisitors in the new lands of the Christian conquest. Presumably, the perverse logic of the Inquisitor's decree was that someone who refused one of these biscuits could be denounced as a Muslim or Jew.

At the same time that the use of sweet biscuits was being employed as a slightly absurd means of ethnic cleansing by the Inquisition against Jews and Muslims, many Christian monastic orders began to dominate the cultural and economic landscape of Spain. Whether or not these powerful Christian monastic institutions conspired to control the confectionary and sweet biscuit market is unknown. However, it is an interesting coincidence that many sweet biscuits (and pastries) have religious names and many are associated with specific Christian feast days. Thus the manufacture of many of these (originally Moorish or Sephardic Jewish) sweet biscuits became an important activity for convents and monasteries throughout Spain and especially in the last Moorish outpost in the country, Andalucía. It has been suggested that the ultra-Christian conquerors of Spain, under the control of the "Catholic Monarchs" Isabel and Ferdinand, deliberately encouraged the monastic orders to gain control of the sweet bakery market in order to associate something delicious with public adherence to their fundamentalist Christian practices of the time. To this day, some of Spain's best biscuits come from convents founded after the Christian conquest, frequently made with ingredients from their own farms, elaborated by hand, and packed with unambiguously Christian motifs and sold to celebrate Christian feasts.

Perhaps the Spanish sweet biscuit is one of the world's first attempts by a government to use sugar as a means of social and religious persuasion and control, in a similar way that the monastic orders of Belgium (and Germany) have for centuries produced dozens of the best (and strongest) beers in Europe!

ALFAJORES ANDALUCES DE MEDINA-SIDONIA
Spiced Bread of Medina-Sidonia

This is a sweet with a very clear history. It has descended almost unchanged from the Hispano-Arabic era. The alfajor (sometimes also called alajú) is a traditional sweet from Andalucía, but the most well known producers come from the old town of Medina-Sidonia in the province of Cádiz.

The word alfajor is believed to derive from the Arabic for "excellent," or perhaps from the Arabic 'al-hasú' meaning "filled". The Arabic cookbook "tabīkh Kitāb al-Maghreb" mentions a very similar spicy sweet bread using honey. There is quite a bit of written evidence that this sweet was well known in this part of southern Spain during the twelfth and thirteenth centuries and it pops up again after the Christian invasion of the area. The ingredients described in these accounts are pretty much the same ingredients that are in use to the present day.

Today, the town of Medina-Sidonia is considered the authentic source of this sweet biscuit and has a regulating council to protect the name and excellent quality of the "Alfajor de Medina-Sidonia". This is very much a Christmas sweet and, despite its origins in deepest Andalucía, it is known and loved throughout Spain.

Ingredients (for 40):

Biscuit Dough:

> 120 g sugar
> 120 ml water
> 400 g breadcrumbs
> 200 g raw whole hazelnuts
> 300 g whole, blanched, peeled almonds
> 20 g whole aniseed
> 75 g sesame seed
> 1 g ground coriander seed (optional)
> 10 g cinnamon powder
> 0.5 tsp of ground cloves
> 450 g honey

Syrup for coating:

> 200 ml water
> 200 g sugar

<u>Sugar for coating:</u>

Icing sugar for coating

Preparation:

1. Make a syrup: Pour the water into a small saucepan and add the sugar. Put the pan on medium-high heat. Stir until the sugar is completely dissolved. Bring to the boil and then reduce to a simmer until the mixture has thickened into a syrup. Remove from the heat and allow it to cool.

2. Toast the almonds and hazelnuts. Finely grind the nuts, aniseed, sesame and coriander seeds in a blender. Place in a medium-sized bowl. Add the ground cinnamon and cloves and mix with a wooden spoon.

3. Measure the honey into a heatproof bowl and heat it in a water bath until almost boiling.

4. Pour the syrup into the bowl with the nuts, breadcrumbs and spice mixture. Stir well. Whilst mixing, gradually add the warm honey. Combine all the ingredients thoroughly.

5. Whilst the mixture is still warm, form it into small sausage-shaped rolls by hand and place them on greaseproof paper to cool.

6. Make another syrup in a saucepan. Remove from the heat and leave to cool for 5-10 minutes. Roll the alfajores in this syrup and then roll them in icing sugar. Cool on greaseproof paper.

7. When they are cool, wrap them in absorbent paper. Ready to serve!

AMARGUILLOS

Almond and Sweet Potato Biscuit

This little almond biscuit is made in several parts of Spain, but in particular in Medina-Sidonia and Grazalema in Cádiz, Villoldo in Palencia, and Sahagún in León. Traditionally (and to the present day), these biscuits are baked in and sold by convents. The type that comes from Medina-Sidonia is made with sweet potato as in the following recipe. Despite some regional variations, the amarguillo is always topped with an almond.

Ingredients:

> 250 g ground almonds
> 250 g icing sugar
> Juice from half a lemon
> 1 egg
> 100 g cooked sweet potato
> Icing sugar to decorate
> Whole almonds for garnish

Preparation:

1. Mix the sweet potato with the icing sugar, egg and lemon juice into a consistent paste.

2. Next, mix in the ground almonds. The result is a slightly sticky dough that is easier to work using a pastry / piping bag.

3. Preheat the oven to 200°C.

4. Line a baking tray with baking paper. Squeeze out little rounds of dough on the baking paper. Keep them small - with the diameter about 2 or 3 times the length of an almond.

5. Place a raw whole almond in the centre of each biscuit and use a sieve to shake some icing sugar over them.

6. Bake for a few minutes (five to seven minutes is enough) just until they begin to become golden. Remove from the oven and allow to cool.

CARAJITOS DEL PROFESOR DE SALAS DE ASTURIAS

Hazelnut Biscuits of the Professor of Salas, Asturias

The rather complicated name of this biscuit derives from a café-restaurant in the Asturian town of Salas that was opened in 1918 and run by "Pepin the Professor", a musical maestro. He named the café the "Casa del Profesor" (House of the Professor). Little by little, he specialised in baking biscuits and cakes made from hazelnuts and other dried fruits in the traditional Asturian way. The bakery continues to this day and these famous Asturian biscuits are still a speciality of the Casa del Profesor and are made fresh every day.

Ingredients:

> 250 g ground hazelnuts
> 130 g sugar
> 3 egg whites (90 g)

Preparation:

1. Preheat the oven to 180°C using lower and upper heating.

2. Prepare a baking tray with baking paper.

3. Shell, skin and grind the hazelnuts in a food processor or coffee grinder.

4. Mix the ground hazelnuts in a bowl with the sugar, stirring well so that the two ingredients are well combined.

5. Add the egg whites one at a time, whisking them into the mixture with a fork.

6. The objective is to achieve a soft dough so, depending on the ground hazelnuts, you may need more or less egg whites.

7. Use two tablespoons or a small ice cream scoop to place equal portions of the dough on the baking paper. Allow for some expansion during baking.

8. Bake at 180°C for twenty minutes or until golden.

9. Remove from the oven and leave for 5 minutes before placing them on a rack to cool completely.

CORDIALES DE MURCIA

Filled Almond Sweet of Murcia

These are almond biscuits, typical of Christmas in Murcia, and made in most homes in the region. They are believed to be from the town of Pacheco but can now be found in most of Murcia. They have a long tradition as a sweet biscuit in several Murcian convents.

Ingredients:

>500 g ground almonds
>350 g sugar
>6 eggs
>Grated peel of 1 lemon
>Angel hair
>Baking wafers

Preparation:

1. Put all the ingredients in a bowl (except for the angel hair and wafers), mix and knead into a consistent dough.

2. Preheat the oven to about 150°C.

3. In the meantime, place pieces of wafer large enough to take a piece of dough 6-8 cm wide on a baking tray.

4. Form small balls of dough, fill each with a portion of "angel hair", and close up the dough ball again and flatten a little. Place each cordial on a piece of wafer on the baking tray.

5. When the tray is filled, place it in the oven for 15 to 20 minutes until the cordiales are golden coloured.

6. Remove from the oven and allow them to cool completely before serving.

CORTADILLOS DE ANÍS

Christmas Anís Biscuits

This is another popular Christmas biscuit still made in several convents in Andalucía, particularly in the province of Sevilla. It is simple to make.

Ingredients:

>250 g lard (or butter / margarine)
>3 egg yolks
>0.5 glass of sweet anís liquor
>125 g sugar
>Juice of 1 lemon
>500 g flour
>Almonds and walnuts, raw, shelled and peeled
>Sugar to decorate

Preparation:

1. Preheat the oven to 250°C.

2. Separate the egg whites from the yolks.

3. Thoroughly mix the egg yolks with the butter (at room temperature).

4. Add the anís liquor, sugar, lemon juice and, finally the flour. Beat each ingredient into the mixture, one by one, to form a dough.

5. Roll out the dough on a work surface until it is about 1.5 cm thick.

6. Use a dough cutter of your preferred shape to form the biscuits (traditionally star-shaped) and place them on an oven tray lined with baking paper.

7. Place an almond slice or piece of walnut on the centre of each biscuit.

8. Bake for about 10 minutes, remove from the oven and allow to cool.

9. When almost cool, coat with sugar.

CRESPELLS DE MALLORCA

Easter Biscuits of Mallorca

Crespells are a simple traditional sweet biscuit of Mallorca in the Balearic Islands (Islas Baleares). They are most often made for the celebration of Christmas and Easter. Traditionally the dough is shaped into stars, flowers, moons and other figures using a dough cutter.

There are some variants in different parts of the Baleares, one of which uses orange juice. Crespells are simple to make and generally made with the active help of the children of the household who delight in cutting out their favourite shapes. One version suggests dipping the biscuits in melted chocolate.

Ingredients:

    100 g lard (or butter / margarine)
    100 g sugar
    20 ml olive oil
    60 ml orange juice
    1 egg yolk
    500 g flour
    Icing sugar to decorate

Preparation:

1. Mix the olive oil with the lard using your hands, until creamy. Add the remaining ingredients except the flour and mix until consistent.

2. Finally, add the sifted flour. Knead by hand (or in a food processor) until you have a smooth dough (to make it smooth you may need to finish kneading by hand). Allow the dough to rest for about 15 minutes.

3. Roll out the dough with a rolling pin and cut out biscuits using shaped dough cutters.

4. Bake in a preheated oven for 10-15 minutes at 180°C until they begin to brown.

5. Remove from the oven and sprinkle with icing sugar.

FEOS DE ZAMORA

Almond Biscuits of Zamora

The name of this biscuit is hardly complimentary - it translates as the "Uglies of Zamora". Despite the name, these almond biscuits are a local speciality and are delicious. They originate in the province of Zamora in North-West Spain. The tiny, old village of Cerecinos de Campo is famous for these biscuits though the larger towns of Benavente and Villalpando are also well known for their "Feos". These villages are situated in the fertile and pretty district known as Tierra de Campos ("land of fields"). The area is also known as the "Gothic Plains" because it was a zone long settled by the Visigoths during their colonisation of Northern Spain.

The origin of the name of this biscuit appears to be around the end of the 19th century when a local baker made an error in his almond dough recipe. The dough apparently resembled that of the Guirlache nougat, which is known as "ugly dough".

Despite the name, the biscuits are eaten throughout the year but are especially popular in this part of Zamora during the fiesta of the local patron saint San António de Padua on June 13.

Ingredients:

> 250 g sugar
> 250 g raw almonds, peeled and chopped
> 125 g flour
> 2 egg whites (use 3 if the eggs are small)

Preparation:

1. Preheat the oven to 180°C.

2. Mix the sugar, chopped almonds and flour in a large bowl. Put aside.

3. In a separate bowl beat the egg whites and add this to the sugar, almond, and flour mix.

4. Use a fork to blend the dough until all the ingredients are well incorporated and the dough takes on a pasty and sticky consistency.

5. Place a sheet of baking paper on an oven tray. Wet your hands and place small portions of dough on the baking paper, level them and keep the portions separate by a couple of centimetres to allow for expansion during baking.

6. Finally, place the tray into the oven and bake for about 20 minutes or until golden brown.

7. Take the tray out of the oven and use a spatula to remove the biscuits. Place them on a rack to cool.

8. Once cooled, the biscuits can be served. They can be safely stored for several weeks in an airtight container.

GALLETA CAMPURRIANA

Almond Shortcake Biscuit

This rustic crispy biscuit is named after an area of Cantabria in the North of Spain called Campoo, but this biscuit is now found throughout Spain. It is a popular biscuit to be taken at breakfast or for merienda.

Ingredients (25 or 30 biscuits):

125 g butter
125 g sugar
1 egg
450 g flour
60 g ground almonds
8 g dried yeast

Preparation:

1. Chop the butter into small pieces in a large bowl and allow it to soften at room temperature for about twenty minutes. Add the sugar and beat until it is consistent and creamy.

2. Break the egg and add to the bowl whilst continuing to mix until completely incorporated.

3. Add the sifted flour, the ground almonds and the yeast and stir slowly with a spatula, until the dough is smooth and consistent.

4. Preheat the oven to 200ºC.

5. Line a baking tray with baking paper.

6. Make small balls with the dough and crush them lightly with the palm of your hand, but do not make them too flat - they should be rounded on top.

7. Place each on the baking tray making sure to leave a space between them.

8. Bake for 12-15 minutes until they start to become golden brown.

9. Allow the biscuits to cool on the tray before serving. When cool, they can be stored in an airtight box to keep them crispy.

GALLETAS DE ANÍS

Anís Biscuits

Anís is one of the typical Christmas flavours in Spanish seasonal baking. It's use originated in Arabic times, when aniseed was added to various heavy dishes to aid digestion. In post-Moorish Spain, the use of strong anís liquor became common.

Ingredients:

100 g flour
150 g sugar
40 g butter at room temperature
A teaspoon of sodium bicarbonate
2 tablespoons of anís liquor
1 tablespoon of milk
Icing sugar (for decoration after baking)

Preparation:

1. Put all the ingredients into a bowl, mix well and then knead until you have a ball of consistent dough.

2. Preheat the oven to 170°C. Roll out the dough to about 1 cm thick and cut out the biscuits with star-shaped or round biscuit cutters. Place each biscuit on an oven tray lined with baking paper.

3. Put the tray in the middle of the oven and bake for about 15 minutes or until the biscuits are golden brown and crispy.

4. Allow them to cool on a rack, lightly sprinkle with icing sugar and serve.

GALLETAS DE PASAS DE MALAGA

Moscatel Raisin Biscuits

Moscatel raisins come from an area of Málaga province known as the Axarquía. Apart from their use in wine production, they are also extensively dried for use in cooking and baking. Here is a local recipe that uses the raisins in a biscuit. The raisins are rehydrated using the local wine or a strong spirit such as brandy or rum.

Ingredients:

150 g raisins (Moscatel)
3 eggs
100 g butter
125 g sugar
200 g flour
120 ml brandy, rum or Málaga Virgen wine

Preparation:

1. Soak the raisins in the Málaga Virgen wine (or brandy or rum) and put aside until they have swollen.

2. Leave the butter to soften at room temperature. Mix it with the sugar into a smooth paste. Add the beaten eggs one by one.

3. Add the raisins, the Málaga Virgen and the flour, gradually working it into a dough until it has a consistent texture, neither too liquid nor too thick. Preheat the oven to 180°C.

4. Line an oven tray with baking paper.

5. Use a spoon to place little balls of dough onto the baking tray. Make sure to keep them separate, because when they start to bake they will expand.

6. Put the biscuits to bake in the upper part of the oven for 20 to 30 minutes.

7. When they are golden brown, remove them from the oven and allow them to cool before eating.

GALETTE DE PÉROUGES DE CATALUÑA

Catalan Sugar Cake

This rich, sweet tart is eaten as a Christmas dessert in Cataluña.

Ingredients:

> 220 g flour
> 125 g butter
> 30 g sugar
> Grated peel of half a lemon
> Pinch of salt
> 100 ml water
> 1 egg
> 7 g dried yeast
> 100 g butter
> 70 g sugar

Preparation:

1. Mix the flour, the 125 g butter (in pieces), lemon peel, the 30 g sugar and the pinch of salt in a bowl. Crumble the ingredients together.

2. Add the egg and the yeast (dissolved in water) and knead the mix to form a dough. Add more flour if necessary.

3. Put the dough aside and let it rise until it has doubled in volume. Preheat the oven to 220°C.

4. Roll out the dough into a very thin circle. Put this on a greased ovenproof plate and mark an edge with your finger all around the circle.

5. Place some small pieces of butter on the surface and sprinkle the surface with sugar. Bake immediately at 220°C for about15 minutes.

6. Remove the cake from the oven, coat the surface with the remaining butter and then place it under a hot grill for a final quick caramelisation of the surface sugar, taking care not to burn it.

7. Finally, remove and set aside to cool before serving.

GALLETITAS DE VAINILLA

Vanilla Biscuits

Vanilla biscuits are a Christmas favourite in many European countries, but especially in Spain (and in most of Latin America). No Christmas is complete without vanilla biscuits and they are simple to make. In parts of Spain, they are sometimes baked using lard rather than butter.

Ingredients:

> 100 g butter
> 350 g flour
> 1 tsp. of vanilla essence
> 1 tsp. of baking powder
> 150 g sugar
> 2 eggs

Preparation:

1. Allow the butter to soften at room temperature for a few hours.

2. Mix the butter with the sugar. Add the eggs and the vanilla essence. Stir until thoroughly blended.

3. Add in the sifted flour together with the baking powder. Mix well until it becomes a smooth dough.

4. Leave the dough to rest in the refrigerator for about 30 minutes. Preheat the oven to 180°C.

5. Remove the dough from the refrigerator, roll it out, cut the biscuits and bake at 180°C for about 10 to 15 minutes.

6. Let them cool on a rack before serving.

HOJALDRINAS

Wine and Orange Christmas Shortbread

This is another popular Christmas sweet similar to the mantecados, but based on wine, grated orange peel and orange juice - thus giving them a completely different flavour. This recipe uses butter, but more traditionally, the recipe used pig lard. These are also sometimes called "Mantecados Hojaldrados".

Ingredients:

> 600 g flour
> 400 g butter
> 50 ml orange juice
> 50 ml white wine
> 3 grated orange peels
> Icing sugar

Preparation:

1. Soften the butter in a bowl. Add the filtered orange juice and the white wine. Mix well until the butter is well incorporated.

2. Add the 600 g of flour through a sieve and then the grated peel of 3 oranges.

3. Stir it all together with a spoon until the ingredients are well blended. Form the dough into a ball with your hands.

4. Cover the dough and leave it in the refrigerator for one hour.

5. On a smooth surface sprinkled with flour, roll out the dough thickly (2 or 3 cm) with a rolling pin and then cut it into rectangles of about 4 cm x 6 cm.

6. Place the pieces of dough in an oven tray lined with baking paper. Put the tray in the fridge for a while. In the meantime, preheat the oven at 180°C. When the dough is cold, place the tray into the oven and bake for 30 minutes.

8. Remove from the oven and leave the hojaldrinas to cool on a rack.

9. When cool, dust them with icing sugar and serve.

MANTECADOS DE ACEITE DE NAVIDAD

Almond and Olive Oil Christmas Shortbread

This typical Andaluz shortcake has many variations using, for example, cinnamon, almond, and chocolate. However, one thing that all of these varieties have in common is calories - because their main ingredient is lard. Here we have suggested a traditional recipe that substitutes the lard with olive oil to make them healthier but just as delicious.

Ingredients:

> 100 g chopped roasted almonds
> 620 g flour
> 220 g sugar
> Cinnamon powder
> Grated peel of 2 lemons
> Salt
> 250 ml mild olive oil
> Sesame seeds and icing sugar to decorate

Preparation:

1. Mix the flour, sugar, cinnamon, lemon peel and a pinch of salt in a bowl.

2. Gradually stir in the olive oil and the almonds, and mix well to make a dough.

3. Form the dough into a ball and put it into the fridge for 2 hours.

4. Preheat the oven to 180°C.

5. Remove the dough from the fridge and roll out to a thickness of about 2 cm.

6. Use a biscuit cutter to cut out the biscuits and place them on a baking tray lined with baking paper.

7. Shake the sesame seeds on top of the biscuits.

8. Bake for about 20 minutes.

9. Remove from the oven and allow to cool. Sprinkle with icing sugar before serving.

MANTECADOS DE ALFARNATE

Christmas Biscuits of Alfarnate

This is another variation on the mantecado recipe and typical of the many delicious Andalusian sweet Christmas specialities. This one originates in an old Arab village in a mountainous part of eastern Málaga province. Alfarnate is well known for its traditional sweet bakery. This is a catering-sized recipe for Christmas. You may want to adjust the quantities for a smaller household!

Ingredients:

    1 kg butter
    1 cup olive oil (heated up and then cooled)
    2 egg yolks
    Egg white for coating
    Icing sugar to coat
    500 g sugar
    3 shots dry anís liquor
    15 g ground cinnamon (according to taste)
    15 ground cloves
    3 kg flour

Preparation:

1. Make a dough with all the ingredients - it should not be sticky; add a little more flour if it is.

2. Preheat the oven to 180°C.

3. Roll out the dough to a thickness of 2 to 3 cm and use a round biscuit cutter to cut out the biscuits.

4. Baste the tops with beaten egg whites and icing sugar.

5. Place the biscuits on baking paper on an oven tray. Bake in the oven at 180°C for about 15 minutes.

5. Allow to cool - remember that they will be quite delicate and very crumbly.

MANTECADOS MANCHEGOS

Shortbread biscuits of La Mancha

Here is another regional version of mantecados; this time with both wine and anís liquor flavour.

Traditionally, the dough for the mantecados was prepared at home and then brought to the local bakery or village oven to bake. Families had large tins with a capacity some four times larger than the capacity of a domestic oven. These were filled with the uncooked mantecados and brought to be baked as soon as the baker's ovens were empty. These same tins were also used to carry red peppers for roasting, or for baking other homemade biscuits or cakes in large quantities.

The mantecados of this recipe are very easy to prepare, with very simple ingredients. You can then add flavourings to taste, such as, for example, anise, or grated orange/lemon peel and juice.

Ingredients:

> 500 g lard (can be substituted with butter / margarine)
> 600 g flour
> 200 ml white wine (La Mancha)
> 1 small glass anís liquor
> Ground aniseed to taste
> 1 pinch of salt
> Icing sugar to decorate

Preparation:

1. Leave the lard to soften at room temperature for a few hours.

2. Beat the lard, the wine and the aniseed / anís liquor together.

3. Sift the flour and salt into the whipped lard and wine mix. Add just enough flour without having to knead the dough (the dough should not be overworked).

4. Make a ball of the dough and leave it in a covered bowl to cool overnight (or refrigerate the dough for at least 1 hour to harden).

5. Preheat the oven to 180-200°C. Roll out the dough using a rolling pin until it has a thickness of about 3 cm or a little more. Cut out the shortbread with a star-shaped biscuit cutter (about the size of 2 bites).

6. Place the mantecados slightly separated from each other on an oven tray lined with baking paper. Put the tray in the oven and reduce the temperature to 100°C.

7. Bake for about 60 minutes. The mantecados should NOT be very brown, just baked.

8. Remove the tray from the oven and leave the mantecados to cool on the tray (they are very fragile when hot). When cool, shake some icing sugar on them. Serve when completely cold.

MANTECADOS DE NAVIDAD

Almond Christmas Biscuits

Mantecados are a traditional Christmas confectionary of Andalucía. A visit to the town of Estepa in Sevilla province during the months leading up to Christmas reveals an entire town busy making a vast array of traditional Christmas confectionary - based usually on the almond - including their famous mantecados. The area around the town supplies the almonds, olive oil and lard that are the basic ingredients for many Andalusian confectionaries. The mantecado and the aroma of cinnamon are very emblematic of Christmas in Spain and no Christmas would be complete without them.

Ingredients :

150 g lard (can be substituted with butter / margarine)
200 g sugar
100 g ground almonds
300 g flour
4 g cinnamon powder

Preparation:

1. Put the flour in a frying pan and toast it over a very low heat, stirring all the time with a wooden spoon.

2. When the flour starts to brown, remove it from the heat and place it in a bowl with the ground almonds. Allow to cool.

3. In another bowl, whisk the lard until very smooth and creamy. Then add the cinnamon and sugar and stir well until all is thoroughly mixed.

4. Add the flour and almond to the mix, stirring constantly until it forms a dough and is dry enough not to stick to the bowl. Preheat the oven to 150°C.

5. Dust a smooth work surface with flour to prevent sticking and place the dough on it. Use a rolling pin to flatten the dough well until you obtain a sheet of about 2 cm thick. Divide the dough into equal parts, forming small balls to get the basic shape of the mantecados.

6. Put these on a baking tray lined with baking paper and bake them in the oven at 150°C for about 10 minutes or until golden. Remove from the oven and allow them to cool.

8. Sprinkle a little icing sugar on them before serving.

MARAÑUELAS DE CANDÁS DE ASTURIAS

Easter Biscuit of Candás, Asturias

The marañuela is a typical Asturian sweet biscuit eaten at Easter. It is traditionally part of the giving of gifts by godparents to godchildren on Easter Sunday and is sometimes accompanied with a jug of spicy wine. They have existed for a very long time; at least since the middle ages. Because the marañuelas keep well, they were especially popular amongst the pilgrims on the Camino de Santiago.

The two towns most famous for the marañuela are Candás and Luanco. There are slight differences in the recipes from the two towns and a certain amount of rivalry about whose is the best! Here we give the recipe from Candás. Some recipes suggest adding a pinch of cinnamon to the dough.

Ingredients (20 marañuelas):

> 4 eggs (at room temperature)
> 350 g butter
> 500 g sugar
> 1 kg bread flour
> Grated peel of 1 lemon
> 1 shot anís liquor
> 16 g baking powder

Preparation:

1. Clarify the butter (see below).

2. Preheat the oven to 200°C.

3. Whisk the eggs, adding one at a time until they are well blended.

4. Add in the sugar and continue to whisk. Add the clarified butter (see below), lemon peel and anís liquor and mix thoroughly.

5. Combine the flour and baking powder in a bowl. Make a little hole in the pile of flour and gradually add the butter and egg mix to it, stirring continuously.

6. When the dough is consistent, knead it until it is elastic using a little more flour if required.

7. Now, mould and cut the dough into strips and use the strips to make the biscuits by plaiting the 2 or 3 strips together or rolling the strips into spiral shapes.

8. Bake for 20 to 30 minutes, until just golden brown.

9. Allow to cool on a wire rack.

How to clarify Butter:

Butter is clarified traditionally to increase the fat content and help to preserve it. To clarify butter, follow these simple instructions:

1. Put the butter in a saucepan in a double boiler ("bain-marie") over a low heat so that it slowly melts.

2. Once melted, pour the butter carefully into a glass bowl and let it stand for a while until it separates into three layers.

3. Use a spoon to remove the foam from the top (which are the impurities). Some people sieve the melted butter but then it has to settle again.

4. Carefully pour the clarified butter into another container, taking care to leave the bottom layer that is mostly water. This should be discarded.

5. Allow the butter to cool and solidify before use. Store the butter in the refrigerator.

MOSTACHUDOS

Sephardic Spicy Biscuits

These spicy biscuits originated in the bakeries of the Sephardic Jews and Moors who lived in Spain in the Middle Ages. Both groups were amongst the most important influences in Spanish and indeed Northern European food especially spicy sweet bakery.

This recipe has some very distant connection with the Roman spicy sweet "mustaceum" which was made with "mosto" - young wine and spices but it is essentially a Sephardic-Moorish spicy biscuit. The recipe survives in Ourense in Galicia to this day where the biscuits are still made in the traditional way by a local baker.

Ingredients (for 15 mostachudos):

> 225 g peeled walnuts
> 80 g sugar
> 1 large egg (65 g)
> 1 teaspoon of ground cloves (or cinnamon powder, or a mixture of both)
> 1 teaspoon of grated orange peel
> Icing sugar to decorate

Preparation:

1. Preheat the oven to 190°C with heat top and bottom.

2. Line a baking tray with baking paper.

3. Finely grind the walnuts, sugar, cloves and orange peel in a food processor or mincer. Put in a mixing bowl.

4. Add a beaten egg and mix until you have smooth, consistent dough.

5. Moisten your hands, take pieces of the dough and form them into balls of about 3cm in diameter, place them on the baking paper about 3cm apart. Flatten the balls slightly by hand.

6. Bake at 190°C for 10 to 12 minutes. They do not need to brown too much because when they cool they will become crispy.

7. When baked, place on a wire mesh to cool and sprinkle with icing sugar to your taste.

8. When completely cooled, store in an airtight container with kitchen paper between the layers of biscuits.

NEVADITOS DE CANTABRIA

Snow Cakes of Cantabria

Nevados, also called nevaditos, which means "snow-capped" is an apt name given to a type of small, soft Christmas biscuit / cake. These traditional, snowy-white cakes are covered in icing sugar, and have become popular throughout Spain. The recipe is thought to have originated in Cantabria, in the far North of the country.

Ingredients (for approximately 40 cakes):

> 200 g lard (can be substituted with butter or margarine)
> 500 g flour
> 125 ml white wine (Moscatel wine works well)
> Half a teaspoon of salt
> 50 g sugar
> Icing sugar for coating

Preparation:

1. Preheat the oven to 180°C.

2. Put the flour in a mixing bowl, make a hollow in the centre and add the lard (at room temperature), wine, salt and sugar. Mix until a dough starts to form. Knead thoroughly for a few minutes until it becomes a workable dough.

3. Roll out the dough with a rolling pin, making it about 1 cm thick. Cut out shapes such as stars, circles or other festive shapes with a biscuit cutter.

4. Place the nevaditos on a baking tray lined with baking paper, separating them slightly.

5. Bake them for about 30 minutes at 180°C until they are lightly browned.

6. Take the nevaditos out of the oven and coat them with icing sugar when they are still hot. Leave to cool on a rack.

7. When they are cooled, sprinkle them again with icing sugar and serve.

PACIENCIAS DE CATALUÑA

Mini Biscuits of Cataluña

Several regions of Spain claim to be the origins of these little biscuits such as Castilla y Leon and Extramadura. Barcelona claims they were invented by an Italian pastry chef. They have various names including "nun's pet", "nun's chest" and some even more vulgar nicknames!

Regardless of the origins, these little biscuits have a similar recipe in general although in Castilla they are also made using a little anís liquor to flavour. They are simple to make and are eaten cold like any biscuit at any time.

Ingredients:

> 3 eggs
> 150 g sugar
> 250 g flour approximately
> Grated peel of 1 lemon

Preparation:

1. Beat the eggs in a bowl and then add the sugar and grated lemon peel.

2. Add the flour whilst mixing continuously. The amount of flour will vary depending on the size of the eggs. The resulting dough should have a fluffy texture, be thick but still suitable for putting into a pastry bag with a small nozzle.

3. Preheat the oven to 180° C.

4. Put a sheet of oven paper on a baking tray. Use a pastry bag to make the little biscuits on the baking tray. Each should be round and about 2cm in diameter although they may be a little larger and about 0.5cm thick.

5. Bake them until they become a light golden colour. Remove from the oven and allow them to cool before serving or storing.

PASTAS ALMENDRA DE LA RIOJA

Almond Biscuits of La Rioja

This is an almond biscuit especially popular in the region of La Rioja in Northern Spain. They are sometimes referred to as "Almendrados". It is a very simple recipe with just three main ingredients and is easy to make. Traditionally, these pastas are made around Christmas but they are now also found at other times of the year. There are several variants, one of which uses grated lemon peel, but this is the basic recipe.

Ingredients:

> 250 g of ground almonds
> 250 g of sugar
> 4 egg yolks (one of them to coat the biscuits)
> Sliced almond to decorate

Preparation:

1. Preheat the oven to 180°C (top and bottom, without the fan).

2. Stir the ground almonds and sugar together in a bowl and thoroughly mix in the three egg yolks to create a thick dough.

3. Line a baking tray with baking paper.

4. Use a spoon to form small balls of dough on the baking paper and flatten them slightly with your hand. Leave a centimetre or two between the biscuits to allow for expansion during baking.

5. Coat each with egg yolk and decorate the tops with sliced almond.

6. Bake for 12 to 15 minutes until they start to brown. Take the tray out of the oven and allow the biscuits to cool and harden completely before removing them from the tray.

PASTAS DE ALMENDRAS - BOCADITOS DE CIELO
Heavenly Almond Biscuits

As the name implies, these almond biscuits are traditionally baked in various convents in Spain. They are also referred to in the book entitled "Dulces y postres de las monjas" (ISBN: 9788492520008) ("Sweets and Desserts of the Nuns") which is considered one of the best collections of Spanish monastic sweets and dessert recipes in existence.

Despite its monastic credentials in Spain, there is an almost identical traditional recipe popular in Morocco, without using lard, of course. There are several variants on this recipe that are quite similar and often baked during Christmas and around the "Reyes Magos", Epiphany on the 6th January, when the three kings come to bring Spanish children their gifts.

Ingredients:

> 100 g butter
> 70 g sugar
> 200 g flour
> 50 g almond (half as almond flour and half finely chopped)
> 1 egg
> 15 g lard or margarine
> 1 tablespoon baking powder
> Icing sugar to decorate biscuits

Preparation:

1. Preheat the oven to 200°C.

2. Put the sugar, egg, butter and lard (or margarine) in a bowl. Mix all these ingredients until you have a consistent dough.

3. Add the almond flour first and then the chopped almond, little by little. Continue to mix thoroughly.

4. In a separate bowl, combine the baking powder with the flour. Make a hollow in the middle of the flour and add the almond, sugar, egg, butter mix.

5. Work into a dough. Empty onto a floured work surface to knead.

6. Knead the dough well and finally roll it out until about 1 cm thick.

7. Use a small round or star shaped biscuit cutter to cut the dough. Put these on an oven tray, lined with baking paper with a bit of space between each to allow expansion during baking.

8. Place in the oven at 200ºC for 18 to 20 minutes.

9. When removed from the oven sprinkle immediately with icing sugar. Allow the biscuits to cool before eating.

PASTAS DE NARANJA Y MIEL

Orange, Cinnamon and Honey Biscuit

This is a simple and traditional biscuit found throughout rural Spain. It is based on locally available ingredients but given a slightly exotic taste by adding a little cinnamon. This is a common technique in Spanish rural bakery, derived from Moorish traditional use of spices in the bakery - where a cake or biscuit is made with readily available local materials (in this case flour, orange juice and honey) but then given an additional spicy flavour. Spain was, after all, on one of the main European spice routes from the Far East and Africa. These biscuits are simple to prepare and have a delicious aromatic taste.

Ingredients:

> 125 g pastry flour
> 125 g ground almonds
> 50 g butter
> 1 tablespoon of honey
> Half a teaspoon of cinnamon powder
> 50 ml orange juice (strained)
> A little grated orange peel
> 100 g of sugar

Preparation:

1. Preheat the oven to 180°C.

2. Mix the ground almonds with the flour.

3. Melt the butter (can be done in a microwave) and beat together with the sugar, honey and orange juice. Stir well over a low heat until the sugar is completely dissolved.

4. Take the mixture off the heat and add the flour and almond, the cinnamon and the orange peel. Mix all the ingredients thoroughly.

5. Use a pastry bag or a teaspoon to put equal portions of the dough onto an oven tray covered with a sheet of baking paper (approximate diameter 6 cm each). Leave space between each portion of dough so that the biscuit can expand during baking.

6. Bake for between 5 to 7 minutes, until golden brown.

7. Let the biscuits cool completely before removing them from the baking paper.

PASTAS DE SANTA ISABEL

Almond Biscuits of Saint Isabel

This is a typical convent biscuit originating from the region of Castilla y León in Central-Northern Spain. It was first documented in the famous work of monastic bakery entitled "Los dulces de las monjas. Un viaje a los conventos reposteros de Castilla y León" ("The sweets of the nuns: A voyage to the baking convents of Castilla y León").

It is still popular to this day; made, and sold in several famous old convents in the city of Valladolid, including the Convento de Santa Isabel.

Ingredients:

> 0.5 kg lard (or butter / margarine)
> 3 eggs (one whole and two yolks - keep the remaining egg white aside)
> 500 g sugar
> 1 kg flour
> 75 g ground roasted almond
> Cinnamon powder
> Lemon essence
> Vanilla essence

Preparation:

1. Preheat the oven to 200°C.

2. Mix the eggs thoroughly with the butter (one whole and two yolks).

3. Next the flour is added and finally the ground almond, then a little of each of the essences and some cinnamon powder to taste. Mix thoroughly into a smooth, consistent dough.

4. Roll out the dough with a rolling pin.

5. Cut out shaped pieces of dough (they are often triangular) and paint them top and bottom with some slightly beaten egg white.

6. Bake at 200°C until golden brown. Allow to cool before serving.

PERRUNILLAS DE CONVENTO DE ESTREMADURA

Anís and Lemon Biscuits of Extremadura

Perrunillas are a type of dry, sweet biscuit found in many parts of Spain. It generally has a rough texture that crumbles in the mouth. There are many variants, made with a combination of cinnamon, anís, lemon, almond, or brandy. Traditionally they were and still are baked and sold by nuns in their convents.

Originally, the perrunillas are thought to have come from the remote Western region of Extremadura. Many convents in the towns of Badajoz and Trujillo, for example, still make and sell their own varieties of this local biscuit. These biscuits are eaten with coffee or hot chocolate for breakfast and for the evening merienda.

Ingredients:

> 125 g pig lard or margarine (at room temperature)
> 125 g anís liquor
> 250 g sugar
> 4 whole eggs
> 1 egg white
> 1 tablespoon of grated lemon peel
> 500 g flour
> 15 g baking powder

Preparation:

1. Put the lard in a bowl, add the anís liquor and whisk together.

2. Add the sugar, 2 egg yolks, 2 whole eggs, and the grated lemon peel. Beat all the ingredients again.

3. Add the flour mixed with the baking powder and knead into a dough on a floured work surface. The dough needs to be uniform and rather firm. It should not stick to your hands and you may need to use more or less flour. Leave the dough to stand for 30 minutes

4. Whisk the egg whites until they are stiff and put aside.

5. For each biscuit, take a portion of dough and form a ball, then flatten the ball into a circle about 1.5 cm thick and 8 to 12 cm in diameter. Make an indentation in the centre of the dough with your finger.

6. Lightly beat another egg white and use a brush to coat all the perrunillas.

7. Now, using the previously whisked stiff egg whites, place a teaspoonful in the indentation in each perrunilla.

8. Place some sugar on a plate (optionally with some cinnamon powder to taste) and very carefully coat each perrunilla completely with sugar being careful not to lose the egg white.

9. Preheat the oven to 200°C. Bake the perrunillas a light golden brown, but no more.

10. Remove from the oven and allow to cool on a rack before serving.

POLVORONES DE CHOCOLATE

Chocolate Shortbread

One of the most delicious Spanish Christmas biscuits is definitely "polvorones de chocolate", i.e. chocolate shortbread.

Ingredients:

> 250 g flour
> 80 g icing sugar
> 125 g butter
> 60 g of ground roasted almonds
> 25 g cocoa powder (pure, not sugared)
> Cocoa powder for decoration
> Half a teaspoon of cinnamon
> Icing sugar for decoration
> A pinch of salt

Preparation:

1. Preheat the oven to 180°C. Spread the flour on a baking tray lined with baking paper. When the oven is hot, place the tray into the oven and toast the flour for about 15 minutes. Take care not to burn the flour, so stir it occasionally. When the flour is toasted, take it out and let it cool.

2. Mix the flour thoroughly with the butter, cocoa, icing sugar, salt and cinnamon. Add the almonds and continue kneading until it becomes a consistent, smooth dough.

3. Increase the oven temperature to 220°C and in the meantime prepare the shortbreads by rolling out the dough to a thickness of about 1.5 cm. Cut out the shortbreads with a circular biscuit cutter and place them on an oven tray lined with baking paper.

4. Put them in the oven until dark golden brown.

5. Remove the tray from the oven and let the shortbreads cool. Sprinkle with icing sugar and/or cocoa powder to taste.

POLVORONES DE ESTEPA
Shortbreads of Estepa (Sevilla)

The polvorón is a typical Christmas confectionery in Spain and particularly in Andalucía. The most famous ones are made in Estepa, an old Arabic town in the province of Sevilla. The polvorón is a type of shortbread. There are quite a lot of variations on the basic recipe, including one aromatic variety - "polvorones de limón" - that is very popular. It uses a paste made with whole grated lemons, skin and all. Many traditional Christmas varieties of polvorón use a small quantity of ground almond flour in the recipe.

In all these variations, the smell of cinnamon and anís from freshly baked polvorones at Christmas is guaranteed to imbue everyone with festive spirit!

Ingredients (makes 45):

> 400 g flour (optionally substitute 10% with almond flour)
> 225 g lard (can be substituted with butter)
> 150 g icing sugar
> 2 tablespoons of anís liquor
> Half a teaspoon of ground cinnamon
> Grated lemon peel (or 2 lemons grated into a paste, if making the Polvorones de limón)
> Flour and icing sugar for dusting

Preparation:

1. Preheat the oven to 150°C. When it is at temperature, toast the flour. To do this pour the flour in a baking tray and spread it out with a spatula. Put the tray in the oven for 6 minutes to toast slightly. Then remove from the oven, stir it with the spatula and toast it again for another 6 minutes.

2. Sift the flour into a bowl. Add the cinnamon, sugar, and some grated lemon peel (or the lemon paste). Add the lard or butter and anís and knead well.

3. Dust a smooth surface with a little flour, place the dough on the surface, sprinkle with some more flour and then roll out the dough to a thickness of about 1.5 cm. Use a round biscuit cutter to cut the shortbreads and place them on an oven tray lined with baking paper.

4. Bake at 170°C for 15 minutes. Allow the polvorones to cool before sprinkling them with icing sugar. Serve on Christmas morning!

REQUEMAOS DE MURCIA

Cinnamon and Lemon Biscuits of Murcia

This biscuit recipe comes from the northwest of Murcia where many old sweet recipes are still made in the traditional way.

This "requemao" recipe gets its name because the oil that is used is previously heated to a very high temperature - "quemao" meaning, "burned". This recipe uses sunflower oil but olive oil can also be used.

Ingredients:

> 0.5 L sunflower oil
> 1 kg flour
> 500 g sugar
> 1 grated lemon peel
> 1 egg
> Cinnamon powder (to taste)

Preparation:

1. Heat the oil until it is very hot and then remove from the heat. Allow it to cool completely.

2. When cold, pour the oil into a bowl and add the sugar, stirring until it is dissolved. Next, add the grated lemon peel and mix again. Then add the flour, little by little, mix and then knead until a consistent dough is formed.

3. Preheat the oven to 180°C (top and bottom).

4. When the dough is ready, roll it out on a lightly floured work surface to a thickness of about 0.5cm.

5. Use a biscuit cutter (the shape is up to you) and cut out portions of dough and place on baking paper on a baking tray.

6. Coat each biscuit with the beaten egg, sprinkle with sugar mixed with a little cinnamon powder.

7. Bake the biscuits until they start to brown (about 15 or 20 minutes). Scatter a little more sugar on them, let them cool and they are ready to eat.

ROSCOS DE SAN ANTÓNIO

St. Anthony Rings

There are literally dozens of types of "Roscos" in Spain that range from small flaky biscuits like this one to full sized fruit cakes for Christmas. They are all ring-shaped, some with a dent or hole in the centre. There are many flavours for this biscuit. Different flavours include using lemon peel or anís liquor.

This rosco is dedicated to Saint Anthony - the patron saint of lovers and those who have lost something! The following is a simple traditional recipe for the saint's day on June 13th. It uses traditional lard but for vegetarians this can be substituted with margarine or butter. Some recipes use olive oil, which is even better.

Ingredients (for 30 biscuits):

> 500 g lard (or margarine / butter)
> 250 g granulated sugar
> 3 egg yolks
> 2 large eggs
> Granulated sugar for dusting
> 1 kg flour

Preparation:

1. Beat the lard and sugar together in a large bowl.

2. Add one whole egg and all 3 egg yolks, beating until smooth. Stir in the flour little by little until a dough is formed.

3. Preheat the oven to 180°C.

4. Knead the dough manually.

5. Take a quarter of the dough at a time, put it on a lightly floured work surface and roll it out with a rolling pin.

6. Use a biscuit cutter or glass to cut out around 30 biscuits in total from the dough. Place them on oven tray(s) lined with baking paper. Make a depression in the centre of each circle of dough.

7. Beat the remaining egg, and brush the dough with it. Sprinkle each with some granulated sugar.

8. Bake the biscuits in the middle of the oven until golden brown, which takes approximately 15 minutes.

9. When baked, remove the tray from the oven, and allow the biscuits to cool on a rack.

10. When completely cool, store in a tightly sealed container in a cool place.

SUSPIROS DE PAJARES, ASTURIAS

Butter Biscuits of Pajares, Asturias

Pajares is a small, mountainous village, bordering León, which has around 140 inhabitants. The name of the village derives from the valley in which it is located, the river that runs through it and the better known "Puerto de Pajares", which for centuries was the main route between Asturias and the rest of Spain.

These biscuits have a long tradition in the area. The translation of the word "suspiros" is "sighs" and local folklore says that the biscuit's name was the result of the sighs of the women waiting for their men to return home from the long days in the fields.

Ingredients:

> 500 g flour
> 400 g butter
> 1 egg
> 200 g sugar
> 50 g icing sugar to decorate

Preparation:

1. Melt the butter and let it cool to room temperature.

2. Whisk the butter with the sugar, until thoroughly mixed. Blend in the egg and, little by little, add the flour, mixing continuously until you have soft dough.

3. Preheat the oven to 180°C. Use butter to grease an oven tray or line a tray with baking paper. Place small amounts of dough on the tray, make them round and flatten them slightly.

4. Place the oven tray in the oven at 180°C for about 15 minutes until the suspiros are golden brown.

5. When they are ready, remove the tray from the oven. Let the biscuits stand for 5 minutes. Sprinkle them with the icing sugar and serve.

TEJAS DE TOLOSA

Almond "Tile" Biscuits of Tolosa

This simple almond biscuit is shaped like a traditional roof tile (hence the name) and is thought to have been created in 1924 by the famous Pastelería Eceiza in the town of Tolosa in el País Vasco (the Basque region). The town was on an important trading route and since the Middle Ages was a ready source of almonds. Thus, almonds became incorporated into recipes for many of local sweets and cakes. The biscuits are generally eaten with coffee or with the famous local Basque cider. A variant of this biscuit uses pine kernels instead of almonds.

Ingredients:

> 100 g icing sugar
> 100 g egg whites
> 100 g butter
> 100 g flour
> 50 g finely chopped almonds

Preparation:

1. Preheat the oven to 180°C.

2. Stir the icing sugar into the softened butter.

3. Gradually mix the unbeaten egg whites with the butter and sugar

4. Add the sifted flour and mix thoroughly until you have consistent dough.

5. Line an oven tray with baking paper. Put a tablespoonful of dough on the tray and shape the biscuit into an oval a couple of millimetres thick. Repeat for the rest of the dough.

6. Sprinkle the chopped almonds on the "tiles" and place the tray in the oven.

7. Bake for 6 to 8 minutes or until the biscuits begin to brown around the edges.

8. Remove the tray from the oven and, whilst the biscuits are still warm, mould them, one by one, around a glass to make the traditional curved tile shape. Place aside to cool before serving.

TORTAS DE ACEITE DE ALGARROBO

Spicy Biscuits from Algarrobo

These very nice, very famous spicy biscuits are one of the best-kept secrets of the village of Algarrobo in the Axarquía. They are delicious dipped into a good coffee!

Ingredients:

> 60 g fresh yeast
> 1 kg flour
> 500 g sugar
> 0.5 litre olive oil
> 2 tablespoons of aniseed
> 1 glass of brandy
> 100 g whole roasted almonds
> Water

Preparation:

1. Dissolve the yeast in a little warm water and mix with the flour and sugar.

2. Heat a little olive oil in a frying pan. When it starts to fume, remove the pan from the heat and add the aniseed, stirring to toast the seeds evenly. When cool, pour over the flour mix.

3. Finely chop the almonds.

4. Gradually add the remaining ingredients to the dough, kneading continuously. Add a little water if the dough gets too dry.

5. Let the dough stand for at least 24 hours in the refrigerator.

6. Preheat the oven to 180°C. Divide the dough into round "cakes" of about 100 g each (not too thin) and place on a baking tray lined with baking paper.

7. Bake these cakes for about ten minutes at 180°C, making sure that they do not burn, but are baked through.

8. Leave to cool on a rack before serving.

TORTAS DE ACEITE DE CASTILLEJA DE LA CUESTA

Olive Oil biscuits of Castilleja de la Cuesta, Sevilla

These famous crispy biscuits originate in the town of Castilleja de la Cuesta in the province of Sevilla and the modern recipe dates from just 1910. The most famous producer is the bakery of Inés Rosales (considered the creator of the original torta) but there are many small artisan bakeries in the town producing their own version.

These tortas are easy to make and you can easily tailor the ingredients to your own taste, or bake them a little longer if you prefer them to be crispier. The original recipe and its local importance means that this biscuit is now officially recognised by the EU as a traditional product of this region.

Ingredients (for 21 biscuits):

500 g flour
100 g olive oil
150 ml water (or water mixed with around 60 ml anís liquor)
50 g orange juice
15 g fresh yeast or 5 g dried yeast
5 g salt
8 g aniseed
10 g sesame seeds
White sugar for dusting

Preparation:

1. Preheat the oven to 200°C

2. Put all the ingredients into a bowl, mix thoroughly and then knead together into a consistent dough.

3. Take pieces of dough of around 40g each and form them into balls. Put aside and allow them to rest for about 30 minutes.

4. Roll out the pieces of dough as thinly as possible and shape them into rounds. You can also use a dough cutter if you find it difficult to maintain the round shape.

5. When you have enough biscuits to fit on one standard size baking tray (probably about 6), place them on a sheet of baking paper on the tray. Sprinkle the dough rounds with a generous amount of sugar.

Optionally, you may paint the dough with some egg white before adding the sugar.

6. Bake the tortas for 10 to 15 minutes.

7. When they are turning golden, remove them from the oven and place them on a wire rack to cool completely before serving.

8. The tortas can easily be stored for several days in a biscuit tin.

TORTAS DE ALCÁZAR DE SAN JUAN DE LA MANCHA
Lemon and Cinnamon Biscuits of La Mancha

Alcázar de San Juan is an old Arabic town in Castilla-La Mancha and is the area in which Cervantes' Don Quixote is set. The town was a garrison of the Christian knights of St. John after the Christian conquest of the Arab city and its name reflects both its Arab and Christian History (Alcázar means fortification, castle or palace in the original Arabic).

Although the biscuits probably originated with Arabic or Jewish bakers, using typical flavours such as lemon and cinnamon, they became famous when the Franciscan nuns of the convent of Santa Clara de Alcázar began to make them in the town. Queen Isabel II visiting the town in 1854 was so taken by the tortas that she ordered that the town supply the royal household thereafter. The biscuit is now a famous product of Alcázar de San Juan.

Ingredients (16 biscuits):

> 8 medium eggs
> 200 g sugar
> 200 g flour
> 2 grated lemon peels
> Cinnamon powder
> 1 pinch of salt
> Butter at room temperature
> Sugar for dusting

Preparation:

1. Grate the lemon peels and put aside.

2. Separate the egg whites from the yolks and mix the whites with the grated lemon peel and a little cinnamon powder.

3. Whisk the egg whites with a pinch of salt until they are very frothy and then add in the sugar until you have a smooth texture but don't make them too stiff.

4. Add the egg yolks to the mixture and blend them in with a few strokes of a spatula.

5. Now fold in the flour and gently mix until you have completely consistent dough.

6. Preheat the oven to 160°C. Place the dough in a pastry bag with a wide nozzle.

7. Put baking paper on a baking tray and coat it thinly with butter. Squeeze out around 16 thin flat circles of dough onto the paper.

8. Sprinkle each biscuit with sugar and cinnamon to your taste.

9. Place the baking tray low down in an oven at 160°C for 10-15 minutes until the biscuits are golden brown at the edges.

10. When ready, remove from the oven and place the biscuits on a rack to cool before serving.

TORTAS DE PASCUA DE MURCIA

Murcian Christmas Almond Biscuits

This is a recurrent combination of tastes for Christmas biscuits in Murcia: almond, anís and orange. This recipe is based on the traditional recipe still used by the nuns of the old Convento de San António in Murcia.

Ingredients (for 30 biscuits of around 8 cm diameter):

200 g almonds
60 almonds for decoration
500 g flour
250 g granulated sugar
1 teaspoon of baking powder
125 ml anís liquor (or mix vodka with 1.5 teaspoon of anise extract)
125 ml orange juice
100 ml olive oil
100 ml honey to coat biscuits

Preparation:

1. Warm the olive oil in a small saucepan on very low heat for 1-2 minutes. If using unpeeled almonds, blanch and skin the almonds.

2. Put 60 almonds aside to use as decoration. Put the rest of the almonds in a blender and very finely chop.

3. Stir the ground almonds and flour together in a bowl. Add the sugar, baking powder, anís and orange juice, and mix well.

4. Pour in the warm olive oil and mix until the oil is absorbed into the dough.

5. Preheat the oven to 180°C. Line an oven tray with baking paper. Use a spoon to place a small amount of dough on the tray. Flatten it slightly.

6. Press a few peeled almonds or almonds slices into the top of each biscuit.

7. Bake for approximately 30 minutes or until the biscuits have turned a deep golden colour.

8. Remove from the oven and allow to cool.

9. Pour a little honey on top of each biscuit and serve.

TOSTADITAS DE PIÑONES DEL CONVENTO

Cinnamon Pine Nut Biscuits of the Convent

This crunchy cinnamon biscuit is made in several Andaluz convents and is a simple but delicious biscuit using pine nuts as a base and it is made entirely without added fat.

Ingredients

> 250 g pine nuts
> 150 g flour
> 150 g sugar
> Cinnamon powder to taste
> 100 ml water (approx.)
> Icing sugar to decorate

Preparation:

1. Preheat the oven with the grill on to 170°C.

2. Roughly crush the pine nuts with a mortar and pestle.

3. Put the crushed pine nuts into a large bowl. Add the sugar and a pinch of cinnamon. Sift in the flour.

4. Mix the ingredients thoroughly and add the water little by little.

5. Knead until you get a consistent biscuit dough.

6. Line a baking tray with baking paper and coat it with oil.

7. Roll out the dough on a lightly floured work surface and cut out the biscuits. Any shape is fine: circles, squares, rectangles etc. Place the pieces of dough on the tray.

8. Place the tray in the middle of the oven, and bake until the biscuits are golden brown.

9. Remove the tray from the oven and allow the biscuits to cool completely.

10. Sprinkle the cold biscuits with plenty of icing sugar and serve.

---oOo---

2.3 Sweet Pastries and Cakes

There is an immense wealth of sweet pastries and cakes in Spain. Many have romantic, evocative or funny names reflecting their chequered history. Some sweet pastries and cakes are very simple; some are complex, elaborate and time-consuming.

The use of puff pastry is very common in Spanish traditional sweet bakery and the advent of frozen / chilled puff pastry makes the task of home baking a lot less work these days. Similarly, traditional fillings like angel hair can now be bought ready-made so no need to stand over a pot of boiling pumpkin to be able to use this popular and delicious ingredient.

As usual, it is quite difficult to say when a pastry or cake is something eaten with tea or coffee or is a dessert as part of lunch or dinner or just one sweet part of breakfast. Many of these sweets are interchangeable and the Spanish are not so worried about how their baked products are classified. If you eat it after lunch, it is a "postre" (dessert). If not it may well be a "torta" or "pasta" depending, of course, on where you are in Spain! Trying to define rigid rules is a complete waste of time - just enjoy the end product!

AGUARDENTAOS DE MURCIA

Christmas Anís Cakes of Murcia

The villages of the Northwest of Murcia have a very particular gastronomy. Many villages have a wealth of ancient domestic recipes based on local produce. As usual, many recipes are centred on religious festivities such as Christmas and Easter.

These small cakes are quite like biscuits and are often baked at Christmas time and spiked with a glass of anís liquor to add flavour and warm the eater!

Ingredients:

> 500 ml olive oil
> Lemon peel
> 1 kg of flour
> 50 g of sugar
> Half a glass of anís liquor

Preparation:

1. Heat the oil in a saucepan with the lemon peel to infuse the flavour of the lemon into the oil.

2. Preheat the oven to 180°C. Pour the flour into a bowl and make a hole in the centre. Pour the hot oil into the flour and stir well with a wooden spoon.

3. Next, add the sugar and anís liquor. The liquor will make the dough contract slightly. Put the dough out on a work surface, and start kneading the dough manually to make it malleable. Add enough flour to allow the dough to be kneaded and rolled out.

4. Use a rolling pin to roll out the dough and then cut out the biscuits with a dough cutter. Place them on a baking tray lined with baking paper.

5. Bake the aguardentaos at 180°C until they start to turn golden brown.

6. When baked, remove them from the oven and coat the biscuits with a mixture of sugar and cinnamon.

7. Serve cold.

AHORCADITOS DE LA RIOJA

Almond Pastries of Santo Domingo de la Cazada

These sweet pastries are filled with cream and almond paste and shaped like a shell with the figure of a man in the centre. The scallop shell shape is an old crusader symbol and connected with the pilgrim route to Santiago de Compostela. This was hugely important during the Middle Ages and still used to this day.

These pastries are absolutely typical to the village of Santo Domingo de la Calzada in La Rioja and the village is famous for them. The modern pastries were developed in 1953 in the bakery of Saint Isidro and the recipe is still a secret but the pastry is sold throughout the region of La Rioja. It has become a local treat for passing pilgrims on the Camino de Santiago. The following recipe creates a reasonably similar copy of the original.

The name and shape of the pastry comes from the legend of a miracle that happened in the village. The legend tells us that a young German pilgrim was unjustly hanged in the village after a bitter love affair with a local girl went wrong. His parents continued their pilgrimage after his execution but on their return found their son hanging from the gallows but still alive and demanding for the mayor to take him down. The incredulous mayor, about to start his chicken dinner, responded to the news, saying, "That boy is as alive as these two roast chickens we are about to eat". Suddenly, the chickens on his table sprung to life, sprouted feathers and beaks and began to crow! So, to this day there is a saying about the town that runs, "Santo Domingo, where the roosters crow after being roasted". The town still has a 15th century henhouse close to the cathedral to keep a hen and a rooster in memory of this famous miracle. Indeed, there are documents from Pope Clemente VI from 1350 allowing these chickens to live in the cathedral.

Ingredients:

> 30 g of mashed boiled potato
> 1 tablespoon of angel hair
> 2 tablespoons of sugar for the filling
> 50 g sugar for syrup and a little more for dusting the pastry
> 50 ml water
> 2 sheets of puff pastry
> Chopped almonds
> 100 g of almond flour

Preparation:

1. Prepare the mashed potato.

2. Lay out the pastry and sprinkle sugar on top. Roll out until smooth.

3. Cut the pastry into an even number of scallop shell shapes about the size of the palm of your hand. If you do not have a pastry cutter this shape, you can make a template for this using baking paper and then cut around it.

4. Preheat the oven to 200°C. Make the filling: Add two tablespoons of sugar and the almond flour to the mashed potato and mix into a smooth paste whilst adding the angel hair.

5. Place half the pastry shells on baking paper on an oven tray and spread some of the filling on each shell base. Leave a border around the filling, and then cover with another piece of pastry shell dough. Seal the edges with water.

6. Use the leftover pastry to create a simple man's figure for each pastry. Attach this to the top of each pastry with a little water. Prick each shell with the tip of a knife to avoid swelling when baked.

7. Bake in the oven at 200°C for about 10 minutes (with both lower and upper heat on).

8. When baked, remove the tray from the oven and leave the pastries to cool.

9. Meanwhile, prepare the syrup: Mix the sugar with the water in a saucepan. Bring to the boil and then immediately remove from the heat.

10. Pour the syrup generously over the pastry shells and then sprinkle the chopped almonds on top.

11. Allow the ahorcaditos to cool completely before serving.

ALMENDRADOS DE ALLARIZ (GALICIA)

Almond Macaroon of Allariz

This little macaroon is traditionally eaten as a dessert in Galicia. It has its history in the thirteenth century when the Jewish community of the pretty village of Allariz were famous for their sweet baking. Galicia is too cold for large-scale almond cultivation but the Moors introduced almonds into Southern Spain where they thrive to this day. The arrival of almonds and sugar in Galicia in the early Middle Ages triggered many new sweet cake recipes using almonds, including the almendrado.

Many such recipes were adopted by Christian religious orders. In this case, the local convent of the Poor Clares had contact with the local Jewish bakers and eventually took over the recipe and commercialised these popular macaroons for themselves. This is a very simple and fast recipe with a delicious result and makes between 12 and 15 macaroons. Almendrados are baked on wafers with three little macaroons on each wafer.

Ingredients (to make 12-15 almendrados):

    250 g ground almonds
    200 g sugar
    3 egg whites
    12-15 wafers 8-10 cm in diameter

Preparation

1. Grind 250 g of almonds or buy ready ground almonds. If you decide to grind your own almonds then it is best to do this in 2 steps (ideally in a blender). The first half of the whole almonds should be ground almost to flour; the second half should be left a little coarser. After grinding, place the almonds on a tray in the oven at about 120°C for around 10 minutes to reduce their moisture and release the almond flavour. Allow them to cool before using.

2. Preheat the oven to 180°C (top and bottom heat with fan).

3. Separate the egg whites from the egg yolks. (Keep the egg yolks for some other purpose).

4. Stir the ground almonds and sugar together in a bowl. Add the egg whites and mix into a smooth paste.

5. Line an oven tray with baking paper and place the wafers on top.

6. Put three little heaps of the paste on each wafer keeping them slightly apart - remember they will expand a little during baking and will fuse together. Sprinkle a little sugar over each one.

7. Put the tray in the oven and bake at 150°C for 20-25 minutes, until slightly golden. Do not over-bake them - otherwise they will be very hard.

8. When they are just brown, remove the macaroons from the oven and place them on a wire rack to cool before serving.

ALMENDRILLOS DE LAS MONJAS

Almond Sticks of the Nuns

This is another monastic pastry recipe, documented in the famous monastic recipe book "Dulces y Postres de las Monjas" (Sweets and Desserts of the Nuns - 2008). It is very simple to make. Despite being a favourite "monastic" recipe, this sweet is almost certainly of Arab origin with its telltale use of cinnamon.

Ingredients:

300 g ground almonds
500 g flour
250 ml water
250 g sugar
6 tablespoons of olive oil
32 g baking powder
Cinnamon to taste
 Grated peel of half a lemon
4 eggs
Egg for coating

Preparation:

1. Preheat the oven to 150°C.

2. Mix all ingredients thoroughly and allow the mixture to stand for a few minutes

3. Put the mixture in a pastry bag with a large nozzle. Squeeze out strips of the mixture onto a baking tray lined with baking paper. Paint them with egg.

4. Place the almendrillos in the oven for about 30 minutes until golden brown. Allow them to cool before serving.

ALMOJABÁNAS DE VALENCIA

Honey Doughnuts of Valencia

This recipe is just one version of the almojabána, served with honey and is closely related to the original Moorish dish. A more modern variation is known as "Rollo de amor de Jumilla" (Rings of Love, from Jumilla in Murcia). The recipe was originally recorded in Spanish cookery books dating from the 13th and 16th centuries.

This is essentially a baked doughnut coated in honey that is often filled with cream. Traditionally it was filled with fresh cheese. Indeed the name derives from the Arabic word, "almuyábbana", which means a mixture made with cheese. Cheese and honey are still a popular taste combination in Spain.

This pastry is typical throughout the area known as the Vega Baja del Segura in Valencia close to the Murcian border. It is an especially popular pastry eaten during the religious holidays of San José (March 19), All Saints' (November 1), and at Christmas.

Ingredients:

> 300 g white flour
> 5 medium eggs
> 100 ml olive oil (mild)
> 275 ml water
> 1 teaspoon of salt
> 100 ml honey
> 2 tablespoons of water

Preparation:

1. Heat the 275 ml of water, the olive oil and salt together in a large saucepan until the liquid starts to boil.

2. Remove from the heat and add all the flour to the mixture. Stir well until a dough is formed that does not stick to the walls of the saucepan. Depending on the flour used, you may need to heat the mixture again whilst stirring in order to get the correct consistency.

3. Take the dough out of the pan, put it in a bowl and leave it to rest for about 5 minutes to cool down and then knead it by hand.

4. Using a wooden spoon (or an electric mixer) add the eggs into the dough one at a time. Make sure each egg is thoroughly mixed in before adding the next one.

5. Preheat the oven to 200°C.

6. Place small rounds of dough onto a baking tray lined with baking paper. Keep the mounds well separated to allow for expansion during baking. Wet your finger and press the centre of each to make a hole in it. Traditionally the dough is allowed to remain roughly shaped to maintain its "rustic" charm!

7. Bake for about 25 to 30 minutes at 200°C until golden brown.

8. Remove from the oven and allow them to cool completely.

9. Make a honey syrup by heating up the honey with 2 tablespoons of water until it begins to boil. Coat the top of each doughnut with the warm honey. Serve warm or cold.

ALPISTERAS DE SANLÚCAR DE BARRAMEDA (CÁDIZ)

Sweet Anís Cakes of Sanlúcar de Barrameda (Cádiz)

Sanlúcar de Barrameda is a fishing village in North West Cádiz province in Andalucía. The village is famous for many culinary delights and "alpisteras" are certainly their most famous traditional sweet, though they are only baked during Lent and Easter.

Alpisteras became internationally famous when the English romantic author Richard Ford (1796-1858) wrote about them in his two books that he called "Handbook for Travellers in Spain", published in 1844. He suggested that alpisteras were the perfect accompaniment to the famous local Manzanilla wine of Sanlúcar. He even gives his readers a recipe for the cakes.

Ingredients (for 8 alpisteras):

For the dough:

>   4 egg yolks
>   Flour (the same amount as the weight of the egg yolks)
>   Grated peel of a quarter of a lemon
>   1 teaspoon of aniseed

For the glaze:

>   2 tablespoons of water
>   2 teaspoons of lemon juice
>   70 g sugar

Preparation

1. Preheat the oven to 180°C and line a baking tray with baking paper.

2. Separate the egg yolks and whites. Weigh the yolks and put the same weight of flour into a bowl with the egg yolks, grated lemon peel and the aniseed. Mix the ingredients together to form a consistent dough.

3. Roll out the dough on a lightly floured work surface. Use a diamond shaped pastry cutter with sides of around 5 or 6 cm to cut out the dough and place the pieces of dough on the baking paper.

4. Put the tray in the oven and bake until the edges of the cakes begin to brown and the corners begin to bend slightly.

5. Remove from the oven and allow the cakes to cool completely on a rack.

6. Prepare a glaze by mixing the water, sugar and lemon juice in a saucepan. Bring the mixture to the boil. You can tell if the syrup is ready by dropping a little into cold water. It should solidify into a ball. Remove from the heat and keep stirring until the syrup turns white.

7. Glaze the cold alpisteras with the syrup and allow the glaze to cool and dry before serving.

ARNADÍ DE VALENCIA

Easter Pumpkin and Almond Cake of Valencia

Arnadí is a traditional sweet cake of Valencia, particularly from the old Arab town of Játiva. Indeed, Arnadí has its origins in the Moorish period. The Andalucian Arabs used the word "garnadí" to refer to those who lived in the Moorish kingdom of Granada and as the word evolved into modern Spanish, the 'g' was lost. An almost identical cake, called Sellou is made in Morocco to this day and served during Ramadan and other special occasions.

Arnadí is usually made during Lent and Easter. It is also known as "Calabaza Santa", meaning "holy pumpkin", because it is now normally made with pumpkin, although other versions of the cake are made with sweet potato. Arnadí is eaten as a dessert, often baked in individual earthenware bowls.

Ingredients:

A pumpkin of 2.5 to 3 kg
900 g sugar
360 g almond flour
30 g peeled almonds and pine nuts
4 eggs
1 lemon
Cinnamon powder

Preparation:

1. Roast the pumpkin and then peel it and remove the seeds.

2. Drain the pumpkin overnight in a colander or cotton bag to remove excess moisture.

3. Separate the eggs and beat the yolks well in a bowl. Grate the peel from the lemon and put aside.

4. When the pumpkin is fully drained, add the sugar to it and blend pumpkin and sugar together. Then incorporate the almond flour and egg yolks into the mixture, together with some cinnamon powder (to your taste) and the grated lemon peel.

5. Preheat the oven to 140°C. To create a fine dough, put the mixture in a saucepan on a very low heat for 20 minutes, stirring continuously to avoid sticking.

6. Once cooked, place the dough into an ovenproof (earthenware) bowl and shape the dough into a conical shape. Sprinkle the top with a little sugar and press the tips of peeled almonds and pine nuts long ways into the dough so that they protrude all around the cake.

7. Bake at 140°C until golden brown but without burning the almonds and pine nuts. Remove from the oven and serve when cool.

BESITOS DE SANTA CLARA DE SEGOVIA

Little Kisses of Saint Clare from the Convent of St Clare of Segovia

This recipe comes from the 13th century Royal Convent of Saint Clare in the tiny village of Rapariegos in the province of Segovia. It is a universal favourite but no one actually seems to know its origins.

Ingredients:

  500 ml pastry cream (you can make your own)
  1 large egg or 2 small eggs
  50 ml olive oil (preheated with lemon peel to flavour and cooled)
  75 ml milk
  75 g sugar
  250 g flour
  16 g baking powder
  Grated coconut to decorate
  Syrup made with equal amounts of water and sugar, and a glass of sweet wine

Preparation:

1. Beat the eggs with the sugar until the mix begins to whiten.

2. Add the cold olive oil, milk and flour together with the baking powder.

3. Mix everything thoroughly and put the dough into a pastry bag with a smooth nozzle.

4. Preheat the oven to 180°C and line an oven tray with baking paper

5. Use the pastry bag to extrude circles of dough of roughly the same size on the tray, leaving enough space between them for expansion.

6. Bake them for 7 minutes at 180°C until golden brown.

7. Meanwhile, make the syrup by boiling the water, sugar and sweet wine together.

8. Remove the besitos from the oven when ready. To finish, take each two besitos and sandwich pastry cream between them and put aside. When completed, use the syrup to moisten them and then coat with coconut. Leave to cool overnight (in a refrigerator) before serving.

BICA GALLEGA

Galician Butter Sponge Cake

Bica is a very rich buttery sponge cake originating in Galicia. It is very popular in the area, especially around the time of carnival and other fiestas, but has come to some international attention and is considered one of the classical European pastries.

The cake originates in the village of Puebla de Trives, which is famous for its bica and actually hosts a festival of bica on the last Sunday of July. Bica was first mentioned in the nineteenth century but is thought to be older than this.

The key to the popularity of the cake is its rich texture that results from the butter content and sugared top. It is eaten at breakfast or with coffee but it is also often eaten with cheese and mulled wine.

Ingredients:

400 g flour
200 g butter (at room temperature)
200 g sugar (plus some to coat the bica)
200 ml cream
4 large eggs
15 g baking powder

Preparation:

1. Preheat the oven to 170°C with lower and upper heating.

2. Sift the flour together with the baking powder and put aside.

3. Use a whisk to beat the eggs together with the sugar until it is very foamy and has doubled in size. This will take at least 5 minutes.

4. To melt the butter: put the butter in a microwave for a few seconds or use a double boiler ("bain-marie") until the butter has almost melted and then stir with a spoon until completely smooth.

5. Gradually add the melted butter to the egg and sugar mixture, beating all the while.

6. Next, slowly add the cream and continue beating.

7. Add the flour in three or four stages and incorporate it well into the mixture with a spatula.

8. Line a baking tin with baking paper and coat the paper lightly with some oil Pour the mixture into the tin. With these quantities, a square tin of 26 cm x 26 cm is sufficient.

9. Sprinkle the top of the mixture with sugar according to your taste and place the tin in the oven for a total of 40-50 minutes.

10. Do not open the oven door before at least 35 minutes has passed. After 35 to 40 minutes test to see if the sponge is baked. Do this by inserting a skewer or fork into it. If the skewer comes out clean, then it is baked, otherwise wait a few minutes and try again.

11. When the cake is baked, remove it from the oven and let it cool before taking it out of the baking tin. Serve cool.

BIENMESABE ANTEQUERANO, MÁLAGA

Almond Cake of Antequera, Málaga

"Bienmesabe" roughly translates into English as "Tastes good to me". It is a sweet cake traditionally made with eggs, honey and almonds from the ancient city of Antequera in Andalucía, though there are versions of the cake in both the Canary Islands and the Balearic Islands. A cake of the same name is also made in Córdoba and its recipe is very similar. Another almost identical variant is found in several villages in the province of Jaén such as Porcuna.

Bienmesabe is often eaten as a dessert or with merienda. In the Canary Islands, the dish may include rum. Some contemporary versions of the cake use sugar rather than honey. Although it is not actually baked, we included it here because it is such a popular sweet.

Bienmesabe is believed to have its origins in the Arab culinary tradition and indeed Antequera was a prominent Arab town during the Moorish period and is still dominated by a beautiful Arab fortress.

There are many recipes for bienmesabe that vary from a sauce to a cake. However, the nuns of St Claire in the Convento of Bélen in Antequera have been using the same recipe for bienmesabe since 1635 and are still selling this sweet dish to passers-by in the city through a little wooden shutter opening onto the street from the convent.

Ingredients:

> 250 g raw almonds
> 425 g sugar
> 250 ml water
> 125 g ladyfinger biscuits
> 500 g angel hair
> 6 Eggs
> Cinnamon powder
> Icing sugar

Preparation:

1. Roast the almonds in a frying pan, taking care not to let them burn. When they are roasted, grind the almonds but not too finely. Put aside for later.

2. Use the ladyfinger biscuits to cover the base of a shallow cake mould.

3. Dissolve the sugar in the water in a saucepan and let it simmer to produce a syrup. Pour half of this syrup over the ladyfinger biscuits in the cake mould, covering the biscuits. Keep the remaining half of the syrup.

4. Cover the biscuits and syrup with a thin layer of angel hair.

5. Whisk the eggs well.

6. Put the ground almonds into the remaining syrup and add the beaten eggs (you can also add some cinnamon to this mixture according to your own taste).

7. Mix the almonds, eggs and syrup until they form a smooth paste. Put the mixture on a low heat to thicken. When it is thick enough, pour the mixture over the biscuits, syrup and angel hair in the cake mould.

8. Finally, decorate the cake with a thin layer of icing sugar and cinnamon. Allow it to cool before serving.

BIZCOCHÓN DE GOFIO (CANARIAS)
Gofio Sponge Cake of the Canary Islands

Before the arrival of the Spanish in the Canary Islands, an aboriginal society occupied these islands, whose people are known today as Guanches. They were closely related to the Berbers of North Africa. The impact of Spanish colonisation of the islands meant that few survived. However, parts of their legacy continue to this day and "gofio" is one example. The Guanches made a type of flour from a mixture of roasted barley and the roots of various ferns in a very similar way to the roasted flours of Morocco. This "gofio" formed an important part of their staple diet.

Over the years the composition of gofio on the islands has changed somewhat and gofio now refers to several types of flour made from roasted grains and beans including maize, wheat, rye, barley, chickpeas and lupin beans.

In the past, the roasting of the grains served several purposes: it destroyed potentially dangerous mould toxins, thus allowing poor quality grain to be used. The process also breaks down starches and proteins making them more digestible. These days Canarian foods using gofio in various ways are famous on the islands and each island has its own version of gofio.

Here is a sponge cake recipe, using the gofio from the small island of Gomera, which is made with maize, wheat, barley, oats and chickpeas, ground in a traditional way with natural stone mills.

Ingredients:

>   200 g butter (at room temperature)
>   300 g sugar
>   Icing sugar to decorate
>   1.5 teaspoons of vanilla essence
>   4 large eggs
>   320 g flour
>   80 g Canary gofio (Gofio Gomero 5 grain)
>   1.5 teaspoon of baking powder
>   240 ml milk (at room temperature)
>   Rectangular mould of 30cm x 11cm x 5cm

Preparation:

1. Preheat the oven to 180°C (with heating from above and below).

2. Use a blender or mixer to beat the butter until smooth and creamy. Add the sugar and vanilla to the butter and continue to beat until it becomes fluffy.

3. Add the eggs one at a time, whilst beating continuously. When each egg is thoroughly blended in, add the next one.

4. Sift the flour, gofio and baking powder together and add to the eggs and butter. Do not mix too long but just so that the ingredients are well combined.

5. Pour the mixture into the mould but only to about two thirds full because the cake needs space to expand. It should not be allowed to overflow during baking.

6. Place the mould in the oven and bake for 60 to 75 minutes. Test to see if the cake is baked by inserting a fork. If it comes out clean, it is ready.

7. When baked, remove the cake from the oven and take it out of the mould. Allow to cool and sprinkle with icing sugar before serving.

BIZCOCHO DE LAS CARMELITAS DE SEVILLA

Carmelite Sponge Cake of Sevilla

This is an ancient and rather strange recipe from the Carmelite nuns of Sevilla. It takes 10 days to prepare, so this is definitely not a recipe for someone in a hurry. It has various nicknames including "10 day sponge cake" (in Spanish).

Traditionally, this cake was made by hand and was shared with neighbours who in turn would make the same cake from the shared sourdough.

There is no precise history or explanation for the lengthy preparation, although some people attribute religious significance to it and it is generally believed to bring good luck and health to the baker and to those who share their sourdough. In any case, it has a very rich taste. Just do not be in a hurry!

Firstly, you must create a sourdough ("masa madre", in Spanish) or work with a sourdough that has been given to you. Do note that all the measures in this traditional recipe are "glasses" (or cups). How big your glass is will determine the size of your sponge cake! However, "a glass" in Spain is generally considered to be a coffee glass, which is 200 ml.

You will note that for the making of the cake, we are being true to the original recipe and showing the ingredients, as they are added, not in a separate list of ingredients.

If you are not lucky enough to have been given a sourdough by a friend, you must create your own. Below we give you a very basic recipe.

Ingredients:

Sourdough only:

> 1 cup flour
> 1 glass milk
> Half a glass of sugar
> 3 g dried yeast

Preparation:

Sour dough:

Mix everything together in a bowl with a wooden spoon and then cover, leave to ferment for 24 hours, ideally in a warm place.

Cake recipe:

Day 1: Take a glass of the sourdough you have made and pour into a large bowl. Add 1 glass of sugar and 1 glass of flour. Do NOT mix them.

Day 2: Mix the ingredients together with a wooden spoon.

Day 3: Do not touch the mixture - leave to rest.

Day 4: Do not touch the mixture - leave to rest.

Day 5: Add 1 glass of milk, 1 glass of sugar and a glass of flour. Do not mix.

Day 6: Mix well with a wooden spoon.

Day 7: Do not touch the mixture - leave to rest.

Day 8: Do not touch the mixture - leave to rest.

Day 9: By now, the dough will have risen considerably. Separate the dough into 3 equal parts. It is traditional to give two parts away to bring good luck to the recipients. With the third part, you will make the cake as follows:

1. Mix the dough with a glass of milk and two eggs. Add a pinch of cinnamon and 6 g of dried yeast.

2. Add a glass of olive oil and half a glass of sugar and mix with a wooden spoon.

3. Add two glasses of flour and mix until you have a consistent dough.

4. Preheat the oven to 180°C.

5. Add some chopped nuts, raisins and/or apple. Mix well.

6. Grease the baking tin with a little butter and pour in the dough.

7. Bake for 45 minutes at 180°C.

8. When it is baked and cooled, remove it from the tin and the cake is (finally) ready to serve.

BIZCOCHO - BIZCOCHADA DE LAS MONJAS

Lemon Sponge Cake of the Nuns

Another monastic recipe, this one is an aromatic lemon sponge, documented in the famous traditional monastic bakery book "Dulces y postres de las monjas" (Sweets and desserts of the nuns) by Sr. Isabel de la Trinidad and published by Styria. It is easy to make and is often taken at breakfast or with coffee.

Ingredients:

> 4 eggs
> 250 ml milk
> 375 g flour
> 300 g sugar
> 250 ml olive oil
> Grated peel of 1 lemon
> 1 tablespoon of baking powder
> 40 g icing sugar

Preparation:

1. Separate the eggs and beat the egg yolks in a bowl with the grated lemon peel and 175 g of the sugar. Add the milk and oil, beating thoroughly until it has a consistent texture.

2. Sieve the flour and baking powder together and add to the mixture little by little until thoroughly incorporated.

3. Whisk the egg whites with the remaining sugar until stiff. Add this slowly to the dough mixture and continue mixing until you have thick consistent sponge cake batter.

4. Preheat the oven to 170°C.

5. Put the batter into a baking tin and bake for 30 to 40 minutes.

6. When baked, coat with icing sugar. (Some people use melted chocolate or jam instead.)

7. Cut into squares to serve when fully cooled.

BIZCOCHO DE PASAS Y RON

Raisin and Rum Cake

Using strong spirits to preserve fruit is a common and traditional means of long-term storage in Spain. However, alcoholic spirits are also used to rehydrate dried fruits and simultaneously imbue them with the taste and smell of the spirit being used. This is a typical example where raisins are soaked in rum for some time (overnight will be fine - longer is even better!) and then used in a cake recipe.

Ingredients:

150 g flour
8 g baking powder
1 egg
1 tablespoon of honey
100 ml milk
100 g butter (room temperature)
50 g sugar
Grated peel of 1 orange (to taste)
50 g peeled walnuts
1 handful of raisins soaked in rum
Mint leaves for decoration

Preparation:

1. Preheat the oven to 180°C.

1. Put the sugar in a bowl, add the soft butter and beat together. Grate a little orange peel into the mixture and then add the honey, egg and milk. Continue beating until you have a smooth mixture.

2. Mix the baking powder with the flour. Drain the soaked raisins, dry them and add them to the flour.

3. Add the flour mix to the previous one. Gently fold the two mixes together until a completely consistent dough is formed.

4. Chop the walnuts and add them into the mixture.

5. Pour the dough into a baking tin (use a small bread tin) and bake for about 35 minutes at 180°C.

6. Remove the cake from the oven and allow it to cool. Serve garnished with some mint leaves.

BIZCOCHO DE CABELLO DE ANGEL Y ALMENDRA

Almond and Angel Hair Sponge Cake

The Spanish are fond of sponge cake and there are many different types. This one uses the traditional favourite ingredients of almonds and angel hair. It is typically eaten with breakfast or merienda.

Ingredients:

> 3 eggs
> 125 ml olive oil
> 100 g sugar
> 125 ml milk
> 125 g flour
> 150 g almond flour
> 400 g angel hair
> 16 g baking powder

Preparation:

1. Preheat the oven to 180°C.

2. Mix the eggs, oil, sugar, milk, flour and almond flour in a bowl.

3. Add the baking powder and mix again.

4. Add the angel hair and mix again thoroughly.

5. Put the mixture into a baking tray of about 20cm x 30cm lined with baking paper.

6. Bake for about 35 minutes. Test by pricking with a cocktail stick - it is baked if the cocktail stick is still dry after pricking the sponge.

7. Let the cake cool before serving it.

BOCADITOS DE ALMENDRA

Almond Scones

This type of sweet scone, based on almond flour, is one of many traditional variants of almond pastries in southern Spain It is simple to make, popular and usually eaten with coffee / chocolate at merienda or with breakfast.

Ingredients:

> 170 g ground raw almonds
> 150 g sugar
> 2 eggs
> 1 egg yolk
> Grated peel of 1 lemon
> Juice of half a lemon
> 1 tablespoon of butter

Preparation:

1. Preheat the oven to 170°C.

2. Beat the 2 eggs with the 1 egg yolk in a bowl.

3. Add the remaining ingredients whilst mixing continuously until you have obtained a smooth, homogenous dough.

4. Cover the bowl with plastic film and place it in the fridge for 1 hour.

5. Grease and flour small individual baking moulds and fill these with the dough.

6. Place the scones in the oven and bake until golden brown. To check if they are baked, insert a toothpick or fork into one or two of them. If it comes out clean, then the cakes are ready to be removed from the oven.

7. Allow to cool.

BOCADITOS DE HOJALDRE Y CABELLO DE ÁNGEL

Christmas Angel Hair, Almond and Cinnamon Pastry

This small sweet snack is very easily prepared and especially popular around Christmas. It is based on angel hair, it is made with puff pastry, and therefore quick to make, which is useful in the case of unexpected visitors. This is as close as pastry baking comes to fast food! Several convents make a similar pastry commercially.

Ingredients:

> 1 pack of puff pastry
> Angel hair (filling)
> 1 egg
> Almonds (coarsely chopped)
> Cinnamon powder

Preparation:

1. Preheat the oven to 200°C.

2. Roll out the pastry and cut it into strips of about 2 cm wide.

3. Line an oven tray with baking paper and powder it with flour.

4. Place the strips of pastry on the tray. On each strip of pastry place a little angel hair and cover with another strip of puff pastry.

5. When all the strips have been filled and covered, beat the egg and glaze the pastry. Finally cut the strips into rectangles and scatter some almonds on top.

6. Place in the oven at 200°C for 10-15 minutes, until the pastry starts to brown.

7. Before serving, allow to cool and sprinkle with cinnamon.

BOLLITOS DE SANTA INÉS DE SEVILLA

Sweet Sesame Buns - Convent of St. Inés, Sevilla

These sweet buns are the most famous sweet product of the old convent of St Inés in Sevilla. They are simple to make.

Ingredients:

> 500 g flour
> 1 teaspoon of dried yeast
> 1 glass of water
> Pinch of salt
> Icing sugar to coat
> Sesame seed to coat

Preparation:

1. Preheat the oven to 180°C.

2. In a bowl, mix the flour with the yeast, water and salt.

3. Knead the mixture until it becomes a dough, adding water or flour as needed.

4. Place a sheet of baking paper on a baking tray

5. Divide the dough into small pieces and make little rolls with them then form each one into an "S" shape, sprinkle with sugar and sesame seed.

6. Bake for around 15 minutes until they are golden brown.

BOLLO ESCARCHADO DE AVILÉS

Easter Cake of Avilés, Asturias

Every year in the town of Avilés in Asturias the local people hold the "Fiesta de Bollos" on Easter Sunday and Monday. This colourful festival originated in the 19th century and celebrates the arrival of spring and the end of Lent. It is an important cultural event and centres on a rich local sponge cake.

Traditionally, godparents gave these cakes to their godchildren and the cake is shaped as a four-pointed star and served in two or more layers with a large star at the bottom with a smaller star placed on top of it and so on. Most have just two stars as in our recipe below.

The baking tins for this cake are readily available in that part of Asturias, but it may not be so easy to find them elsewhere, so you may have to compromise on the shape.

The cake is usually eaten (by the adults anyway) with a glass of white wine, normally a local wine from the area of Nava del Rey.

Ingredients:

Cake:

> 9 medium-sized eggs (about 500 g in the shell)
> 500 g sugar
> 500 g flour
> 500 g butter
> Grated peel of 1 lemon

Coating:

> Water
> Icing sugar
> Few drops of lemon juice

Preparation:

1. Preheat the oven to 180°C.

2. Warm the butter in a pan or double boiler until it melts. Remove any froth.

3. Let the butter cool a little and then add the sugar and grated lemon peel. Mix well and next stir in the flour, mixing continuously.

4. Knead the mix with your hands until it becomes a consistent dough.

5. Grease the star-shaped baking tins with butter. One should be a large star and one a smaller star (in the traditional practice in Avilés) and fill them with the dough.

6. Bake for at least 50 minutes. Use a toothpick to test if the cake is baked. When the toothpick comes out clean, it is ready.

7. Remove from the oven and allow to cool. Then remove the cake from the baking tins.

8. Prepare the icing by mixing some icing sugar with a couple of teaspoons of warm water and a few drops of lemon juice. Coat each sponge with the sugar mix and place the smaller star sponge on top of the larger star sponge. When the coating is dry, the bollos are ready to serve.

9. Traditionally, the bollos of Avilés are decorated with all kinds of Easter symbols, such as chocolate flowers and figurines but that is up to you.

BOLLOS DE MIEL

Honey Buns

This is another favourite in monastic kitchens and bakeries throughout Spain. However, many households and local bakeries traditionally make these simple and economical sweet buns as well. There are many variations; for instance, using molasses instead of honey or adding finely chopped nuts.

This is really a type of bread but we have included it in this chapter of sweet pastry because it is normally served as a sweet for breakfast or merienda. Bollos can be eaten as they are, but some people also eat them with a sweet filling and others with a savoury filling.

Ingredients (4 to 6 buns):

190 g white flour
70 g wholemeal flour
1 teaspoon of dried yeast
Half a teaspoon of salt
45 g honey
145 ml lukewarm milk (25-30°C)
15 g butter (at room temperature)
25 g egg (half an egg approximately)
Beaten egg or melted butter to coat the buns

Preparation:

1. Sift the white flour into a large bowl and add the wholemeal flour, salt and dry yeast (add separately). Add the honey and the warm milk. Slightly beat the egg and add. Mix and knead until the dough does not stick to the bowl. Add the butter little by little and continue kneading until you have a consistent, smooth dough.

2. Make the buns about 8 cm in diameter, either forming balls or rolling the dough slightly and cutting them out with a dough cutter or a glass.

3. Put the buns on a baking tray lined with baking paper. Let them sit in a warm place to rise until they double in volume (an hour or more). You can also put them in an oven preheated to 25-30°C for an hour if the kitchen is cold.

3. When the buns have risen, coat them with beaten egg. You can optionally sprinkle a little sesame seed on top of the buns.

4. Preheat the oven to 180ºC and then bake for about 10-20 minutes, until the buns are golden brown.

5. After baking, coat the buns with a little melted butter.

BOLLOS DE SEMANA SANTA DE ARCOS DE LA FRONTERA

Easter Anís Doughnuts of Arcos de la Frontera

This is a traditional Easter pastry from the pretty town of Arcos de la Frontera in the province of Cádiz in Andalucía. As with many Easter pastries, it is flavoured with anís. Alternative local recipes also add some cinnamon powder to the dough mix. These baked doughnuts are eaten for both breakfast and merienda, often dipped in chocolate or coffee.

Ingredients (for 6 doughnuts):

> 85 ml olive oil
> Half a heaped teaspoon of sesame seed
> 100 ml water
> 15 g fresh yeast
> 25 g sugar
> 250 g pastry flour
> Half a teaspoon of aniseed
> 1 pinch of salt
> Sugar and almonds to decorate

Preparation:

1. Warm the olive oil with the sesame seed and aniseed on a moderate heat to avoid burning for a few minutes until the seeds release their aroma.

2. Meanwhile, crumble the yeast into the water with the sugar and a little flour.

3. Strain the now scented, lukewarm olive oil into the yeast mix and add the remaining ingredients (except the final sugar and almonds). Mix well and knead the dough thoroughly until it has a smooth, soft and moist consistency. It should not be sticky.

4. Divide the dough into 6 portions of about 80g each. Roll each into a ball and flatten. Make a hole in the centre of each so that it has the shape of a doughnut. Make the hole large enough, remembering that the dough will rise.

5. Place the doughnuts on a sheet of baking paper on an oven tray, leaving plenty of space between each doughnut. Decorate the tops with

the raw almonds and sugar, slightly moistened with water. Allow them to rise until they have almost doubled in volume.

6. Preheat the oven to 200°C and bake the bollos for about 18-20 minutes, or until they are golden brown.

7. Allow the doughnuts to cool on a wire rack before serving. Store them in an airtight container.

BRAZO DE GITANO DE ARAGÓN

Rolled Chocolate Sponge Cake of Aragón

Literally translated, the name of this cake is "Gypsy's Arm" and it has many variants. In its modern form it looks like a Swiss roll but its origins are believed to be in an Egyptian monastery. It is thought that a medieval monk from Bierzo in the province of León discovered the recipe in Egypt and brought it back to Spain. For some time it was called an "Egyptian arm" but gradually the name was corrupted into "Gypsy's arm" because gypsies, in those days, were thought to have originated in Egypt.

This cake is basically a rich filling rolled into a pastry that may be decorated or coated. The filling is often jam, cream or chocolate and the cake is then decorated with sugar, chocolate, whipped cream or meringue. One variation "Brazo de gitano de queso y membrillo" uses a filling of cream cheese and quince jam scattered with grated almond. Yet another modern version, "Gitanitos de chocolate" uses slices of the roll coated in melted chocolate. There are many variations!

The brazo de gitano is very popular in Aragón (especially in the municipality of Colungo) but variants of it are now to be found throughout Spain.

Ingredients:

> 6 eggs
> 250 g flour
> 250 g sugar
> 75 g butter (at room temperature)
> 250 g cream
> 75 g dark cooking chocolate
> 25 g jam of your choice
> 1 spoonful of a fruit liquor of your choice
> Fruit in season to decorate (strawberries, red currants)
> Icing sugar, to coat

Preparation:

1. Beat the eggs together with the sugar until frothy.

2. Add the softened butter little by little to the flour and stir together. Add the egg and sugar mix to the flour and continue to stir vigorously until you have a consistent dough.

181

3. Place buttered baking paper into a large, shallow baking tin and pour the mixture in. (The sponge cake must be flat and thin).

4. Bake for about 20 minutes at 180°C.

5. When the sponge is ready, allow it to cool.

6. Whip the cream, melt the chocolate in a double boiler (or microwave). When the chocolate has cooled a little, mix it with the whipped cream.

7. Soak the sponge cake with the fruit liquor, spread the jam over it and then cover it with the chocolate and cream mixture.

8. Roll the sponge cake to enclose the filling and then dust it over with icing sugar. Decorate with strawberries or other seasonal fruit.

9. Allow to cool and serve in slices.

BUÑUELOS DE ALMENDRAS

Almond Fritters

One of many traditional buñuelo recipes that can be found throughout Spain, this one is made with almonds. They are simple to prepare and delicious. They are often to be found around Easter time, although the origins of buñuelos are almost certainly 16th century Arabic and Jewish. This recipe comes from the old Arab village of Zagra in the province of Granada. The quantities can easily be scaled up if you like them!

Ingredients (for about 12 buñuelos):

> 65 g natural yoghurt
> 3 tablespoons of honey
> 1 egg yolk
> 60 g butter
> 80 g flour
> 50 g chopped almonds
> Icing sugar
> Olive oil

Preparation:

1. Mix the butter together with the beaten egg yolk, the yogurt and a teaspoon of honey. Continue to mix until it becomes a consistent paste.

2. Sift the flour into the mix little by little and mix well. When a dough has formed, start kneading it by hand. If the dough is still sticky, add a little more flour.

3. Wrap the dough in kitchen film and let it stand for about two hours at room temperature.

4. For the filling: mix the chopped almonds with the rest of the honey whilst stirring until fully blended.

5. Put the dough on a floured work surface and roll it out evenly but not too thinly. Cut out twelve circles of dough.

6. On each circle of dough, spoon a small portion of the almond mixture. Fold the edges over the filling by pressing carefully to seal them well. Form into a ball shape with your hands.

7. Fry the buñuelos in plenty of hot oil until they are evenly browned.

8. Leave the fritters to dry on absorbent kitchen paper to remove the excess oil and then sprinkle them with a little icing sugar.

9. Let the buñuelos cool completely and finish them off with another sprinkling of a little more icing sugar just before serving.

BUÑUELOS DE CUARESMA

Lenten Anís Doughnuts

A buñuelo is basically a fried dough ball, so not strictly speaking a pastry. However, it has a long history in Mediterranean and Roman cuisine and has a tradition at the culinary heart of Sephardic Jews, Muslims and Christians.

Buñuelos were very popular during the Moorish period in Spain, when the poor, especially in the South of Spain, supplemented their income by selling these fried doughnuts on the street. In Sevilla and Granada, buñuelos were a typical dessert eaten covered with honey. The dish became popular with the gypsy community and after the expulsion of the Moors and Jews, the buñuelo survived. Buñuelos of all kinds are still very popular in many parts of Spain.

There are many versions of buñuelo, often finished with a different topping or sauce. This version is traditionally eaten during Lent when meat was officially forbidden under church law.

Ingredients:

> Pinch of salt
> 75 g icing sugar
> Splash of anís liquor
> Grated peel of 1 lemon
> Olive oil for frying
> 1 teaspoon of fresh yeast
> 100 ml milk
> 50 g butter
> 2 eggs
> Icing sugar
> 250 - 300 g flour (approx.)

Preparation:

1. Dissolve the yeast in warm milk in a cup, stirring it with a wooden spoon.

2. Beat the butter with sugar and eggs with a whisk, until creamy. Add a pinch of salt and mix in the dissolved yeast.

3. Gradually add the flour to the mix and stir with a wooden spoon, until very thick. Grate the lemon peel and add this to the mix together with the anís liquor.

4. Place the dough on a work surface and kneading until smooth.

5. Take small portions of dough and shape them into balls about the size of a walnut. You can optionally flatten each ball slightly and make a hollow in the middle to form a doughnut or just leave them as a ball.

6. Allow to stand for 15 minutes in a cool place.

7. Fry the buñuelos in oil (not very hot), allow them to swell and turn golden brown.

8. Remove them from the oil and let them drain on kitchen paper. Sprinkle with icing sugar and serve.

BUÑUELOS DE CALABAZA

Pumpkin Fritters with Cinnamon

These fritters are really doughnuts but may be simply shaped in a ball. Here we present a recipe using pumpkins and cinnamon but they are also often prepared with ginger and / or nutmeg (with similar quantities as the cinnamon in this recipe). Buñuelos can be eaten warm or cold and are often accompanied with hot chocolate. They are a very traditional favourite of Valencia and eaten especially during the spectacular Fallas Festival in March when huge effigies are paraded around various Valencian towns and then ceremonially burned. The festival is an ancient one celebrating the spring equinox but is now timed to celebrate St Joseph's day.

Buñuelos are very easy to prepare and come from a long culinary history of sweet Mediterranean fritters, which are popular to this day. Cato (the Elder), the Roman historian, wrote enthusiastically about them in the second century AD and even gave recipes in his book "De Agri Cultura".

There are so many variations of the buñuelo that it is impossible to document them all. The Sephardic Jews of Spain during the 10th century created many variants of their own to celebrate Hanukkah. After the Christian expulsions of Moors and Jews from Spain during the 15th and 16th centuries, the Jews brought their recipes to France and elsewhere. There is also many a good yarn about the Arabic origins of the buñuelo, including the one about the siege of Almogía, Málaga, in 1090, when buñuelos were reportedly fried in the boiling oil being prepared to defend the town against attack.

However, the culinary concept of buñuelos also existed in pre-Hispanic South American cultures where an almost identical dish was made by the Mayans and Aztecs using cassava. In reality, many cultures have similar sweet and savoury dishes made with fried dough.

The cross-pollination of ingredients and recipes between Latin America and Spain meant that buñuelos are often made with a combination of sweet ingredients and staples such as pumpkins or sweet potatoes. The use of pumpkins in buñuelos became popular with their widespread cultivation in Spain. Pumpkins can be of immense size and traditionally provide an important source of carbohydrates, fibre and vitamins in rural Spain. They can be easily stored and used over the winter.

Ingredients (25 fritters):

> 75 g flour
> 25 g sugar (or more to taste)
> 200 g pumpkin pulp (already cleaned and chopped)
> 1.5 teaspoon of baking powder
> Half a teaspoon of ground cinnamon
> 2 eggs
> A pinch of salt
> Grated peel of half a large orange
> Olive oil (mild) for frying
> Icing sugar mixed with cinnamon powder

Preparation:

1. Cook the pumpkin in a steamer, a microwave or by boiling it in a pan with a very small amount of water. Whichever way you choose to cook the pumpkin, ensure that after it is cooked it is very well drained. After draining the pumpkin mash it with a fork until it is smooth and consistent.

2. Mix the mashed pumpkin with the flour, the baking powder, cinnamon, salt, orange peel, sugar and egg yolks. Stir well until the mixture becomes a smooth dough. The dough should have the texture of a thick béchamel, i.e. it should remain slightly firm when stirred with a spoon. If the dough is too thick, add a little water and if it is too fluid, add a little more flour.

3. Whisk the egg whites until stiff. Fold them into to the dough and mix gently.

4. Use two tablespoons to form balls of dough. You can also use an ice cream scoop to form the buñuelos.

5. Fry the buñuelos in warm olive oil on a medium heat until they are cooked through.

6. Place the fried buñuelos on absorbent kitchen paper to drain. Sprinkle with a mixture of icing sugar (or granulated sugar) and cinnamon powder. Serve hot or cold.

BUÑUELOS DE MANZANA A LA CANELA

Apple and Cinnamon Doughnuts

The origin of doughnuts is thought to be Arabic. In the great Moorish capital of Granada, they produced fritters made with honey, water and flour, which were then dipped into very hot honey. The first written recipes for doughnuts originated in 16th century Spain. The recipes were for both sweet and savoury doughnuts, filled or unfilled.

In Spain, doughnuts are traditionally eaten during celebrations. For example, in Cataluña they are eaten during Lent, in Madrid and Andalucía during holy week, and in Valencia during the "Fiesta de Fallas". There are many more examples. In many Northern areas, where apples are grown, apple doughnuts are a favourite snack during the Christmas festivities.

Here we have a very simple and quick-to-prepare recipe. The original recipe calls for the addition of cognac, but you can also use Moscatel wine. It depends on your taste.

Ingredients:

> 2 rennet apples (for example, Golden Reinette)
> Moscatel wine (or cognac)
> 160 g flour
> 160 g sugar
> 200 ml water
> Olive oil for frying
> A mixture of cinnamon powder and icing sugar to coat

Preparation:

1. Core and peel the apples. Cut them into rings of no more than 1 cm thick. Make sure the core hole is in the middle of the ring if you want to form a doughnut!

2. Place the apple slices in a tall glass or in a jar. Cover them with Moscatel wine (or brandy if you choose this option) and marinate for 4 or 5 hours.

3. Prepare the batter by mixing the flour, sugar and water until it is a creamy paste. It should be of a consistency that will coat the apple slices.

4. Dip the apple slices into the batter and fry them immediately in hot olive oil.

5. Once they are golden coloured, remove them from the oil, put them on a plate covered with absorbent kitchen paper and sprinkle them with the cinnamon and sugar mixture.

6. Serve hot.

BUÑUELOS DE MONJA

Nuns' Fritters

This is a very simple and economical traditional recipe from Alcoy in Alicante. Its origins are certainly Moorish - fried dough recipes are still popular in the Levant and are found in many traditional Jewish and Moorish recipe books. However, the recipe was taken over by the nuns as a tempting dish and there are several variations, including one version which uses a little Moscatel wine and cinnamon.

Ingredients:

> 300 g pastry flour
> 200 g sugar
> 50 g butter
> 250 ml milk
> 3 eggs
> Grated peel of 1 lemon
> Oil for deep-frying
> Icing sugar

Preparation:

1. Separate the egg yolks from the whites.

2. Grate the lemon peel.

3. Melt the butter in a saucepan. When the butter has melted, mix in the sugar. Then add the milk and lemon peel and stir well. Leave it on a low heat for about 5 minutes until it starts to boil, and then remove the pan from the heat.

4. Continue mixing until the mixture has cooled, then little by little add the flour whilst still mixing constantly.

5. When the dough does not stick to the sides of the pan put aside.

6. Beat the egg yolks and egg whites each in a separate bowl.

7. Add the beaten egg yolks and egg whites to the mixture and continue to stir until the dough is consistent.

8. Pour the dough into a large bowl.

9. Then put plenty of oil for frying into a pan (about 2 or 3 cm deep) on the heat.

10. When the oil is hot, use a large spoon to take the dough from the bowl and drop into the oil. Turn the fritters to make sure they are evenly fried on both sides. They brown very quickly.

11. When browned, remove each buñuelo from the hot oil and place them on kitchen roll to dry.

12. Whilst still hot, sprinkle them with icing sugar (optional) and serve.

BUÑUELOS DE NARANJA

Orange Fritters

This is another variant of the traditional and popular buñuelo, this time with orange filling. Often eaten as a breakfast sweet, it is also served as a "postre" (dessert) after a main course lunch or dinner. They come in various shapes, as balls, rings or flat circles.

Ingredients:

> 250 g flour
> 2 tablespoons of baking powder
> 3 eggs
> 125 g of natural yoghurt
> 225 g sugar
> Pinch of salt
> 1 large orange
> Olive oil

Preparation:

1. Peel the orange, remove the bitter white pith and cut up the fruit and peel.

2. Put the orange into a blender and add the eggs, yoghurt, a tablespoon of oil and a pinch of salt. Blend the ingredients well.

3. Put this mixture into a bowl and add the baking powder. Sift the flour in and mix thoroughly until you have a consistent dough.

4. Let the mix stand for an hour.

5. Heat a deep frying pan with plenty of olive oil until the oil is quite hot.

6. Form the dough into small balls and fry these until golden brown.

7. Remove each one and place them on absorbent kitchen paper to remove excess oil.

8. When dried, roll the buñuelos in sugar and they are ready to serve.

CAÑAS FRITAS DE O CARBALLIÑO, GALICIA

Cream Filled Fritters of Galicia

This is a very typical cinnamon sweet from the old town of O Carballiño in Galicia. They are particularly popular during the carnival celebrations. Traditionally the tubes of dough were shaped using pieces of wild cane (caña, in Spanish) collected around riverbanks. Nowadays, there are steel moulds used to shape the tubes of dough, which can remain with the dough when it is deep-fried.

Cañas are often taken with merienda and hot chocolate or tea or they are sometimes just eaten on the street during the carnival fiestas. However, they are also eaten at breakfast or as a formal dessert.

Ingredients:

Dough:

> 400 g flour
> 100 ml milk
> Pinch of salt
> 225 ml mild olive oil or sunflower oil for the dough
> Sunflower oil to fry the cañas

Pastry Cream:

> 500 ml milk
> 4 eggs
> 40 g flour
> 75 g sugar
> 1 vanilla pod

Decoration:

> Cinnamon powder
> Icing sugar

Preparation:

1. Prepare the dough: Mix the flour, a pinch of salt, milk, and oil. Knead into a smooth dough.

2. When thoroughly kneaded, cover the dough with kitchen film or a cloth and let it rest for about 2 hours.

194

3. Prepare the pastry cream: Heat the milk with the vanilla seeds in a saucepan until it boils. Set aside. Remove the vanilla pods just before using the milk.

4. Thoroughly mix the sugar and flour in a bowl, adding a little cold milk.

5. Beat the eggs with a splash of warm milk and add them to the sugar / flour mix. Stir well and then add the mix to the vanilla-flavoured milk.

6. Put the saucepan on the heat and stir continuously until the pastry cream thickens. When it has thickened enough, remove from the heat, put it aside and let it cool.

7. Uncover the dough and roll it out on the work surface.

8. You are now going to use the stainless steel cylindrical moulds for the cañas.

9. Cut the pastry into squares and roll them diagonally around the cylindrical moulds.

10. Heat the sunflower oil in a deep frying pan and as soon as it is hot lower the cañas into the hot oil (with the moulds still in place). Fry until golden brown and then remove them from the oil and place them on a plate covered with kitchen roll to absorb the excess oil.

11. When the cañas are cold, carefully remove the steel moulds.

12. Put the pastry cream into a pastry bag and use it to fill the cañas.

13. When the cañas are all filled, scatter them with a mixture of sugar and cinnamon.

14. They are ready to eat!

CARBAYONES DE ASTURIAS

Sherry and Almond Pastry of Asturias

Carbayones are a typical Asturian pastry and especially famous are those from Oviedo. The name derives from the Asturian word for the famous oak (carbayu) which used to stand in front of the Campoamor Theater in the city. The pastry was invented in 1924 for the First International Exhibition of Gijón. A legendary master pastry chef of the town's most famous confectioner Camilo de Blas created the pastry. The pasteleria Camilo de Blas still exists and is still famous for its quality sweet pastries. It is a very rich pastry but needs a little patience to finish.

To make these you will need small rounded, oblong, grooved cake moulds about the size and shape of what is called an éclair in English.

Ingredients (makes 6):

Pastry:

> 1 sheet puff pastry
> 125 g finely ground almond
> 125 g sugar
> 1 large egg, separated into yolk and white
> 1 pinch of grated lemon peel
> 30 ml sweet sherry
> Butter for cake moulds

Egg Cream:

> 4 egg yolks
> Same weight of sugar as the weight of the egg yolks
> Same weight of water as the egg yolks

Sugar Glaze:

> 4 tablespoons of icing sugar
> A few drops of lemon juice
> 1-2 tablespoons of water

Preparation:

1. Mix the finely ground almond, sugar and egg yolks in a bowl.

2. Add the grated lemon and the sweet sherry and mix well.

3. Whip the egg white until it becomes white but not stiff and add it to the almond mix with a spatula.

4. Preheat the oven to 200°C.

5. Grease the cake moulds thoroughly with butter.

6. Roll out the puff pastry thinly, cut out shapes a bit larger than the moulds and line the bottom of each mould. Cut off the excess pastry.

7. Fill the moulds with the almond paste mixture and place them on a baking tray.

8. Reduce the oven temperature to 180°C (from the bottom only) and put the tray in the oven. Bake until golden brown, which takes around 25-30 minutes. It is best to place the tray at the bottom of the oven in order to brown properly and slow down the baking. Place some aluminium foil over the moulds to avoid burning.

9. Allow the pastries to cool slightly on a wire rack and then remove them from their moulds.

10. Whilst cooling, prepare the egg cream as follows:

11. Put the egg yolks in a bowl and beat a little.

12. Make the syrup in a saucepan with the water and sugar. Heat for about 6 minutes until it starts to thicken. Remove from the heat and leave to cool for a short time.

13. Prepare another pan for a bain-marie (double boiler) and place the syrup pan into it - the cream sticks very easily when heated directly.

14. Pour the syrup over the egg yolks whisking vigorously to ensure that the mixture remains fluid and the yolks do not solidify.

15. Place the sauce into the bain-marie, again stirring constantly until the sauce thickens to the consistency of a thick custard. Allow to cool for a short time.

16. Cover each cake with a generous coating of the sauce using a spoon. Allow the sauce to cool on the cakes by placing them in a fridge for 2 hours.

17. When the cakes are cooled, prepare the sugar glaze: Put the icing sugar in a bowl and add 3 or 4 drops of lemon juice. Then gradually add the water and mix to a uniform consistency.

18. Carefully cover each cake with a generous coating of the glaze and allow it to dry, preferably overnight. They are then ready to serve.

CARMELAS DE CREMA DE JEREZ

Cream Éclairs of Jerez

Carmelas de crema de Jerez are actually sweet buns filled with bakers' cream and coated in icing sugar. They are a very typical sweet of Jerez de la Frontera in Andalucía but there are many local variants to be found in Sevilla province and as far away as Córdoba. Some variants have fillings that use chocolate and other sauces.

Ingredients:

For the dough:

>325 g bread flour
>100 ml water
>1 large egg
>12 g sugar
>38 g sugar
>50 g fresh yeast
>0.5 ml vanilla paste or equivalent in vanilla sugar / essence
>10 ml sunflower oil
>5 g salt
>15 g milk powder

For the filling:

>500 ml water (divide into 2 portions of 250 ml each)
>2 egg yolks
>125 g sugar
>65 g flour
>0.5 ml vanilla paste or equivalent in vanilla sugar / essence

Preparation:

Start by making the cream filling.

Cream filling:

1. Pour 250 ml of water into a saucepan and bring it to the boil.

2. Meanwhile, thoroughly mix the flour and sugar together in a bowl. Add the second 250 ml of water to this and blend well until there are no lumps.

3. Beat the egg yolks and blend them into the flour and sugar mix.

4. When the water in the saucepan begins to boil, gradually add the mixture in the bowl to the water whilst stirring continuously. Bring the mixture to the boil again. Then pour the mixture into another bowl and allow it to cool.

Pastry Dough:

5. Place all the dough ingredients in a large bowl and mix thoroughly with a wooden spoon until you have a consistent, smooth dough. Knead the dough by hand and then form it into a ball, cover it and allow it to stand for an hour or so, away from draughts.

6. Knead again to let out the gas and then cut the dough into 30 g portions shaped like a small bun. Place each one onto a baking tray lined with baking paper. Allow enough space for them to increase in size (depending on your oven it may be better to use two trays to allow for expansion).

7. Allow the dough to rise again until the buns have doubled in size. Preheat the oven to 200°C.

8. Brush the buns with milk and then bake them for about 10 minutes at 200°C, or until they begin to brown.

9. When baked, remove them from the oven and place them on a wire rack to cool completely.

10. Cut the rolls in half with a sharp knife, fill them with the cream filling and sprinkle the tops with icing sugar. The Carmelas are ready to serve.

CANUTILLOS DE PESTIÑO
Filled Pestiño Cones

Pestiños are a traditional fried sweet found in Andalucía and other parts of Southern Spain. The pestiño has a history. It was mentioned in the 1528 novel entitled "La Lozana Andaluza" (known in English as "The Portrait of Lozana") by Francisco Delicado. However, pestiños are closely related to the Moroccan "shebbakiyya" so in all probability pestiños originated during the Andalusí period of Arab culture in Spain.

Generally, pestiños are prepared during Christmas and Easter whereas the shebbakiyya is made during Ramadan and is a high-energy way of breaking the daily fast. It is similar to other fried sweets prepared during Jewish Passover.

Canutillos de pestiño are a variant on the pestiño. They are made into the shape of a conical hollow tube and are sometimes filled with various sweet contents such as chocolate or a cream paste. To make canutillos of any kind you need small conical ovenproof moulds. These are readily available in Spain but in other countries, you can improvise by rolling aluminium foil into conical forms.

Ingredients:

> 200 ml olive oil
> 200 ml white wine (some people use Oloroso, the sweet sherry from Jerez)
> 1 tablespoon of sesame seed
> 1 tablespoon of aniseed
> 500 g flour
> A pinch of salt
> 1 egg (beaten)
> Sugar for coating

Preparation:

1. Heat the olive oil and when hot put it aside for two minutes to cool a little. Add the aniseed and sesame seed to the oil. Note that the seeds should not burn or fry, so ensure that the oil is not too hot. Allow the mix to cool down until luke-warm.

2. Put the wine into a bowl and add the almost cold oil and seeds with a pinch of salt. Mix and then start gradually adding all the flour until you get a smooth dough, being careful to avoid lumps forming.

3. Put the dough into the refrigerator for two hours.

4. Roll out the dough on a lightly floured work surface, using a rolling pin, until it is 2 to 3 mm thick. Use a pastry cutter to cut the dough into rectangular strips of the same size and sufficiently long to cover your conical canutillo mould.

5. Preheat the oven to 200°C.

6. Cover the conical moulds with the strips of dough starting at the pointed tip of the conical mould and rolling the dough around the mould, allowing the strips to overlap a little but advancing to the top of the mould to form a cone of wrapped dough.

7. Line an oven tray with baking paper and place the canutillos slightly apart on the tray.

8. Paint each canutillo with the beaten egg.

9. Bake them in the oven for 25 to 30 minutes at 200°C ensuring that they do not burn. You know when they are ready when the moulds detach from the baked pastry. Take them out of the oven and cover them quickly with sugar.

10. Allow the canutillos to cool before filling or serving.

CARACOLA DE HOJALDRE CON PASAS

Cinnamon and Raisin Whirl

Literally translated, the name of this pastry is "puff pastry snail with raisins". Of course, the "snail" refers to the shape of the pastry and is not an ingredient! Variants of this pastry are found in other countries but you can find them in almost every bakery in Spain. The recipe uses a sheet of puff pastry rolled up with a filling. The roll is then sliced and each slice placed on a baking tray. When baked they expand and the expanded pastry roll gives the impression of the snails shell.

The Spanish versions are, of course, uniquely Spanish in taste. There are many types to be found but the most traditional ones use cinnamon and the raisins are soaked in a sweet wine, such as Moscatel, or in strong liquor, such as brandy, before using them in the pastry. Some recipes use cream or honey instead of butter.

Here is a typical traditional recipe.

Ingredients:

>1 rectangular sheet of frozen puff pastry dough
>2 tablespoons of melted butter
>Cinnamon powder
>Brown sugar
>Soaked raisins (use brandy or a sweet wine like Moscatel for soaking)

Preparation:

1. Paint the surface of the dough with melted butter. Sprinkle brown sugar, cinnamon powder and the soaked raisins evenly across the sheet of pastry.

2. Loosely roll up the pastry like a Swiss roll. Seal the roll closed with a little water.

3. Cut this roll into slices of about 1.5 cm thick. Place these slices, a little apart, on a baking tray covered with baking paper. Flatten the slices slightly by hand so that they do not open too much during baking and brush them with beaten egg.

4. Bake at 190°C for 15 to 20 minutes or until golden brown.

5. After they are half-cooled, paint the pastries with a sugar glaze and then allow them to cool fully before serving.

COCA DE LLANDA DE VALENCIA

Valencian Sugar Sponge

Coca de llanda is a typical and well-liked sugar sponge cake of Valencia. In the province of Alicante, these cakes are also known as "boba coca" (meaning that they are easy to make). This is a cake that expands quite a lot but it is also quite dense.

The sponge is made on a baking tray, which is called a "llanda" in Valencian. The recipe below is for a cake that is rectangular and about 25cm by 30cm and 5cm high.

Variants of coca de llanda are made with almonds, cream, apple, nuts, raisins or chocolate. In some places, bakers decorate the crust with pictures created with sugar and cinnamon.

Coca de llanda is eaten both as a dessert and for merienda. Here is a basic recipe.

Ingredients (for a 25 x 30 x 5cm baking tray):

3 eggs (about 180 g)
350 g sugar (plus some for sprinkling on the top)
Grated peel of 1 lemon
220 ml sunflower oil (or a mild olive oil)
500 ml milk
500 g flour
17 g baking powder

Preparation:

1. Preheat the oven to 180°C.

2. Break the eggs into a large bowl, add the sugar and beat together until the mix has doubled in volume. Add in the freshly grated lemon peel, sunflower (or olive) oil and milk and continue to mix.

3. Sift in the flour together with the baking powder and gradually incorporate this into the mix until you have a smooth dough without lumps.

4. Line a rectangular baking tray with baking paper, covering the bottom and sides. Pour the cake batter into the tray and spread it until the tray is uniformly covered and the top of the sponge is smooth.

5. When the oven has reached temperature, place the tray below the middle of the oven and bake for about 30 minutes.

6. Check that the sponge is baked by sticking a fork into it. If it comes out dry then the cake is done. Remove the tray from the oven.

7. Sprinkle the cake immediately with sugar and allow it to cool before serving.

COCA DE MOLLITAS DE ALICANTE

Crumble Pastry of Alicante

The coca de mollitas is one of Alicante's most traditional dishes and the basic recipe has remained unchanged for generations. It has a characteristic flavour and texture but there are now many variants on this original recipe, mostly sweet. Therefore, we include this recipe in the sweet pastry chapter. Some variations use a crumble made with bread, some substitute wine for the original beer and some sweet varieties add chocolate or hazelnut cream to the topping. The contrast between chocolate and salty tastes is interesting and pleasant. Some new varieties use puff pastry as a base.

This original recipe is very simple to make and is slightly salty. It is served as a snack often with a beer and also served as street food during festivals or pilgrimages.

Ingredients:

Base:

> 375 g bread flour
> 225 g olive oil
> 125 ml beer
> Salt to taste

Crumble topping:

> Salt to taste
> 112 g olive oil
> 300 g plain flour

Preparation:

Base:

1. Sieve the flour with a teaspoon of salt into a bowl. Make a hole in the centre of the flour and pour in the olive oil. Stir well with a spatula (or use an electric mixer).

2. When you have a consistent dough, add the beer and continue to mix and knead for 10 minutes. You can add more or less salt, according to your taste.

3. Line a baking tray with baking paper and sprinkle with flour.

4. Manually spread the dough over the baking paper into a rectangle.

5. Preheat the oven at 200°C (with heat top and bottom).

Crumble topping:

6. Mix the sifted flour and two pinches of salt together with the olive oil. (Most recipes make the crumble a little saltier than the base). Mix thoroughly with a spatula.

7. Put the dough into a plastic container with a lid and shake vigorously until it starts to form small balls of dough - the crumble. You can also coarsely grate the dough to create the crumble.

8. Spread the crumbled dough over the base dough in the tray.

9. Before baking, cut into rectangular portions (it is much easier to do this before baking than after).

10. Bake for at least 20 minutes until the crumbs turn golden but not brown.

11. Remove the coca from the oven and allow it to cool for 5 minutes. Then place the portions on a rack to cool completely and they are then ready to serve.

COCA DE SANT JOAN DE CATALUÑA

St. John's Mid-Summer Fruit Cake of Cataluña

The Coca de Sant Joan (St. John in Catalan) is a famous traditional Catalan fruitcake made for the feast of Saint John. St John's is traditionally considered the shortest night of the year. It is celebrated on the night of the 23rd of June. The 24th June is the birthday of John the Baptist, hence the name of the festival.

In Cataluña, this traditional cake has been made since at least the 13th century. The festival of Saint John (which is also really the pagan summer solstice) is celebrated in all of Spain and often with ceremonies involving fire. The fire is said to give the weakening sun strength.

This is an ancient festival and long precedes Christianity. Even in small villages and rural areas, bonfires are built and nighttime ceremonies are held.

In Cataluña, every village has its own recipe for Coca de Sant Joan with many variations and different toppings. These toppings include pine nuts, candied fruit, angel hair and cream. The traditional recipe here uses candied fruits and pine nuts.

Ingredients (for a 40 cm x 30 cm baking tray):

> 400 g bread flour
> 175 ml milk
> 2 eggs
> 75 g brown sugar
> Grated peel of 1 lemon
> 30 g fresh yeast
> 50 g butter
> 5 g salt

To cover the coca:

> 100 g candied fruits
> 50 g pine kernels
> 1 egg yolk
> Olive oil
> 25 g sugar

Preparation:

1. Warm the milk, pour it in a bowl and mix in the yeast. Add a little flour, stir and let the mixture stand for 15 minutes.

2. Sift the remaining flour into another bowl. Add the eggs, butter, grated lemon peel, salt and sugar. Mix and knead the ingredients until the butter is well incorporated.

3. Combine the contents of the two bowls and mix well until you have a soft (rather sticky) dough.

4. Preheat the oven to 175°C.

5. Coat the baking tray with olive oil and spread the dough evenly onto the tray. Use a brush to paint the surface of the dough with egg yolk. Scatter pieces of candied fruit and pine nuts on top of the dough. Sprinkle the top with olive oil and scatter with sugar. Leave to stand for 15 minutes.

6. Place the tray in the oven and bake for 20-25 minutes or until golden brown.

7. When baked, remove the coca from the oven and allow it to cool before serving.

COCADAS DE LAS CLARISAS DE MARCHENA

Coconut Sweets of the Poor Clares of Marchena

This recipe is for a very famous and well-liked pastry from the monastery of the Poor Clares in the town of Marchena in Sevilla province. It is made with potatoes, which may seem strange to Northern Europeans. We associate potatoes with savoury dishes, but, in fact, many sweet dishes in Spain use potatoes as a base. Potatoes have a neutral taste. Thus, they can be made into either sweet or savoury dishes.

Ingredients:

> 1 kg grated coconut
> 2 eggs
> 1 kg sugar
> 1 kg potatoes
> Grated peel of 1 lemon

Preparation:

1. Boil the potatoes.

2. When they are cooked, mash them (in a blender). Preheat the oven to 220°C.

3. Place the potatoes in a bowl, add the sugar and mix. Then add the eggs and lemon peel and finally the coconut.

4. Continue to mix until you have a consistent dough.

5. Make small balls with the dough, place on a paper lined baking tray and bake for 18 minutes in an oven at 220°C to 240°C until golden brown.

6. When baked, remove the cocadas from the oven and allow them to cool before serving.

CORBATAS DE UNQUERA

"(Bow) Tie" Pastries of Unquera, Cantabria

This is an interesting and easy to make pastry from the small town of Unquera in Cantabria. It is known as a "corbata" because it is formed into the shape of a tie or bow tie. It is made with puff pastry, coated with almonds. The apparent reason for the shape (and name) seems to be that the pastry was invented to use up excess puff pastry and a bow tie seemed a convenient shape.

Corbatas have become popular throughout Spain and are now quite widely available but the original is still produced by three bakeries in Unquera. Generally, it is eaten with breakfast but is also served as a dessert or with merienda, with afternoon coffee, tea or chocolate.

Ingredients (for about 16 corbatas):

1 or 2 rectangular sheets of puff pastry (depending on size)
1 egg white
1 teaspoon of lemon juice
100 g icing sugar
Chopped raw almonds to decorate

Preparation:

1. Preheat the oven to 190°C (heating from above and below).

2. Prepare the glaze: Put the icing sugar, egg white and the teaspoon of lemon juice in a bowl. Stir well with a whisk until completely mixed and without lumps.

3. Roll out the puff pastry and cut it into strips. To make a bowtie shape, twist the pastry in the middle (you can also make a necktie shape by twisting the pastry at one end if you want!)

4. Place each "(bow) tie" on a baking tray lined with baking paper.

5. Paint the glaze onto the pastry and sprinkle with the chopped almonds.

6. Place the tray in the oven (at the top) and bake for about 10-12 minutes at 190°C. Keep an eye on progress after about 8 minutes. Turn the pastries, if necessary, to make sure they are thoroughly baked.

7. When baked to a light golden brown, remove the pastries and allow them to cool on a rack.

CORDIALES DE MURCIA

Almond Christmas Macaroons

The cordiales de Murcia (also known as "puñetitas") are a very traditional Christmas cake of Murcia, made with almonds and angel hair. They are round and shaped with a little pointed top and are usually the size of a magdalena (cup cake) but can be bigger or smaller.

Like many Spanish Christmas sweets, cordiales have their origin in Moorish confectionary. The sweet has found its way into the Christmas diet through the many convents that still manufacture them.

Cordiales are eaten as a dessert.

Ingredients:

> 250 g almonds
> 200 g icing sugar
> 1 grated lemon peel
> 3 eggs
> 250g angel hair

Preparation:

1. Finely chop the almonds.

2. Beat the eggs.

3. Mix all the ingredients (except the angel hair) well in a bowl, cover it and leave it to stand in the refrigerator for two hours.

4. After two hours, take the mix out of the fridge and add the angel hair

5. Preheat the oven to 170°C.

6. Use the dough to make the small round macaroons with a point on top of each. Place each in paper baking cups or on wafers on a lined baking tray.

7. Bake in a preheated oven at 170°C until golden brown on top.

8. Shake a little icing sugar onto the cordiales, allow to cool and serve.

COSTILLAS DE HOJALDRE DE MURCIA

Angel Hair Puff Pastries of Murcia

The combination of puff pastry and angel hair is very popular in many regions of Spain, often in combination with cinnamon, almonds or other fillings. This very simple recipe comes from Murcia and is a popular sweet made at Christmas. The pastry has many humorous local nicknames such as "herradura" - horseshoe, or "orejas de fraile" - friar's ears, or "costillas" - ribs.

There are plenty of variations on the basic recipe, which include sliced almonds as a topping. Some recipes add strong liquors, such as anís, to the filling but the recipe below is for the most basic version.

Ingredients:

>Puff pastry
>Angel hair
>Cinnamon powder to taste
>Icing sugar to decorate
>Egg to coat

Preparation:

1. To make the costillas, simply cut pieces of puff pastry. You can make them square and small or larger and rectangular.

2. Mix the angel hair with a little cinnamon powder. Spread this on the puff pastry and cover with another piece of puff pastry of the same size.

3. Preheat the oven to 200°C.

3. Paint the tops of the pastries with egg and a little sugar and put them in the oven.

4. Bake until the puff pastry rises and browns.

5. Remove them from the oven and sprinkle with a little icing sugar to decorate.

6. Allow the costillas to cool and they are ready to serve.

COSTRADA DE ALCALÁ DE HENARES

Almond and Meringue Pastry of Alcalá de Henares

Despite the common misconception, meringues are not unique to France, Italy, Switzerland, or Morocco. Traditional meringue dishes were found in Mexico (and predated Columbus), and old recipes were documented in Germany, Poland and Spain.

This particular recipe uses meringue as an ingredient but for the rest is typical of a sweet with Arabic origins using puff pastry, chopped almond, sugar and lemon. The tart consists of several layers of puff pastry, baker's cream, meringue and almond.

The confectioners and royal pastry chefs Salinas created the modern version of the costrada in the 19th century. This pastry is particularly popular in the town of Alcalá de Henares in the province of Madrid.

The pastry is served in individual pieces, sometimes as a dessert. It is also just taken with a coffee.

Ingredients:

General:

> 3 sheets of puff pastry
> Flour for dusting work surface
> Chopped, roasted almonds

Meringue:

> 4 egg whites (about 170 g)
> 6 drops of lemon juice
> Pinch of salt
> 150 g sugar
> 1 teaspoonful of cream of tartar

Pastry cream:

> 4 egg yolks
> 600 ml milk
> 120 g sugar
> 60 g corn starch
> 1 teaspoonful vanilla sugar
> 30 g butter

Preparation:

General:

1 Preheat the oven to 200°C.

2. Gently roll out the puff pastry on a floured work surface.

3. Place each sheet of puff pastry flat in a baking tray lined with baking paper. Puncture the pastry well with a fork. Place a sheet of baking paper on top of the pastry and place another baking tray on top of this. This will stop the puff pastry rising too much.

4. Bake in the preheated oven for about 16 minutes (for each pastry). When baked, remove and put aside.

Meringue:

5. Put all the meringue ingredients in a largish bowl and warm them "au bain-marie" (double boiler) on a medium heat, mixing them together using an electric mixer or whisk, until the meringue forms. It takes a few minutes.

6. Fill a pastry bag with the meringue and place in the refrigerator.

Pastry cream:

7. Put all the ingredients of the pastry cream in a saucepan and use a hand blender to mix thoroughly. Then carefully warm the mixture on a very low heat, stirring continuously until it thickens. Do not allow the mixture to boil!

8. Put the pastry cream into a pastry bag and put it into the fridge for several hours.

Final Preparation:

9. On one of the baked pastry sheets, extract the meringue and sprinkle with ground almonds. Grill until it starts to colour. Be careful that it does not burn. Remove from the oven and allow to cool.

10. Thinly cover each of the other sheets of baked pastry with the pastry cream and place one on top of the other. Now place the meringue covered pastry on top of the tart and put it in the refrigerator.

11. Cut into portions with a sharp fine-toothed knife.

12. The pastry will lasts for at least 2 or 3 days.

CASADIELLES DE ASTURIAS (I)

Walnut Pasties of Asturias (I)

Casadielles is a sweet dish that is very typical during Christmas and carnival celebrations in Asturias. Also called "galletielles", this is yet another variation on the "empanadilla" (filled pastry), which is very similar indeed to the "samosa", which has its origins in India, East and North Africa and the Arab world. The only difference in concept is that samosas tend to be savoury, whereas this is a sweet. Also known as "bollinas", these walnut filled pasties can be fried or baked. Here we give the more traditional fried recipe, followed by the much simpler baked version.

Ingredients (for 10 casadielles):

For the pastry:

> 200 ml wine
> 100 ml olive oil
> Olive oil for frying
> Lemon peel
> Cinnamon stick
> 1 egg yolk
> 100 g butter
> 1 tablespoon of baking powder
> Flour
> 5 g of salt

For the filling:

> 100 g ground walnuts
> 100 g sugar
> 120 ml anís liquor
> 120 ml water
> Sugar to decorate

Preparation:

1. Flavour the frying oil by slowly warming it up with a lemon peel and a stick of cinnamon. After a few minutes remove the oil from the heat and allow to cool again. Just before the casadielles are ready to be fried, remember to remove the lemon peel and the cinnamon from the oil.

2. Mix the olive oil, wine and salt in a bowl, beat it vigorously with a whisk until it emulsifies slightly and becomes white.

3. Next, add the baking powder, egg yolk and butter and continue beating.

4. Gradually, add flour and continue mixing to create a soft dough that does not stick to your hands.

5. Roll out the dough with a rolling pin and then fold it up again, repeat this operation four times.

6. Make a ball with the dough, put it in a bowl and cover it with a damp cloth. Let the dough rest in a cool place for about 2 hours.

7. In the meantime, make the filling. Mix the walnuts, sugar and anís liquor. Gradually stir in the water. Put aside.

8. After the dough has rested, roll it out again with a rolling pin and cut out squares. This quantity should make 10 casadielles, so this should help you determine the exact size.

9. Spread some of the filling in the middle of each square of pastry and fold the edges toward the centre, like a little package. Seal the edges with some water and close the joint by pressing with a fork.

10. Fry the casadielles in the flavoured oil. When browned, take them out and put them to drain on some kitchen paper for a few seconds. Serve them hot, sprinkled with a little icing sugar.

CASADIELLES DE ASTURIAS (II)

Walnut Pasties of Asturias (II)

This is the alternative recipe for casadielles, but this time baked rather than fried. It uses pre-prepared puff pastry, but of course, you can also make your own.

Ingredients:

> 500 g puff pastry
> 400 g walnuts
> 400 g sugar
> Cinnamon powder
> Icing sugar
> 1 "shot" of anís liquor (to your taste)
> 2 egg whites

Preparation:

1. Preheat the oven to 200°C. Grind the walnuts in a mortar or blender and mix together with the sugar, anís liquor and the egg whites to make the filling.

2. Roll out the pastry and cut into rectangles. Place some filling on each piece of pastry, roll it up and bake for 8 to 10 minutes at 200°C.

3. When the casadielles have browned, remove them from the oven and sprinkle them with icing sugar, or icing sugar mixed with a little cinnamon to taste.

CORTADILLOS DE CIDRA SEVILLANOS

Christchmas Angel Hair Cakes of Sevilla

This Christmas pastry is traditionally made in many convents in Sevilla and Cádiz but is said to originate in the town of Écija in the province of Sevilla. In fact, one of the first commercial bakeries making Cortadillos de Cidra was founded in Écija. It is eaten at merienda but also served as a dessert. The cortadillo is now so popular that it can be found throughout Spain.

Ingredients (for 16 portions):

> 200 g lard (or margarine) at room temperature
> 450 g flour
> 100 ml sweet white wine (e.g. Pedro Ximenez)
> 500 g angel hair
> 1 teaspoon of cinnamon
> Grated peel of 1 lemon
> Icing sugar to decorate

Preparation:

1. Preheat the oven to 180°C.

2. Mix the angel hair with the cinnamon and grated lemon peel.

3. In a large bowl, beat the lard until it is soft, and then add the wine and the flour.

4. Keep mixing until you have formed a consistent dough. Then divide the dough into two equal parts. Roll out the dough with a rolling pin.

5. Line a shallow baking dish with baking paper. Spread one sheet of dough onto the baking paper making sure you cover the entire bottom of the oven tray.

6. Pour the mixture of angel hair onto the dough and spread it evenly.

7. Cover with the second sheet of dough and trim.

8. Bake at 180°C for about 30-40 minutes until golden brown.

9. Remove the tray from the oven and allow the cake to cool completely. Lift the pastry out of the oven tray using the baking paper.

10. Sprinkle with icing sugar and then cut into squares. Serve as a dessert or at any time!

EMPANADA DE MANZANA DE GALICIA

Galician Apple Pie

Galicia is famous for its apples (and its many excellent ciders). It is also famous for the many traditional empanadas (pies) that originate there. Whilst empanadas often have savoury fillings, there are some exceptions and this is one of the most famous sweet varieties. It is Galician apple pie.

Every town in Galicia has its own variant on this recipe and they have spread everywhere in Spain. Not only is the Galician apple pie well known and loved throughout Spain but the many Galician emigrants that settled in South America brought this traditional recipe with them. Variants of this and many other Galician empanada recipes are found throughout Latin America.

The Galician apple pie is normally eaten as a sweet dessert but it is also taken with "afternoon tea", merienda!

This recipe is best made with sour apples and the combination with sweet apricot makes for a pleasant contrast of flavours. Some local versions use a little brandy to taste.

Ingredients:

Dough:

>   1 egg
>   1 tablespoon of sugar
>   Pinch of salt
>   2 tablespoons of dry yeast
>   125 ml whole milk (warm)
>   2 tablespoons of unsalted butter (at room temperature)
>   300 g flour

Filling:

>   5 cooking apples, peeled and cored
>   5 tablespoons of sugar
>   3 tablespoons of apricot jam

Etc.

>   1 beaten egg
>   Olive oil for greasing baking tin

Preparation:

1. Beat the egg, sugar and salt together in a large bowl.

2. Dissolve the yeast in the warm milk in a small bowl and leave to rest for 5 minutes or until it begins to bubble.

3. Add the yeast and milk mixture and the butter to the egg and sugar and mix well.

4. Add half of the flour and mix with a wooden spoon. When mixed, add the rest of the flour little by little, stirring continuously.

5. When all the flour has been added, transfer the dough to a lightly floured work surface and knead well until it is elastic but not sticky. This should take about 10 minutes.

6. Place the dough in a large bowl and cover it with a damp cloth. Let the dough rise until it doubles in size, which will take about an hour and a half, depending on the room temperature.

7. Preheat the oven to 230°C and prepare a baking tray (round or square) by rubbing it with olive oil.

8. When the dough has risen, divide it into two pieces for the top and bottom of the pie. One piece should be a bit larger than the other. Roll out the large piece to make it a little wider than the baking tray. Place the dough on the baking tray and lightly press it onto the bottom and up the sides of the tray. Pierce the dough with a fork in a few places to prevent bubbles from forming.

9. Cut the apple into thin slices of about 2 cm thick.

10. Place the apple slices on the dough and sprinkle them with sugar. Next brush the apple with apricot jam.

11. Roll out the second piece of dough and place it over the filling. Seal the edges by pressing the two parts of the dough together. Some bakers decorate the top of the empanada with strips of dough arranged diagonally or make their own designs on the top with leftover dough.

12. Pierce the top of the dough with a fork to allow the steam to escape while it is baking. Paint the top with the beaten egg.

13. Put the pie in the oven at 230°C for 30 minutes or until golden brown.

14. Remove the empanada from the oven and allow it to cool on an open rack before serving.

EMPANADILLAS DE BATATA, PASAS Y NUECES

Sweet Potato Pasties with Raisins and Walnuts

This empanadilla can also be made with filo pastry - a type of dough much beloved in Spain and the Middle East. If you use filo pastry, the pasty can be also be fried in hot oil and should be lightly coated with icing sugar. This recipe is made with puff pastry and is baked.

Ingredients (12 pasties):

> 3 large sweet potatoes
> Grated peel of 1 lemon
> 2 tablespoons of brown sugar
> Half a teaspoon of ground cinnamon
> 2 tablespoons of unsalted butter
> Handful of peeled, chopped walnuts
> 50 g seedless raisins
> 1 dash of sweet anís liquor
> 1 sheet of puff pastry dough

Preparation:

1. Soak the raisins in the anís liquor. When they are thoroughly soaked, drain the raisins well and set both anís and raisins aside.

2. Peel the sweet potatoes and chop them finely. Sauté the pieces of potato with butter, a pinch of salt and the sugar.

3. Add the anís liquor (without the raisins) and let the mixture soften over a low heat. Cover the pan to avoid having to add more water but add a little water if necessary to keep the mixture moist. Cook until all liquid has been absorbed and the mix has the consistency of a thick compote.

4. Preheat the oven to 180°C. Add the raisons, cinnamon, and chopped walnuts to the mixture. Stir well. Let the mixture cool and let it stand until all the ingredients absorb the flavours.

5. Roll out the dough very thinly with a rolling pin and then cut it into circles of 8 to 10 cm in diameter.

6. Fill each pasty with the mixture, fold over in half and seal the edges together well.

7. Place the pasties on an oven tray lined with baking paper and baste with beaten egg.

8. Bake for 10-15 minutes at 180°C until the dough is golden brown.

9. When the empanadillas are baked, remove them from the oven and allow them to cool before eating.

EMPANADILLAS DE CABELLO DE ÁNGEL

Angel Hair, Cinnamon and Aniseed Pasties

There are several versions of this simple sweet pastry. The version we describe here uses homemade pastry dough but a faster method uses pre-made puff pastry. The fillings also vary somewhat but they all use angel hair. Again, you can make your own or buy the filling pre-made. The flavours usually include cinnamon and aniseed and some versions add some baker's cream (pastry cream). Some add a little sweet white wine.

Angel hair pasties are an old and classic sweet pastry, eaten as a dessert but also with breakfast and merienda. They are to be found throughout Andalucía and the Canary islands and are particularly popular around Christmas time. You should also look at a similar dish from Northern Spain called "Pastissets".

Ingredients:

Dough:

>   500 g flour
>   100 ml milk
>   200 ml (approx.) mild olive oil or sunflower oil
>   1 teaspoon of aniseed
>   1 teaspoon of roasted sesame seed
>   A little cinnamon powder to your own taste

Filling / Coating:

>   Icing sugar for coating
>   Angel hair (homemade or ready-made)

Preparation:

1. Mix all the dough ingredients well until you have a uniform and smooth dough. Adjust the amount of flour until the dough is no longer sticky.

2. Roll out the dough with a rolling pin and then cut out circles of around 8-10 cm in diameter. You can also make them smaller, if you prefer.

3. Fill each circle with angel hair and fold over into a semi-circle. Seal the edges of the pasties well to avoid leakage of the filling.

4. Heat oil in a frying pan and fry the pasties until they are golden brown. Avoid burning.

5. Whilst still hot, coat the pasties with some icing sugar and put them aside to cool and drain before serving.

6. The empanadillas can be stored in an airtight container for a few days.

EMPANADILLAS DE MANZANA Y PASAS

Apple and Raisin Pasties

This autumnal pasty is often served as a dessert but is also taken with breakfast or with coffee at merienda. There are several variations on the basic theme but all contain a mixture of apple and raisin and most are flavoured with cinnamon. One version (empanadillas de manzana) is made with just apple and without raisins but the recipe is very similar.

A larger version of this pasty is the apple, raisin pie with grated almonds (called an "Empanada de Manzana"). Some claim that this sweet is the precursor of the famous German and Austrian Apfelstrudel, introduced by the Spanish during their control of the Habsburg Empire.

Ingredients: (16 pasties)

> 16 empanadilla dough circles (See the recipe for "Empanadilla Dough")
> 2 apples
> 2 tablespoons of brown sugar
> 2 tablespoons of white sugar
> 2 tablespoons of raisins
> 40 g butter
> Half a teaspoon of cinnamon powder
> Egg (beaten to glaze the pasties)
> Icing sugar and cinnamon to dust pasties

Preparation:

1. Prepare a baking tray with baking paper.

2. Peel and cut the apples into small pieces. Put the apple into a bowl and coat with a little lemon juice so that the apple does not brown.

3. Put the butter in a frying pan over a medium heat. When the butter is melted, add the apple, both types of sugar and braise the pieces of apple until they are soft and caramelised.

4. Add the raisins and cinnamon and cook for another minute.

5. Remove the pan from the heat. Preheat the oven to 200°C.

6. Place the empanadilla dough circles on a work surface and put a couple of teaspoons of the apple and raisin mix in the centre of each circle.

7. Paint some whisked egg on the edges, fold and close the empanadillas by pressing the edges with a fork to seal them.

8. Place the empanadillas on the oven tray lined with baking paper, paint them with beaten egg and sprinkle sugar and cinnamon on top.

8. Bake for about 15 minutes, until golden brown.

9. Serve warm or allow to cool.

ENSAIMADA

Mallorcan Sweet Bread Buns

This very typical Mallorcan sweet bread is often eaten with coffee or chocolate for breakfast but also during the evening merienda. It is characterised by being shaped in a spiral and being flat. The recipe originates in the 17th century when ensaimadas were made especially for religious celebrations. It is typical of Carnival days, just before Lent, when meat (including lard) was not eaten.

Interestingly, a very similar sweet bread is extremely popular in the Dutch province of Zeeland, which was controlled by Spain (the Habsburgs) until the late 16th century. The "bolus" has a similar shape and is made with bread dough, though is somewhat sweeter. It was introduced into Zeeland in the beginning of the 17th century by migrant Sephardic Jewish bakers from Spain and Portugal who settled in the province. The "bolus", of course, uses butter instead of pork fat and can be found in the whole of the Jewish Diaspora including Jerusalem, Moscow, Paris and the South of France. The word "bolus" derives from the Spanish word "bollo" meaning bun.

Today, there are many variations in most of the Latin American world and in the Philippines. Even in Spain, there are several varieties. The size varies from a small spiral bun to a large pizza-sized version. It is sometimes sliced horizontally and filled with cream and some varieties are made with angel hair. Tallades (literally "sliced") are covered with sobrasada (in Mallorca a kind of sausage) and pumpkin, making for a sweet-savoury taste. Another variant called "Crema" (literally "cream") uses a creamy filling made with eggs. It is also filled with sweet cream, chocolate or turrón paste and can be served covered with apricot jam.

The original ensaïmada of Mallorca was made with flour, water, sugar, eggs, sourdough and a kind of reduced pork lard called saïm (a word derived from the Arab word shahim, meaning 'fat').

Here we have a recipe for a simple ensaimada that attempts to reproduce the original; butter can be substituted for the pig lard. Making ensaimadas is a slightly complicated and time-consuming process because the dough has to be allowed to rise or recover 3 times.

Ingredients (for 2 large or 15 small buns):

> 600 g bread flour
> 200 g sugar (white or brown)

125 g lard (or butter or margarine)
3 eggs
20 g fresh yeast
Olive oil for hands and surfaces
150 ml slightly warm water

Preparation:

1. Put the sugar, eggs and a tablespoon of lard (or butter) in a bowl.

2. Mix the water with the fresh yeast and then add to the other ingredients in the bowl.

3. Gradually begin adding the flour to the mixture using a sieve and blending it into the mixture until you have formed a dough.

4. Manually knead the dough very thoroughly and vigorously. Use a little olive oil on your hands to complete the kneading.

5. Finally, you should have a very elastic dough. Leave the dough overnight at room temperature and out of draughts. (You can leave it inside a switched-off oven, for instance.) The dough should double in size. Bear in mind that in warm weather the leavening of the dough will take a lot less time.

6. Cut pieces of dough according to the number and size of buns you want to make. Place them aside to "rest" for 45 minutes.

7. Prepare an oven tray by oiling it thoroughly.

8. Oil a work surface very well with olive oil to avoid the dough sticking.

9. Take each piece of dough and roll out with a rolling pin into a long, narrow shape.

10. Spread some of the remaining lard (or butter) over each length of dough.

11. Manually stretch the dough as wide as possible until it is almost transparent but do not break the dough, if possible.

12. When fully stretched, roll the dough along its length into a long sausage shape. Now form the dough into the typical spiral shape of the ensaimada by curling the dough from the centre into a spiral.

13. Place each ensaimada on the oiled tray leaving plenty of space in between to allow for the increase in volume (they will double in size).

14. Place the tray in a draft-free space (the switched-off oven is again ideal) until the dough has doubled in volume.

15. When the dough has risen, preheat the oven to 160°C with top and bottom heating.

16. Place the tray of ensaimadas into the oven and bake for approximately 20 minutes or until they are golden brown. Then remove them from the oven.

17. Sprinkle with icing sugar and serve.

FARDALEJOS DE LA RIOJA

Fried Almond Pasties of Arnedo

Fardalejos are a typical pastry from the area of Arnedo in La Rioja. They are considered to be of Arabic origin from the period of the 9th and 10th century AD. They consist of a fried pasty filled with a sweet mixture of ground almond, sugar, eggs and grated lemon. They can be semicircular but traditionally they are rectangular and coated in sugar. They are frequently found during local festivals in Arnedo but these days are often eaten at Christmas in all parts of La Rioja and other parts of Spain. They are popular with breakfast but also as a sweet dessert after a meal.

Despite their Arab origins, like many Spanish festive sweets, after the Christian conquest of Spain, these delicacies were deliberately made with pork lard as a means of identifying closet Muslims or Jews hiding amongst the local population. This was a form of culinary "religious cleansing". However, the same delicacies are just as easily made with a pastry made with oil or butter or, these days, margarine.

Ingredients (for 18 pasties):

Pastry Crust

> 125 g lard (or butter / margarine)
> Pinch of salt
> 125 ml water
> 900 g flour

Filling

> 300 g granulated sugar
> 500 g blanched ground almonds
> 3 eggs
> Grated peel of 1 lemon

Etc.

> 250 - 400 ml vegetable oil for frying
> Icing sugar to decorate

Preparation:

1. Grind the almonds (in a blender or with mortar and pestle). You can also buy whole almonds and blanch and grind them yourself if you want to get the freshest flavour.

To prepare the dough:

2. Put the water, lard or margarine and salt into a small saucepan and place on a high heat. When the fat melts, remove from the heat. Carefully pour the water-lard mixture into a medium sized mixing bowl.

3. Add the flour and stir with a fork until just slightly mixed.

4. Place the dough on a work surface and knead until it is completely smooth. Roll the dough into a ball. Place it in a bowl in a warm place and cover with a kitchen towel to rest.

To prepare the almond filling:

5. Break the eggs into a medium sized mixing bowl. Add the granulated sugar and grated lemon peel and mix together. Add the ground almonds and mix thoroughly.

Final preparation:

6. Scatter some flour on the work surface. Take a handful of dough and roll it out very thinly.

7. Place a heaped tablespoon of almond filling on the dough. Fold the dough over the top of the filling and cut the dough into a rectangle of about 4 cm by 6 cm. (It can also be made into a semi-circular pasty shape like an empanadilla.) Seal the edges all around with a fork. Place aside.

8. Continue rolling the dough and filling the fardalejos until all the dough is used.

9. Pour about 2 cm of vegetable oil into a frying pan. Place on a medium heat.

10. When hot, place the fardalejos in the oil and fry until they are golden brown on both sides. When browned, remove from the oil and place aside on kitchen paper to drain.

11. Allow the fardalejos to cool, dust them liberally with icing sugar and then serve.

FLORES DE SEMANA SANTA

Easter Flowers

Although this recipe comes from Murcia, similar recipes for sweet fritters in the shape of flowers are also found in the regions of Galicia, Extremadura and Castilla-La Mancha. These sweet fritters provided a tasty way of getting through Lent without meat and are a commonly made traditional sweet at Easter time in many parts of rural Spain.

The "flores" are another form of fried dough that was and is a favourite in Spain and originates in both Jewish and Moorish bakery traditions. To make a success of this recipe you will need to buy a flower shaped "rosette iron" on a long handle that can be heated and immersed in hot oil. The iron is made very hot in the oil. It is then dipped into the batter to "seal" the flower to the cutter and it is then transferred to the hot oil to fry. It needs some practise and care to do this well, so expect a few failures when you start.

Generally, the "flores" are eaten with a coffee or tea. They appear at both breakfast and merienda and sometimes as a dessert.

Ingredients (for 12 flowers):

> 250 ml milk
> 1 medium-sized egg
> 1 pinch of salt
> 2 tablespoons of anís liquor
> Grated peel of half an orange
> 200 g flour
> Sunflower oil or mild olive oil for frying
> Sugar and cinnamon to decorate

Preparation:

1. Beat the egg in a bowl. Mix in the milk, anís and grated orange peel. Then slowly add the flour and blend with a fork until the batter is consistent and smooth.

2. Spread the batter on a tray where it can be "cut" with the flower mould. Cover it and allow it to stand for 20 minutes.

3. Heat a deep frying pan of sunflower or mild olive oil. When the oil is hot, submerge the iron in it to heat it up. It needs to be very hot. This makes the batter stick to the mould in the shape of the flower.

4. Uncover the batter, remix it a little and spread again.

5. Press the hot mould iron into the batter so that it is about halfway filled with batter and then immediately place into the hot oil. Shake a little to release the batter into the frying oil.

6. Fry the flower on both sides until golden brown, remove it from the oil and place on absorbent kitchen paper.

7. Coat each flower with a mixture of cinnamon and sugar and allow to cool.

8. Heat the mould iron again and repeat the previous steps until the batter is completely used.

9. The flowers should be eaten the same day but can be kept in a tin for a couple of days.

FOGASETA (TOÑA) DE VALENCIA

Sweet Bread of Valencia

This is a traditional sweet bread / sponge of Alicante, but it can be found throughout the region of Valencia and Murcia. It is also known as "Toña", "Panquemado", "Panou", "Tonya", "Fogassa" or "Pa socarrat", in Valencian. It is often eaten at Easter accompanied with boiled eggs and made with aniseed and cinnamon. Some variants use potato as part of the dough.

The dough is identical to that used in the famous Valencian Easter cake known as Mona. Traditionally such Easter cakes were made for family outings into the countryside on Easter Sunday. Interestingly, the word "Mona" is derived from the Arabic word "munna" which referred to foods prepared by the Moors as presents for their feudal masters.

Ingredients:

> 500 g bread flour
> 250 g pastry flour
> 190 ml olive oil
> 3 eggs
> 1 egg yolk
> 340 ml water
> 23 g fresh yeast
> 240 g sugar
> Grated peel of 1 orange
> A splash of orange blossom water
> 1 beaten egg for coating
> Sugar for coating

Preparation (makes 4 fogasetas):

1. Dissolve the yeast in lukewarm water and add the other ingredients. Mix into a consistent dough (by hand or with a mixer).

2. Continue kneading until the dough is no longer sticky.

3. Place the dough in a bowl, cover it and let it rise in a warm place. It should triple in volume.

4. Place the dough on a floured work surface and cut it into 4 equal pieces. You can also make 2 big fogasetas if you wish.

5. Mould each piece of dough into a round cake shape and allow them to rise again. They should double in volume.

6. Brush the pieces with beaten egg and sprinkle with slightly damp sugar (or just sugar).

7. Preheat the oven to 180°C.

8. Bake the fogasetas for 20 minutes for 2 fogasetas (less time for 4 pieces) until golden brown.

9. Take the breads out of the oven and leave them to cool on a rack. Serve.

GAÑOTES DE UBRIQUE DE SEMANA SANTA

Easter Gañotes of Ubrique

The gañote is a well-known and very old Easter sweet that originates in the area between Ronda in Western Málaga through the rural areas of the Sierras de Grazalema and the Sierra de Cádiz and around the small towns of Ubrique and Algodonales. They have a distinctive spiral shape. Gañotes are generally eaten just before and during Easter. The word "gañote" implies to eat something which is free and overindulge somewhat!

The gañotes of the town of Ubrique are considered the most famous. There, the local population have an annual competition to find the best maker of gañotes.

There are several variations of the basic recipe in the area. In Algodonales, they are made with lemon and orange zest and in Ubrique, they are made with sesame seed. In this recipe, they are made with both. They are often served coated in honey.

The dough is similar to that of the Andaluz pestiño. Traditionally the dough was flattened and wrapped around a piece of cane (caña) in a spiral. Caña is thick cane that grows in riverbeds throughout Spain. It is about 1-1.5 cm thick. These days you can buy stainless steel baking tubes of all sizes that serve as a form for the gañotes.

Ingredients:

550 g flour
150 g sugar
3 eggs (extra large)
95 ml of olive oil approximately
1 tablespoon of ground cinnamon
1 tablespoon of sesame seed
1 tablespoon of aniseed
Grated peel of 1 lemon and 1 orange
Mild olive oil for frying
Honey to coat

Preparation:

Dough:

1. Wash the orange and lemon carefully. Grate the peel avoiding the white pith.

2. Thoroughly mix the eggs, sugar, lemon and orange peel and olive oil in a bowl.

3. Stir the cinnamon, aniseed and sesame into the mix.

4. Use a wooden spoon to add the flour. Mix thoroughly into a dough.

5. Place the dough onto a work surface and knead until it becomes a compact ball that is not sticky.

6. Take small portions of the dough and use a rolling pin to roll them out into long, flat, narrow strips.

7. Roll each of these strips of dough in a spiral around the stainless steel tubes.

Frying and Presentation:

8. Use a mild olive oil to deep-fry the gañotes. Heat the olive oil and place a piece of bread in the oil. When the bread begins to fry, the oil is hot enough. Remove the bread.

9. Place the gañotes (including the moulds) into the hot oil. Regulate the temperature so that they do not burn and are well cooked inside.

10. When the dough starts to brown remove the gañotes from the oil and place them on a tray with absorbent kitchen paper to remove the excess oil.

11. When cooled a little, remove the mould.

12. Gañotes are often served coated in honey. Prepare the honey by heating it with 25% of its volume of water. When warm and well mixed, dip the gañotes completely in the honey mixture one by one and place them on a rack to drain and dry before serving.

HOJALDRES DE ASTORGA DE CASTILLA Y LEÓN

Astorgan Puff Pastries of Castilla y León

This is a typical pastry of the small, ancient city of Astorga, which lies on the old pilgrim route to Santiago de Compostela (Galicia) in the region of Castilla y León. This particular pastry recipe is not thought to be very old. However, it is so popular and typical to this area that the European Union is currently considering its protection as a product of "protected geographic origin".

These pastries are very simple to prepare and are excellent for breakfast or with merienda, served with coffee. Of course, originally, bakers in the area made their own puff pastry but these days, good quality puff pastry can be bought readymade, chilled or frozen. The distinctive taste of honey is important in these pastries, so vary the amount and the type of honey according to your own taste.

Ingredients (30 pastries approximately):

    500 g puff pastry sheets
    375 ml water
    550 g granulated sugar
    3 tablespoons of honey
    Juice from half a lemon

Preparation:

1. Preheat the oven to 190°C.

1. Lay out the (defrosted) puff pastry sheets on a cutting board.

2. Use a sharp knife or pizza cutter to cut the pastry into rectangular pieces of about 4 cm x 5 cm.

3. Use an apple corer to make a hole in the centre of each piece of pastry.

4. Lay each piece on a sheet of baking paper in a baking tray and place the tray in the middle of the preheated oven for about 10-12 minutes, or until the pastries have browned. The pastries become puffy but will not spread out as they bake. Therefore, the pieces of dough may be placed on the tray almost touching.

5. When browned, remove the tray from the oven and allow the pastries to cool on the baking tray.

6. Prepare a syrup by mixing the water, sugar, honey and lemon juice in a saucepan and placing it on a high heat, stirring until all the sugar is completely dissolved. Bring to the boil for about 5 minutes and then reduce to a low heat.

7. When the syrup is slowly simmering, dip each pastry in the syrup for around 20 seconds on each side, allowing them to soak up the syrup. Remove them with cooking tongs and place the pastries on a sheet of baking paper to cool.

8. Serve when cooled.

HORNAZOS DE HUELVA

Angel Hair and Almond Tart of Huelva

Hornazos are a type of pie that is usually savoury. The hornazo de Huelva is, however, one of the exceptions, it being sweet and made with almonds and angel hair. It is very well liked in the province of Huelva and a typical traditional Easter treat in rural areas there. In the past, hornazos were frequently prepared in small villages using communal village ovens. These communal ovens were great places for the people of a village to meet, socialise and exchange recipes.

These days slices of hornazo de Huelva are enjoyed with a coffee during merienda.

Ingredients:

For the dough:

>250 g flour
>16 g baking powder
>1 tablespoon of aniseed
>Grated peel of half a lemon
>100 ml olive oil
>100 ml white wine (at room temperature)
>Salt

For the filling:

>250 g of angel hair
>4 eggs
>200 g sugar
>200 g ground almonds
>Grated peel of half a lemon
>Sliced almonds and sesame seeds
>Salt

Preparation:

For the dough:

1. Mix the flour with the aniseed, and then add the grated lemon peel and the baking powder.

2. Incorporate the white wine and slightly warmed olive oil, mix and then knead everything until you have consistent and smooth dough. Place aside to rest for 15 minutes.

For the filling:

The first layer of the filling is angel hair and the second layer is a creamy lemon-almond mixture made in the following way:

3. Beat the four eggs in a large bowl and then add the sugar, lemon peel, ground almonds and a little salt. Mix all the ingredients well and place aside.

Making the hornazo:

4. Preheat the oven to 180°C. When the dough has rested for 15 minutes, roll it out very thinly and place it on a baking tray lined with baking paper. Turn up the edges of the pastry so that the filling will not leak out or overflow.

5. Firstly, put a generous layer of angel hair on the dough. On top of this, place the almond-egg filling mixture. Keep a slight distance from the edge of the pastry to avoid leaks.

6. Cover the tart with sliced almonds and sesame seed.

7. Bake it in the oven (180°C) for about 35 minutes.

8. Serve cool.

Note: you can also add a little ground cinnamon to the angel hair

MARAÑUELAS DE AVILÉS DE ASTURIAS

Easter Buns of Asturias

Marañuelas are a typical Asturian sweet, made with flour, butter, sugar and eggs. They are normally made as an Easter pastry and are particularly traditional to the coastal Asturian towns of Avilés, Candás and Luanco. Some other versions exist in the area but are more akin to biscuits. If they have a spiral shape, they are called "galleta de marañuela" (marañuela biscuit). If they have a woven shape they are referred to as "bollo de marañuela" (marañuela bun).

The traditional recipe we give here is a bun and is the most popular. It is not dissimilar to an English hot cross bun in appearance and texture.

Ingredients (for 12 small Marañuelas):

> 500 g flour
> 100 g soft butter
> 150 g sugar
> 25 g fresh yeast
> 2 medium-sized eggs
> 125 ml warm milk
> Grated peel of half a lemon
> Pinch of salt

Preparation:

1. Dissolve the yeast in the warmed milk and pour it into a bowl. Add the beaten eggs, the butter, sifted flour, the grated lemon peel and a pinch of salt.

2. Mix and knead until you have a consistent dough. Cover the bowl and place the dough aside in a warm, draft-free place to rise. It should double or triple in volume. Depending on the conditions, this may take some hours.

3. Next, form the marañuelas as follows: Make a ball about the size of a mandarin orange as the marañuela base. Make another ball about the size of a walnut and roll out this dough. Use a pair of kitchen scissors to cut out the shape of a cross. Then place this cross on the marañuela base and press the two pieces together to join the base and cross.

4. Continue to make the remaining marañuelas in the same way until all the dough is used.

5. Line an oven tray with baking paper. Place the marañuelas on the tray, leave them to rise for an hour and then paint the tops with beaten egg. Preheat the oven to 180°C.

6. Bake at 180°C for 15-20 minutes until golden brown.

7. Remove the marañuelas from the oven and allow them to cool. They should be eaten freshly baked, but they can also be frozen.

MASA DE EMPANADILLAS

Empanadilla Dough Recipe

There is a huge variety of empanadillas in Spain in both sweet and savoury varieties. Because of the popularity of empanadillas, the pastry to make them is readily available in supermarkets in the same way that puff pastry is available in other countries. The pastry comes in packs pre-cut in the traditional circular shape, ready to be filled and baked. However, to find these pre-made packs of "masa de empanadillas" outside the Hispanic world will be quite difficult and therefore we provide the recipe to make this simple pastry in your own kitchen.

The empanadilla pastry is very similar to filo pastry and generally, filo pastry can be substituted for empanadilla pastry if several layers are used. But empanadilla pastry is very easy to make and can be rolled out to any thickness - it's not normally as thin as filo pastry - and thus saves having to use multiple layers of pastry for your empanadillas.

There are some variations on this basic empanadilla recipe, with some bakers using part water, part white wine or part beer. This alters the taste a little and you should experiment with this to see if it suits your taste.

Ingredients (for 20 empanadillas):

> 350 g flour
> 150 g mild olive oil
> 150 ml water (some recipes substitute 30% water with white wine or beer)
> 1 teaspoon of salt

Preparation:

1. Put the olive oil and water in a saucepan and heat until it almost starts to boil, then remove it from the heat (about three minutes).

2. Pour the oil and water into a bowl and add the flour and salt.

3. Mix well with a wooden spatula until all ingredients are well incorporated. The dough should not be sticky.

4. Cover the bowl and let the mixture stand for 30 minutes in a cool place.

5. Lightly flour a work surface. Knead the dough and roll it out thinly.

6. Use a circular dough cutter (or a wide glass) of around 10 cm diameter and cut out circles of dough. The size is up to you. Some people like smaller empanadillas, some like them larger.

7. Place the circles of dough between squares of greaseproof paper to avoid them sticking together. They are now ready to use.

MOSTACHONES DE UTRERA

Cinnamon Cakes of Utrera

The mostachón de Utrera is a kind of flat sweet cake typical of the city of Utrera in the province of Sevilla. It is made with flour, honey, eggs, sugar and cinnamon and traditionally made in a wood-fired oven. Generally, it is about 12-15 cm in diameter but some versions are larger.

The origin of this sweet cake is not fully known. Some believe that the origin is Roman and the flavouring probably Arabic. The Latin word "mostaceum" means "round cake". However, the "modern" recipe is first recorded in the 19th century as a traditional cake made by the nuns of the Poor Clares. It is possible that this is where the Latin name originated.

The fame of the cake grew with the prosperity and movement through Utrera caused by the railway junction there. According to a newspaper report of 1897, Utrera stood "at the crossroads of all railway lines of Andalucía and thus the mostachones of Utrera spread far and wide in Andalucía".

Mostachones are normally taken with and dipped in coffee both for breakfast and at the evening merienda.

Ingredients (makes about 18 cakes):

> 6 eggs
> 250 g sugar
> 250 g flour
> 1 teaspoon of cinnamon powder
> Icing sugar and granulated sugar for coating (optional)

Preparation:

1. Separate the egg whites from the yolks.

2. Whisk the egg whites vigorously until stiff and then add the sugar gradually until the mixture begins to thicken. When the mix is consistent add the egg yolks one by one and continue to mix.

3. Finally fold in the sifted flour and cinnamon powder and mix until you have a smooth dough.

4. Spoon the dough into a pastry bag with a large round nozzle. Preheat the oven to 180°C.

5. Cut baking paper into squares and place these on an oven tray. Squeeze out the dough on each square of baking paper. Allow space for expansion during baking and bear in mind the final size should be about 12-15 cm in diameter. Shake some icing and / or granulated sugar over the cakes.

6. Place the tray in the preheated oven for about 10 minutes or until golden brown. Take care not to let them brown too much.

7. When the mostachones are baked, take them out of the oven and leave them to cool on a rack. Serve.

MARQUESAS DE NAVIDAD

Marquesa Christmas Almond Cakes

This is one of the most traditional Christmas almond sweets in Spain and it is one of the most simple to prepare.

Ingredients (For 12):

> 120 g icing sugar
> 120 g granulated sugar
> 250 g almond flour (ground almonds)
> 40 g flour
> 40 g corn starch
> 5 g baking powder
> 4 eggs
> Grated peel of 1 lemon
> Small paper moulds for baking the cakes

Preparation:

1. Grate the lemon skin and mix it with the ground almonds and the icing sugar.

2. Add the lightly beaten eggs and the granulated sugar and mix well.

3. Sieve the flour with the corn starch and the baking powder and add this gradually to the mixture, stirring until you have a consistent, thick dough.

4. Preheat the oven to 180°C. Put a portion of dough into each of the paper moulds (do not fill to the top).

5. Bake for about 12 minutes at 180°C.

6. Remove the cakes from the oven and sprinkle them with plenty of icing sugar.

7. Allow them to cool, and serve.

MELINDRES DE GALICIA

Christmas Doughnuts of Galicia

These small, glazed doughnuts are a typical Galician sweet. They are very popular in winter time and during the Christmas festivities.

Ingredients:

For the dough:

> 3 egg yolks
> 2 egg whites
> 4 tablespoons of melted butter
> 3 tablespoons of sugar
> 250 g flour
> Anís liquor

For the icing:

> 250 g sugar
> 200 ml water
> 1 egg white

Preparation:

1. Mix all the ingredients for the dough in a bowl, but keep some of the flour back, in case it proves to be too much. Knead the dough until it does not stick to your hands. Add more flour as necessary.

2. Let the dough rest for half an hour and then make small dough balls, flatten them slightly and make a small hole in the centre with your finger. Remember to make the hole a bit large because it will close up during baking. When formed, place the doughnuts on an oven tray lined with baking paper.

3. Preheat the oven to 170°C.

4. Bake the doughnuts until they begin to brown. When baked, remove them from the oven.

5. In the meantime, make a thick syrup for the icing with the water and sugar. Whisk the egg white until it becomes stiff. Then gradually add the syrup to the beaten egg white until all is well mixed.

6. Dip the melindres in the icing, making sure that they are well coated, and then let them drain and dry on baking paper.

7. When they are dry and cool, they are ready to eat.

8. If you store them in an airtight container they will remain fresh for several days.

MIGUELITOS DE LA RODA

Cinnamon Puff Pastries of La Roda in Albacete

Miguelitos (literally translated "little Michaels") are a typical pastry of the town of La Roda in Albacete in the region of Castilla-La Mancha. They are made from thin puff pastry, filled with custard and sprinkled with icing sugar. They are actually quite simple to make.

The Miguelito was actually invented in 1960 in La Roda by the famous pastry chef Manuel Blanco. It was called "Miguelito" after the inventor's friend, who was the first to taste it. They are now produced in pastry shops all over the province of Albacete.

During the Feria de Albacete thousands of them are filled and sold at the fairground and are usually accompanied by coffee. However, Miguelitos are also eaten together with cider or the strong spirit known as "orujo" mixed with honey.

This recipe uses milk to make the filling but you can substitute the milk with some cream if you wish to make the filling richer.

Ingredients (for 32 pastries):

Pastry:

> 500 g puff pastry
> 1 large egg
> 2-3 tablespoons of flour
> Icing sugar to decorate

Filling:

> 600 ml milk
> 8 tablespoons of granulated sugar
> 1/4 teaspoon of vanilla extract or half a vanilla pod
> 3 egg yolks
> 3 tablespoons of corn flour
> 1 cinnamon stick
> Peel of half a lemon

Preparation:

1. Prepare the pastry. Be sure not to allow the pastry to warm too much, or it will become difficult to work. It should remain cool. Therefore, thaw the puff pastry for about 20 minutes.

2. Sprinkle some flour on a work surface or pastry board. Roll out the pastry with a rolling pin.

3. Use a very sharp knife to cut the pastry into squares about 4 cm wide. Place the squares onto baking paper in a baking tray.

4. Whisk the egg and brush each square of pastry with the egg. Preheat the oven to 200°C.

5. Place the baking tray in the middle of the oven for about 10 to 12 minutes, or until the pastry has browned on top, and is crispy. Remove the tray from the oven and allow the pastry to cool.

6. Pour half of the milk into a saucepan and add the cinnamon stick, vanilla extract or pod and the lemon peel. Place on a high heat until the milk boils and then immediately reduce to a low heat.

7. Beat the egg yolks and granulated sugar together in a bowl. Add the rest of the milk and the corn flour and continue to mix.

8. Take the cinnamon stick (and vanilla pod) and lemon peel out of the warm milk and add the mixture from the bowl. Stir well until the mixture thickens. Remove from the heat.

9. Remove the pastry squares from the baking paper with a spatula.

10. Carefully, cut each pastry horizontally into a top and bottom, like a sandwich. Add the cream filling, and replace the top.

11. Shake icing sugar over the pastries with a sieve. Store them in a cool place until ready to serve.

MONA DE PASCUA

Easter Sweet Bread with Egg

The mona de Pascua is a very ancient traditional sweet bread originating in Cataluña and Valencia. In Valencia a variant of this bread is also known as "Panquemado", "Panquemao" or "Panou". Similar sweet Easter loaves are also found in Aragón, Murcia, Castilla-La Mancha and Andalucía. Another variant of the bread, with a single egg incorporated, is found in Loja in the province of Granada and is called Hornazo de Loja. The word "Hornazo" is also used for other breads in other regions, so they can be easily confused.

The "Culeca de Navarra" is another famous variant of this sweet bread that is traditionally eaten in parts of Navarra and the Basque country during the festival and pilgrimage of the "True Cross" (on May 3rd). This sweet bread bun has one or two eggs cooked inside the dough. It is typical of the Ribera region and is eaten during the pilgrimage to the hermitage of Santo Cristo. The Order of the Volatín in Tudela has an annual distribution of these sweet breads that is especially popular with the local children. In the area of Cortes, the bun is also eaten on the same feast day in a party referred to locally as the "day of the Culecas".

The mona is normally baked at Easter to break the Lenten fast. The word "mona" comes from the Arabic "munna", which means a gift. Tradition says that a godfather gives a "mona" to his godson on Easter Sunday after mass. It is also said that the Romans made "monus", which is bread with a hardboiled egg.

Generally, the mona is eaten with merienda during the days of Easter, but in the past the sweet bread was often made to be eaten during a family day in the countryside.

Today, there are many variants of the mona but almost all include a hardboiled egg or two. In some cases the eggs are cooked with the dough. Modern variants include those made with chocolate coverings.

Ingredients (For 2 loaves):

For the Sourdough:

     100 g bread flour

     10 g fresh yeast

     60 ml warm water

For the Dough:

      420 g bread flour
      10 g fresh yeast
      3 eggs
      140 g sugar
      80 ml olive oil
      Grated peel of 1 lemon or 1 orange
      2 teaspoons of orange blossom water
      Pinch of salt

For decoration:

      2 Eggs to bake in each loaf
      Sugar
      Chocolate flakes (optional)

Preparation:

For the Sourdough:

1. Make the sourdough the day before you need it.

2. Put the flour in a bowl. Dissolve the yeast in the warm water and add to the flour. Mix well. Cover with shrink wrap and leave it to ferment until the next day.

For the Dough:

3. The dough can be made by hand or using a mixer.

4. Put the flour in a bowl and mix with the crumbled yeast.

5. Lightly beat the eggs and add them to the flour along with the sugar, olive oil, lemon or orange peel, orange blossom water and a pinch of salt. Add the sourdough.

6. Mix all the ingredients very well until it forms slightly sticky dough. Do not over-knead.

7. Grease your hands and the work surface with some vegetable oil and knead the dough into a ball. Place the dough in a lightly oiled bowl, cover with a cloth and let it stand in a warm place until it doubles its volume. This takes between 1.5 - 2 hours.

8. When the dough has risen sufficiently take it out of the bowl and cut it into 2 pieces (to make two loaves).

9. Shape the dough into a ring with a large hole in the centre and place it on an oven tray lined with baking paper. Cover it again with a cloth and allow it to rise again until it doubles its volume.

10. Half way through the rising, place the eggs into the dough.

11. Preheat the oven to 175°C.

12. When the dough has risen again, paint the surface with beaten egg, sprinkle with sugar.

13. Bake the monas in the oven for 15-20 minutes or until they are golden brown. Test they are baked by pricking with a cocktail stick. If it comes out clean, the monas are baked.

14. When baked, remove from the oven and allow to cool. Sprinkle with chocolate flakes (optional)

OREJUELAS DE CARNIVAL

Carnival Anís Fritters

Orejuelas are typical carnival fritters that have become so well liked in some parts of Spain that they are sold year round. They are a descendent of similar Jewish and Moorish fried dough recipes that are still popular today across the Levant. They are simple to make and may be eaten as a dessert but are often sold on the street during carnival.

Ingredients:

250 g flour
15 g butter
2 eggs
5 tablespoons of sugar
Half a teaspoon of baking powder
Pinch of salt
Grated peel of 1 lemon
Half a shot of anís liquor
Oil for frying

Preparation:

1. Beat the eggs and 3 tablespoons of sugar together in a bowl.

2. Add the anís liquor, butter, lemon peel, salt, baking powder and flour, and mix all these ingredients well. Then knead until the dough until it is consistent and smooth. You can also add a little cinnamon to taste.

3. Use a rolling pin to roll out the dough quite thinly.

4. Cut the dough into any shape you like (sometimes triangles or circles, but generally rectangles of about 3cm by 8cm).

5. Fry the shapes in very hot oil until golden brown. Remove the orejuelas from the oil and sprinkle them with the remaining sugar or add some honey.

6. Serve them warm or cold.

PALMERAS DE HUEVO

Egg Palmiers

This well-known pastry is similar to the French pastry called "palmiers" (palms) which has a similar shape. The Spanish version is coated in cream, glazed and thus somewhat richer than the French variety. It is thought to have originated in Moorish Spain at the same time as puff pastry. In those days, puff pastry was made with sheets of pastry coated with olive oil but later butter was used to make it.

Ingredients:

For the pastry:

> 1 sheet of puff pastry
> Sugar

For the egg cream:

> 3 tablespoons of sugar
> 3 egg yolks
> 100 ml water

For the frosting:

> 25 g slightly melted butter
> 100 g icing sugar
> 1 tablespoon of water

Preparation:

Pastry:

1. Preheat the oven to 200°C. Roll out the puff pastry on baking paper, sprinkle generously with sugar, and lightly roll this into the pastry.

2. Now, gently roll up the puff pastry from each side of the sheet towards the middle to form two equal rolls (connected in the middle). Sprinkle the surface of the rolls again with more sugar.

3. Cut across the puff pastry rolls with a sharp knife to make slices of about 1 cm thick. Place each slice on a baking tray lined with baking paper coated with a little sunflower oil. Squeeze each little "palm" together to form the little heart shape.

4. Bake the palmeras at 200°C for about 8-10 minutes until they begin to brown. They burn easily, so take care.

5. Once baked, allow the palmeras to cool until just warm before covering them with the cream and frosting.

Egg Cream:

6. Make a thick syrup with the water and sugar in a saucepan on a medium heat. Allow it to cool.

7. Pour the beaten egg yolks into this syrup through a sieve. Place on the heat again and whisk until the cream thickens. (This can also be done in a double boiler - "au bain-marie").

8. Spread the cream on one side of the palmeras (the less attractive side, usually).

Frosting:

9. Make the glaze by thoroughly mixing the butter, sugar and water until you have a thick white paste (add more sugar if needed).

10. Spread the paste over the pastries and allow it to harden. Serve cool.

PANECILLOS DE SAN ANTÓN

Sweet Cakes of Saint Anthony

Around January 17th, every year, many of Madrid's residents go to the church in Calle Hortaleza to have their pets blessed and celebrate the day of San Antón Abad. He was an Egyptian saint and protector of animals. The parishioners also buy panecillos de San Antón and these are also often blessed on that day.

These little cakes, based on a simple recipe, are an important part of the ceremony and the day's events. Traditionally, the recipe was kept a secret of the church and was always returned to the church by the bakeries that made the rolls for the festival. Nowadays, they can be found in bakeries throughout Madrid, especially after Christmas, but they are particularly common in bakeries near the Church of San Antón. The appearance of the rolls has developed over the years but the traditional panecillos had an Egyptian cross shape placed on them.

The rolls are often eaten at breakfast or for merienda.

Ingredients:

> 700 g flour
> 300 g butter (at room temperature)
> 150 g sugar
> 2 eggs
> 3 egg yolks
> 2 g salt
> Grated peel of half a lemon

Preparation:

1. Cut the butter into small pieces and mix with the flour in a large bowl.

2. Make a hole in the middle of the flour mix and add the remaining ingredients. Gradually and thoroughly mix the flour and other ingredients until you have a consistent dough.

3. Place the dough in the refrigerator for half an hour. Preheat the oven to 200°C.

4. Roll out the dough and cut out circular pieces using a pastry cutter or a glass.

5. Make a symmetrical (Egyptian) cross with dough on top of each circle of dough. Ideally, this should be done with a cross-shaped pastry cutter in one piece but it can also be done by cutting out a cross from pastry by hand although it does not look so attractive.

6. Place the panecillos on a baking tray lined with baking paper and bake them for about 15 minutes until they are golden brown.

7. Allow to cool before serving. They have a low moisture content and can be safely stored for days or even weeks.

PANIZAS DE CÁDIZ

'Paniza' Fritters of Cádiz

Panizas are a very simple fritter, typical of Cádiz and one of many recipes that originated after the Spanish civil war during the long periods of acute food shortages. It is a recipe referred to in Spanish as part of the "Cocina de los tiesos" - the poverty kitchen. With increasing affluence, panizas are not made as often as they were in the past and the recipe is in some danger of extinction.

Despite the privations of the time, the imagination and resourcefulness of many households created some of Spain's most simple, cheap and delicious dishes out of almost nothing! There is some speculation that the recipe was resurrected from that of settlers who arrived in Cádiz from Genoa in Italy in the 14th century.

There are several variants on this simple fritter using honey or sugar as a sweetener but it can be eaten just as it is, without sweetening.

Ingredients:

> 2 water glasses of chickpea flour.
> 3.5 glasses of water
> Salt to season
> Olive oil to fry

Preparation:

1. Mix the flour, salt and water in a blender until it has a thick consistency

2. Pour the mixture into a heated frying pan without oil. Reduce the heat a little and stir until the mix thickens, takes on a consistency of dough and does not stick to the pan. Take the pan off the heat, place the dough onto a plate, and allow to cool.

3. When cooled, cut the dough thinly into rectangles. If the slices are too thick they can be rather heavy to eat. They should be thin and crispy.

4. Heat the olive oil in a frying pan until it is quite hot. Place the slices of dough in the oil and fry them on both sides until browned.

5. You can eat them as they are, hot or sprinkled with sugar. Another popular variation is to dip the fried panizas in a mixture of honey, orange juice and water and eat them cold.

PAPAVIEJOS

Lenten Fritters of Almeria

This is a classic Almerian Lenten recipe. Like many sweet fried dough dishes, it is of Moorish origin but this recipe includes potato. The potato became a common substitute for flour during hard times when cereals were scarce or expensive.

There are several versions of papaviejos, many of which are found throughout Andalucía. Some do not include potato. They are simple to make and especially enjoyable with coffee in cold weather.

Ingredients:

> 250 g flour
> 250 g potato
> 250 ml milk
> 1 tablespoon of baking powder
> Grated peel of 1 lemon (orange is also fine)
> Strip of whole lemon (not grated)
> Pinch of salt
> 2 eggs
> Mild olive oil or sunflower oil for frying
> Sugar
> Cinnamon

Preparation:

1. Boil the potatoes in their skin. When they are cooked, peel and mash them.

2. Grate the lemon peel, avoiding the white pith.

3. Beat the two eggs.

4. Use a fork to mix the potato, the baking powder, a pinch of salt, eggs and grated lemon peel in a bowl with the flour (sifted) to create a dough. The dough needs to be smooth and consistent. It should be mouldable but still slightly sticky.

5. Prepare a frying pan with mild olive oil or sunflower oil and put on the heat. Add the lemon peel to flavour the oil. When the oil is hot, remove the lemon peel.

6. Using two tablespoons, take portions of dough and drop them into the hot oil to fry. Turn around for an even frying until golden brown.

7. Place each fritter on kitchen paper to absorb the excess oil.

8. Make a mixture of sugar and cinnamon and scatter the papaviejos with this mixture. Serve warm or cold.

PASTEL DE CABELLO DE ÁNGEL CORDOBÉS

Angel Hair Tart of Córdoba

This very popular tart can be found in every bakery and café in Córdoba in Andalucía year round. However, it is especially popular on the annual festival of San Rafael, on October 24th.

Modern versions use only angel hair filling but traditionally this tart has a sweet-salt combination of flavours. Some recipes even call for the addition of ham! It seems to have its origins in the 19th century. The tart is sometimes called "Manolete" after the famous bullfighter "El Manolete", who was reputedly so fond of the tart that he had it delivered to his home fresh every day! This tart can also be made using ready-made puff pastry.

It is eaten both as a dessert and with coffee.

Ingredients (for a 24 cm baking tin):

> 500 g pastry flour
> 230 ml water
> A dash of vinegar
> 100 g lard (or margarine) cut into pieces
> 1 pinch of salt
> 200 g melted butter
> 500 g angel hair
> 1 beaten egg
> 3 tablespoons of sugar
> 1 teaspoon of cinnamon powder

Preparation:

1. Mix the flour, water, vinegar, lard and salt until you have a consistent dough.

2. Roll out the dough into a square of about 60 cm.

3. Baste the dough with butter and fold it in half. Repeat the process twice more - roll, baste and fold.

4. Wrap the dough in cling film and let it rest for 30 minutes in the fridge.

5. Preheat the oven to 200°C.

6. Cut the dough in half. Roll out one half of the dough and line a 24 cm diameter round baking tin, greased with butter.

7. Spread the angel hair over this dough base.

8. Roll out the other half of the dough and cover the angel hair.

9. Seal the edges of the dough.

10. Bake for 20 minutes at 200°C.

11. Remove the tin from the oven, paint the tart with beaten egg, sprinkle it with sugar and cinnamon and bake for another 10 minutes.

12. Serve cold.

PASTEL FELIPE DE CARTAGENA

Angel Hair, Wine and Cinnamon Cake of Cartagena

This pastry originates in Cartagena. It is also known as Pastel Romanones and more recently Pasta Flora. It is based on a flavoured shortcrust pastry, filled with angel hair. It is usually eaten as a dessert but also with coffee during merienda.

Ingredients:

> 250 g margarine or butter
> 250 g sugar
> 700 g flour
> 150 ml white wine (or mistela - a spirit-fortified young wine)
> Angel hair (enough to fill the cake)
> Cinnamon powder to taste
> Grated lemon peel to taste
> Egg to coat

Preparation:

1. Mix the sugar and butter (or margarine) thoroughly until creamy. Add the grated lemon peel and cinnamon and finally the white wine and mix well.

2. Add the flour, little by little while kneading to create a loose dough, which does not stick to your hands.

3. Allow it to rest for a few minutes, then separate the dough into two parts (top and bottom of the pastel).

4. Preheat the oven to 180°C.

5. Place one half of the dough in a round baking tin.

6. Mix the angel hair with a little cinnamon powder and cover the dough in the baking tin with it. Place the second piece of dough over the angel hair and coat the surface of the dough with some beaten egg.

7. Bake the cake at 180°C for half an hour, until it is golden and the base is also baked through.

8. Remove the tin from the oven and allow the cake to cool. You can shake some icing sugar on top if you wish. Cut it in portions and serve.

PASTEL RUSO DE ARAGÓN

Russian Pastry of Aragón

This pastry is a famous cake made in the town of Alfaro in La Rioja and in Huesca in Aragón. It is a delicious and very rich pastry made with a sweet almond filling. The original pastry is thought to be of Moorish origin.

It apparently acquired its "Russian" name when Eugenia de Montijo, of Granada, became Empress of France after marrying the Emperor Napoleon III. Her entourage in France included her best Spanish chefs and bakers. During the Paris Exhibition of 1855, a banquet was held with the Tsar of Russia, Alexander II, as guest of honour. The dessert that the Empress chose was the "Pastel of La Rioja". The Tsar was so impressed that he asked for the recipe to be passed to his chefs. The cake has since been renamed as the Imperial Russian Pastel.

Ingredients (for 6 servings):

Almond pastry:

> 150 g ground almonds
> 150 g icing sugar
> 4 egg whites
> 1 teaspoon of white wine vinegar
> Roasted sliced almonds
> Icing sugar for dusting

Ingredients for the filling:

> 150 g sugar
> 125 g butter at room temperature,
> 20 g raw peeled almonds
> 4 egg yolks
> 150 ml milk
> 1 teaspoon of corn starch

Preparation:

1. Preheat the oven to 160°C.

2. Begin by preparing the almond pastry: Mix the ground almonds and icing sugar with a teaspoon of vinegar.

3. Whisk the egg whites until almost stiff. Mix in the egg whites with the almonds and sugar.

4. Spoon the mixture onto a lined baking tray and spread.

5. Bake the pastry for about 20 or 25 minutes at 160°C. Allow to cool.

6. To prepare the filling: Put half of the sugar into a saucepan with a tablespoon of water. Bring to the boil and just as it begins to caramelise, add the 20 g of almonds. Pour the mixture onto an oiled sheet of aluminium foil and allow it to cool and solidify. Then grind this mixture until it has the texture of flour. Put aside.

7. Beat the egg yolks with the remaining sugar. Dissolve the corn starch in 50 ml of milk and add this to the egg yolks. Warm the remaining milk and add to the mixture. Place it into a double boiler ("au bain-marie") and continue stirring until the mixture thickens. Allow it to cool.

8. Beat the butter (at room temperature) in a bowl with a fork or whisk. Add the egg yolk cream and the ground caramel/almond mix to the butter.Mix until all the ingredients are well incorporated and consistent. This is the filling.

9. To finish, cut the baked pastry in two equal rectangular parts. Coat one part with the filling and place the other half on top.

10. Sprinkle with sliced raw almonds and icing sugar and refrigerate until serving.

Note: Some versions of this pastry use three layers rather than two, but the recipe is the same.

PASTEL DE GLORIA O TETILLAS DE MONJA

Gloria Cakes - Almond Meringues

The "Gloria cake" is an exquisite sweet, thought to be of Arabic origin, and known in different regions of the southeast of Spain. Because of their shape and colour, they have been given picturesque popular names, like cow's teat or nun's nipple!

It is quite exotic but simple to make and, with its distinctive almond flavour, nowadays a Christmas favourite in many parts of Spain..

Ingredients (About 10 cakes):

>10 egg whites (large eggs)
90 ml water
40 ml water
850 g sugar
8 egg yolks
250 g ground almonds
Baking wafers (round)
Icing sugar

Preparation:

To make the egg yolk mixture:

1. Put 90 ml of water with 250 g of sugar in a saucepan and let it boil for a minute. Take the pan off the heat and add in the beaten egg yolks.

2. Return the pan to the heat and let it simmer, stirring continuously. When the mixture has thickened, remove from the heat and leave to cool.

To make the almond paste:

3. Make an almond paste by putting 250 g of sugar in a saucepan with 40 ml of water. Bring to the boil, add the ground almonds and mix well until you have a smooth paste. Take off the heat and set aside.

To make the meringue:

4. Pour the egg whites into a large mixing bowl and beat them until stiff. Gradually add the remaining sugar and stir until the mix is consistent.

To make the cakes:

5. Preheat the oven to 250ºC.

6. Line an oven tray with baking paper and place some pieces of wafer on the paper, leaving some space between wafers.

7. On each piece of wafer, put a circle of the almond paste. On top of the almond paste, put a tablespoon full of the egg yolk mixture.

8. On top of the egg yolk mixture, create a little "mountain" of meringue, using a spoon and covering the entire base.

9. Once the cakes are prepared, put the tray into the oven for 10 to 15 minutes, until the meringues are "set" and become slightly browned. Take them out of the oven and sprinkle them with some icing sugar.

10. Allow the "Gloria cakes" to cool and then serve.

PASTELITO DE GLORIA

Little Glory Cakes

This small sweet cake based on marzipan is very typical of traditional Andalucian Christmas baking. This version uses sweet potatoes to create the filling, but other fillings may be used. Like most traditional Andalucian sweets, it has its origins in the era of Arabic Al-Ándalus with its extensive use of almonds in confectionary. These cakes are very, very sweet!

Ingredients:

For the marzipan:

> 300 g finely ground fresh almonds
> 300 g icing sugar
> 3 egg whites

For the filling:

> 200 g sweet potatoes
> 200 g sugar

Preparation:

1. Cook the scrubbed, unpeeled potatoes in plenty of water until tender.

2. Let the potatoes cool slightly and then peel and purée them.

3. Put the potato purée into a saucepan with the sugar and cook over medium-low heat until the mix comes away from the bottom of the pan. Put it in a bowl and leave to cool.

4. In the meantime, make the marzipan by mixing the ground almonds with the icing sugar and egg whites.

5. Mix thoroughly and then spread the mixture on a smooth work surface. Use a rolling pin to flatten it until it is about 2 cm thick.

6. Cut out pieces of about 30g with a biscuit cutter and form each into a little cup to hold the filling.

7. Fill a pastry bag with the filling and use this to put a portion of the sweet potato filling into each circle of marzipan. Then cover this with another piece of marzipan. Seal and coat with egg white.

8. Give the cakes their round shape by carefully rolling in icing sugar until smooth and spherical or cylindrical like a croquette.

9. Toast the cakes under a hot grill for a few minutes until they are slightly firm, being careful not to let them burn. Ten minutes should be enough, depending on the grill.

10. Set the cakes aside, let them cool and sprinkle them with icing sugar before serving.

PASTELILLOS DE CABELLO DE ÁNGEL DE MURCIA

Angel hair Pasties of Murcia

These cakes are a traditional Christmas dish from Águilas in Murcia. It is a very old recipe and very popular in that region.

Ingredients:

> 1250 g flour
> 500 g lard
> 500 g sugar
> 500 g angel hair
> 3 egg yolks
> 250 ml "mistela" (sweet fortified wine)
> Teaspoon of baking powder
> Grated peel of 1 lemon

Preparation:

1. Mix the lard and lemon peel together in a bowl. Add the sugar and continue mixing.

2. Add the lightly beaten egg yolks and continue working the mixture until it is thoroughly blended.

3. Add the wine and keep mixing.

4. Gradually stir in the flour and baking powder. Work the dough on a floured work surface until smooth. Preheat the oven to 200°C.

5. Roll out the dough with a rolling pin and use a pastry cutter (round or star shaped) to cut out the pasty bases and tops.

6. Place the bases in a greased oven tray. Put a spoonful of the angel hair on each base. Then add the top and press the edges together well to avoid leakage.

7. Finally, seal the pasties with some beaten egg and sprinkle with sugar.

8. Bake in a hot oven (about 200°C) until golden brown.

9. Serve when cooled.

PEPITOS DULCES DE MURCIA

Sweet Filled Fritters of Murcia

This is another of the many fried dough desserts that have their origin in Moorish-Sephardic cuisine and indeed are still popular in the Levant to this day. Pepitos have spread throughout much of the Hispanic world and are to be found in Argentina, Venezuela, Guatemala and Peru albeit with their own local names.

It is really a sweet fritter that is cut open and then filled with a sweet cream. There are many variants of the filling (chocolate, chestnut or fruit puree, rum sauce to name a few). Some pepitos are topped with cream, vanilla or chocolate but in its most basic form it is just coated in a little icing sugar and filled with pastry cream.

Pepitos are served as a dessert with a meal or with breakfast or merienda.

Ingredients (for 8 pepitos):

> 250-300 g flour
> 40 g sugar
> 200 ml milk
> 50 g oil or butter (soft)
> 25 g fresh yeast
> 1 egg
> Grated lemon peel
> Olive oil for frying

Preparation:

1. Dissolve the yeast in the slightly warmed milk.

2. Mix the sugar and butter together in a bowl and then add the warm milk with the yeast.

3. Add the egg, and grated lemon peel. Then, little by little sieve the flour into the mixture.

4. Mix all the ingredients thoroughly into a dough that is no longer sticky. Form a ball with the dough and allow it to rest for an hour or two until it rises.

5. When the dough has risen, divide it into 8 equal portions and form these into elongated rolls. Place them aside and let them rise again for an hour.

6. When the dough has risen again, slowly fry the pepitos in plenty of oil (not too hot) until they are golden brown. Take them out of the oil and leave them to drain on a sheet of absorbent kitchen paper.

7. Allow the pepitos to cool. Prepare a pastry cream of your choice - there are many recipes elsewhere in this book.

8. When cooled, slice open the pepitos lengthways and fill them with the pastry cream, sprinkle with a little icing sugar and they are ready to serve.

PIONONOS DE SANTA FE (GRANADA)

Syrup Cake of Santa Fe (Granada)

Santa Fe is the small town outside the city of Granada where, during the end of the fifteenth century, the Christian forces of the Catholic monarchs based their siege of Granada, the capital of the last Moorish kingdom in Spain.

The pionono is a small sweet pastry traditional to the town. They are believed to be named after the Italian version of the name Pope Pius the ninth, "Pio Nono". On the other hand, many food historians believe that the use of honey and cinnamon in this cake almost certainly means it had its origin in the 10th or 11th century Moorish period in Granada. They think that it was later Christianised (with rum) and finally named after a pope! It is very popular around Granada and every bakery has its own version.

A pionono has two parts: a thin layer of sponge rolled into a cylinder, made with different kinds of syrup that makes the pionono sweet. It is topped with toasted cream. It is typically eaten in one or two bites!

In this recipe, the cinnamon in the cream can be complimented by adding vanilla essence (half a teaspoon). It is a slightly complicated recipe but definitely worth the effort.

Ingredients:

Sponge (of 38cm x 25cm):

> 3 large eggs, at room temperature
> 60 g granulated sugar
> 90 g pastry flour
> Pinch of salt

Syrup:

> 150 g granulated sugar
> 160 ml water
> A cinnamon stick
> 2 tablespoons of rum

Cinnamon / Vanilla Cream:

> 4 large egg yolks
> 500 ml whole milk
> 100 g granulated sugar

60 g corn starch

Three quarters of a teaspoon of ground cinnamon

Half a teaspoon vanilla essence (optional)

Icing sugar for decoration

Preparation:

The cream sauce (cinnamon / vanilla) can be prepared the day before baking the piononos if this is convenient. In any case, the sauce should be prepared first.

Cinnamon / Vanilla Cream:

1. Break the eggs in a bowl and add the sugar, corn starch and a little milk. Mix together well with a whisk.

2. Heat the remaining milk in a saucepan with the cinnamon. (If you decide to use vanilla then add the vanilla essence now).

3. Before the milk begins to boil, remove the pan from the heat and add the egg mix, whisking vigorously to prevent curdling.

4. Place on a medium heat and continuously whisk until the mixture begins to thicken. Remove from the heat and allow the cream to cool. Cover the cream.

Syrup:

5. Put the sugar, water and cinnamon in a saucepan and bring it to the boil.

6. Let the mix simmer for 4-5 minutes over a medium heat.

7. Once the syrup is ready, remove it from the heat and set it aside.

Sponge Cake:

8. Preheat the oven to 180°C

9. Grease a shallow baking tray of around 28cm x 35cm with butter and place a piece of greased baking paper in the tray.

10. Put the eggs, a pinch of salt and the sugar in a bowl. Whisk for about 10 to 12 minutes until the mix is thick, consistent and holds its shape.

11. Add in the sifted flour and mix thoroughly.

12. Pour the dough onto the baking tray and spread it evenly with a spatula.

13. Place it in the oven and bake for about 8 minutes until lightly browned.

14. Remove the tray from the oven and use a spatula to lift the paper and pastry from the tray. Place it on a flat surface and cover it with a tray until it cools.

Making the Pionono:

15. Firstly, whisk or blend the cinnamon (and / or vanilla) cream sauce. It will have solidified and needs to be made fluid again.

16. Coat the sponge with the cold syrup using a soft brush. Spread the cinnamon / vanilla cream across the sponge thinly but place a thicker line of the cinnamon cream at the beginning of the sponge using an icing bag. This will be the centre of the rolled sponge.

17. Now, gently begin to roll the sponge into a kind of Swiss roll. Do not use too much pressure or the cream will be forced out.

18. When the whole sponge has been rolled, take a sharp knife and cut the roll into pieces of about 4 cm long. Put them vertically on an oven tray lined with baking paper.

19. Take the icing bag and cover the top of each pionono with a generous amount of the cinnamon / vanilla cream. Sprinkle with icing sugar and grill lightly.

20. Store the piononos in a cool place and keep them covered to prevent drying before serving.

PONCHE SEGOVIANO DE CASTILLA Y LEÓN
Segovian Marzipan Cake of Castilla y León

This is a traditional cake recipe from the old city of Segovia. Its recipe was kept a secret for years, being passed on through families of bakers. The confectioners Frutos García Martín first commercialized it in 1926 in their bakery on the Plaza Mayor of Segovia. At the request of King Alfonso XIII (who was fond of sweet dishes), the cake was presented to the Universal Exhibition of Barcelona in 1929 where it won the gold medal.

Now it is widely known and available in many other parts of Spain. It is quite rich and features marzipan as its dominant ingredient. In Segovia, it comes in small cakes of 600 g up to large versions of 1 kg and 2 kg.

Ingredients (for about 600 g):

The sponge:

> 75 g flour
> 3 eggs
> 30 g sugar

The cream:

> 500 ml milk
> 50 g sugar
> 10 g corn starch
> 3 egg yolks
> 10 g vanilla sugar
> A pinch of ground cinnamon

The marzipan:

> 300 g ground almonds
> 200 g sugar
> Half a shot of anís liquor
> 120 ml of orange blossom water
> 200 ml water

The syrup:

> 150 g sugar
> 150 ml water
> 50 ml of your favourite liquor - brandy, etc.

Preparation:

The sponge:

1. Preheat the oven to 170°C. Beat the eggs until they triple in volume. Add the sugar and flour, and mix well until consistent.

2. Spread the sponge mix evenly on a flat baking tray lined with greased baking paper. Put it in a preheated oven for approximately 10 min at 170°C. It can be considered baked when a fork or toothpick is pushed into the sponge and it comes out clean.

The cream:

3. Mix the corn starch with a little cold milk.

4. In a separate bowl beat the egg yolks together with the sugar until they are fluffy. Then add the corn starch, vanilla and cinnamon. Mix the ingredients very thoroughly.

5. Put the milk in a double boiler ("bain-marie") and little by little add the cream mix to the milk stirring continuously (to avoid curdling the eggs) until the whole mixture has thickened.

The marzipan:

6. Make a syrup by boiling the water in a saucepan and add the sugar, the anís liquor and the orange blossom water. Let the sugar dissolve for about 5 minutes without stirring, until it becomes a syrup. When the syrup starts to form strands, pour it into a bowl with the ground almonds and mix it well until you have a marzipan dough. Knead the marzipan for about 10 minutes on a smooth work surface, until the dough is completely consistent. Wrap it in a piece of shrink-wrap and put it in the refrigerator for 30 minutes.

The syrup:

7. Mix all the ingredients together and boil until you have a thick syrup (about 5 minutes). Do not allow the syrup to caramelise - it should be colourless.

The cake:

8. Slice the sponge into 3 equal sized rectangular pieces (it can be 2 or 4 layers if you prefer).

9. Coat the first layer of sponge with the syrup, then coat with a layer of the cream filling.

10. Cover the filling with a layer of sponge, and then brush on syrup again. Add a layer of cream again to this and then cover with the last piece of sponge.

11. Roll out the marzipan into a fine sheet and cover the top and sides of the sponge and cream cake. Make sure that it is well sealed.

12. Sprinkle the marzipan with icing sugar and you can decorate the top by marking with a red-hot piece of iron. Otherwise, it is ready to eat.

PROFITEROLES DE GIBRALTAR

Profiteroles (Little Choux Pastry Balls) of Gibraltar

The profiterole is a light and delicious sweet pastry (also known as cream "puff" in the US) which is also served as a dessert. It is a widespread European delicacy, ranging from Germany to France, Italy and Spain. In Spain, they are one of the most popular and important local dishes of Gibraltar.

The origin of the profiterole appears to be around the middle of the 16th century with the chefs of Catherine de Medici introducing the idea of "choux pastry" into the French court when she married Henry II of France. Her later family contacts with Spain (her daughter was queen of Spain) are thought by some to have seen the profiterole and many similar dessert delicacies arrived in the Spanish court.

There are many variations of the profiterole with many fillings and coatings including cream, pastry cream, chocolate and sugar.

Ingredients (30 profiteroles):

For the dough:

>250 ml milk
>125 g butter
>Pinch of salt
>250 g flour
>5 eggs
>Icing sugar to decorate

For the cream:

>1 litre milk
>1 lemon peel
>2 cinnamon sticks
>200 g sugar
>6 egg yolks
>10 level tablespoons of corn starch

Preparation:

For the dough:

1. Preheat the oven to 180°C.

2. Put the milk, butter and a pinch of salt in a saucepan and bring it to the boil.

3. When it starts to boil, take the pan from the heat and mix in the flour. Return the pan to the heat and continue mixing until the dough no longer sticks to the side of the saucepan.

4. Allow the dough mix to cool a little. Now add the eggs one at a time, beating vigorously.

5. Use two spoons to make small balls of dough and place these on a baking tray lined with baking paper. Bake at 180°C for about 25 minutes.

6. Remove the tray from the oven and allow the profiteroles to cool.

For the cream:

7. It is best to prepare the cream filling the night before so that it absorbs the lemon and cinnamon flavours.

8. Boil the milk with cinnamon and lemon peel and then leave the mix to infuse overnight. The next day, sieve the milk to remove the cinnamon and lemon peel.

9. Put the milk in a saucepan on a very low heat - it must not get too hot or it will curdle the eggs. Separately, mix the 200 g of sugar, the 6 egg yolks and the corn starch (first dissolved in a little milk). Add a little of the warmed milk to this mix and stir well. Pour this mix back into the saucepan with the luke warm milk. Stir very well to ensure it is completely smooth. Bring to the boil and on a low heat allow the mix to simmer for about 3 minutes, stirring continuously.

10. When cooked, remove from the heat, cover the mix and allow it to cool and thicken.

11. Open the profiteroles with kitchen scissors and fill them with the cream. Finally, sprinkle icing sugar on the tops before serving.

QUESADILLAS HERREÑAS, EL HIERRO, CANARIAS

Sweet Cheesecake of El Hierro, Canary Islands

El Hierro is the smallest of the Canary Islands and is a UNESCO Biosphere reserve. This cheesecake is typical for the island. It is sold as a pastry and usually made in the shape of a flower or a star.

The main ingredient is Herreño cheese. The cake was first created by the owner of the factory Adrian Gutierrez and Hijas in the early 20th century. The factory still produces the quesadillas in the traditional way, using a wood-burning oven.

The cheese of El Hierro is made using a mixture of (mostly) goat's milk with a smaller percentage of sheep's and cow's milk. It is smoked over wood fires to give it its characteristic taste. It is a cheese that melts very well and is delicious.

Quesadillas are simple to make and are often eaten as a dessert as well as with coffee for merienda. Some recipes add a little cinnamon, according to taste.

Ingredients:

> 1 kg unsalted Herreño cheese (or any fresh unsalted goat's cheese)
> 250 g flour
> 3 eggs
> 500 g sugar
> 1 tablespoon of aniseed
> Grated lemon peel

Preparation:

1. Chop up the cheese and blend it in a food processor.

2. Put the cheese into a bowl. Add the eggs, aniseed, lemon zest and sugar.

3. Mix well and gradually add the flour (without kneading) until you have a consistent paste.

4. Preheat the oven to 180°C. Put the mixture into individual star or flower shaped oven moulds, which have been greased with butter and sprinkled with flour.

5. Bake the quesadillas at 180°C for about 25 minutes or until they are golden brown.

6. Take them out of the oven and allow the quesadillas to cool before removing them from the moulds to serve.

REBOJO DE ZAMORA

Sweetbread of Zamora

This is a very typical sweet of the old city of Zamora, which is in Castilla y León, close to the Portuguese border. It is a cross between a sponge cake and bread and has a light crumb and soft crust. It is very simple to prepare. Rebojo is eaten at breakfast or with tea or coffee during merienda.

The rebojo has several variants. For instance, it is often made with orange or lemon flavour and another version uses aniseed or a shot of anís liquor. This is baked in a shallow oval baking tin (4 or 5 cm deep) but if you don't have the traditional shallow oval tin, an ordinary small, shallow baking tin will work fine. The shape does not affect the taste! In Zamora they are also baked in small oval paper moulds.

The origin of this simple cake is unknown but is thought to have been prepared in medieval times. Because it is very simple to make, it is routinely baked in Zamoran households where traditional baking recipes have been passed down through generations and are in daily use.

Ingredients:

> 330 g flour
> 6 eggs
> 5 g baking powder
> 330 g sugar
> Butter
> Grated peel of a medium sized orange or lemon
> Aniseed (optional)

Preparation:

1. Thoroughly sift the flour together with the baking powder

2. Preheat the oven to 180°C (top and bottom).

3. Beat the eggs together with the sugar until it has a consistent, creamy texture. If you want to flavour the dough, add the orange or lemon peel and/or the aniseed according to your own taste.

4. Gradually add the sieved flour / baking powder mix and keep stirring vigorously until you have a consistent dough.

5. The traditional rebojos are baked in shallow oval baking tins with corrugated sides but any shallow oven tin will do if you cannot find these easily.

6. Coat the oven tins with butter and half fill them with dough.

7. Bake for 20 minutes at 180°C until they are golden and the top begins to split as a sponge cake would.

8. Take the rebojos out of the oven, allow them to cool and then remove them from the baking tins. Shake a little icing sugar on top.

ROLLOS DE ACEITE DE MURCIA

Olive Oil Rings of Murcia

Variants of this recipe exist in several parts of Spain, particularly in the South East. For instance the "Rollos de San Blas y de San Antón" are very similar (as you will see in a coming recipe) and are often blessed in collective church ceremonies on the Saints days and then distributed to friends and family to bring good health. Indeed, traditionally they were also given to small farm animals like rabbits and chickens to prevent illness.

The variants include using a little cinnamon with the icing sugar to coat them before baking and flavouring the hot oil with lemon peel. This recipe is for the Murcian version (also known as "Rollos de Vino Blanco") which is eaten at any time of the year. The rollos are quite light and are often taken with coffee or tea for merienda. It is said that it gets its particular texture from the scalding of the flour with hot olive oil.

Ingredients:

    1 L olive oil
    0.5 L white wine
    2 kg flour
    100 g granulated sugar
    32 g baking powder
    Icing sugar to coat

Preparation:

1. Sift the flour into a bowl and add the baking powder and granulated sugar. Mix well. Keep about 200 g of flour aside to add to the dough at the end of kneading.

2. Heat the olive oil but take care not to allow it to smoke. You can verify that it has reached the right temperature by throwing in a piece of lemon peel. The oil is ready to use when we see the lemon peel begin to fry.

3. Preheat the oven to 180°C. Carefully pour the oil into the flour and begin to mix and knead. Add the white wine and continue to mix and knead.

4. Add the remaining flour and continue to knead until the dough does not stick to your hands.

288

5. Make the "rollos" by taking small portions of dough. Roll each piece of dough into a sausage shape and join the ends together so that you have a ring.

6. Bake at 180ºC until they are golden brown.

7. Whilst the rollos are still warm, coat them with icing sugar and serve when cool.

ROLLOS DE AMOR DE JUMILLA, MURCIA (ALMOJÁBANA)

Rings of Love, Jumilla, Murcia

These doughnuts, originally from the famous wine district of Jumilla in the region of Murcia, are particularly popular on St. Valentine's Day, hence the name. The pastry is often served at weddings, baptisms and communions. They are known locally as almojábenas and are also a typical dish in the south of the province of Alicante, and in Aragón. The name derives from the Arabic 'almuyábbana' that means 'mixture made with cheese'. Despite the fact there is no cheese in this variety, there is another "donut" with the same name, made with a dough to which fresh cheese is added and which is typical of the Canary Islands, especially the island of La Gomera.

This particular pastry was first described in 1525 by Rupert de Nola in his cookbook, and in a book of recipes based on a thirteenth century manuscript "Cocina Hispano-Magrebí durant e la época Almohade" ("The Hispano-Magreb kitchen during the Almohad period"). This is not a new pastry invention!

Ingredients:

> 250 ml water
> 100 ml olive oil
> 100 ml sunflower oil
> 250 g flour
> 6 eggs
> Pinch of salt
> Sugar to coat

For the syrup:

> 0.5 L water
> 6 tablespoons sugar
> Grated lemon peel

Preparation:

1. Put both types of oil, water and salt in a saucepan and heat until the mixture begins to boil.

2. Slowly add the sifted flour, stirring continuously and mix over a very low heat until all the flour is blended in and a consistent dough has formed.

3. Remove the dough from the heat and allow it to cool completely to room temperature for at least one hour (the cooling is very important).

4. Now, add the eggs, one at a time, mixing thoroughly after each one before adding the next.

5. Line an oven tray with baking paper. Use a tablespoon to place portions of dough onto the tray. Create a hole in the middle of the dough with your finger dipped in oil. Leave plenty of space between the portions of dough to allow them to expand during baking. You can also make the dough portions using a pastry bag.

6. Preheat the oven to 200°C with fan.

7. Bake the rings for about 20-25 minutes.

8. Remove the rollos from the oven and let them cool on the same tray.

9. Make a syrup by boiling the water with the sugar and lemon peel. Leave to stand for a few minutes. Then dip the rings in the syrup and coat them with sugar.

ROLLOS DE PASCUA DE CARTAGENA

Christmas Orange, Cinnamon and Anís Rings of Cartagena

Murcia has many traditional pastries and sweets, both baked and fried. There are many flavoured rolls, rings and fritters and this is one of the richest, most popular, seasonal and highly flavoured baked Christmas sweets of the region. It is very much an essential Advent and Christmas treat in the town of Cartagena with some of the typical aromas of the Christmas bakery: cinnamon, anís, and lemon.

Ingredients:

> 500 g sugar
> 250 ml orange juice
> Half a litre olive oil
> 125 ml dry anís liquor
> 30 g aniseed
> 60 g pine nuts
> Grated peel of 1 lemon
> 1.5 kg flour
> 24 g baking powder
> Ground cinnamon
> Sugar to decorate
> 2 beaten eggs
> 125 g raw peeled almonds

Preparation:

1. Put the olive oil in a skillet on the heat until it begins to smoke and then put it aside.

2. Bring 100 ml of water to the boil in a saucepan. When it starts to boil, add the aniseed. Let it boil for10 minutes, then remove from the heat and cover.

3. Pour the flour into a large bowl, add the sugar and blend by hand until they are well mixed.

4. Make a hole in the centre of the flour and sugar and add the olive oil, orange juice, anís liquor and 50 ml of the aniseed water and half a handful of the boiled aniseed. Add the baking powder and mix all the ingredients together with the grated lemon peel and pine nuts.

5. Knead the dough by hand until all the ingredients are well incorporated and form the dough into a ball.

6. Put the dough in a bowl and cover it with a clean cloth. Let it stand for 6 hours to rise. The risen dough will be quite oily but this is normal.

7. Before baking, prepare a mixture of cinnamon powder and sugar and beat the eggs.

8. Preheat the oven to 200ºC.

9. Take pieces of dough, kneed and form them into rings, coat them with the beaten eggs and sprinkle with the mixture of sugar and cinnamon. Decorate each ring with 2 or 3 almonds. Place the rings on a baking tray lined with baking paper.

10. Bake until a light golden brown. Remove the rollos from the oven and allow them to cool before serving.

11. They can be eaten when cool but they last for months.

ROLLOS DE SAN ANTÓN DE CARTAGENA

San Antón's Fritters of Cartagena

San Antón is a district (barrio) in the city of Cartagena, Murcia. These fritters are a famous product of that area. They are often made on the feast day of St. Anthony (January 17th) and then brought to the local church to be blessed and sold.

One local custom is to leave one of the blessed fritters next to the housekeeping money so that the house will not be short of cash. The "lucky rollo" is replaced every year with a new one! Another local legend states that any single woman stealing one of the blessed rollos will soon be married.

Ingredients:

> 3 eggs
> 240 ml olive oil
> 1 shot of dry anís liquor
> 250 g sugar
> 500 g flour
> 16 g baking powder
> Olive oil for frying

Preparation:

1. Beat the eggs and sugar together in a bowl. Add the olive oil and anís liquor, and continue mixing thoroughly.

2. Pour the mixture into the heaped flour and mix, and then use your hands to knead it into a consistent dough.

3. Roll out the dough and cut it into quite thick strips.

4. Roll the strips and form them into rings. The rollos are usually made so that they are between 5 cm and 10 cm in diameter.

5. Fry the rollos in plenty of hot olive oil.

6. Remove them from the oil and place the rings on kitchen paper to soak up excess oil.

7. Serve with the local drink "Reparo", which is a mixture of sweet wine and cognac.

ROSCÓN DE REYES

Ring of the Three Kings

Roscón de Reyes (the ring of the kings) is a pastry traditionally eaten to celebrate Epiphany. It is generally 30 cm or more in diameter and there are many different recipes, but usually it is decorated with glace cherries, figs, quinces, and other candied fruits. (A very similar pastry is called Roscón de San Valero).

The Roscón de Reyes is traditionally eaten on January 6, during the celebration of the "Día de Reyes" (The "Day of the Kings") which commemorates the arrival of the three Magi or Wise Men to visit the infant Jesus.

In Spain (and in most other parts of the Hispanic world), this is also the day on which Christmas gifts are given (unlike in other countries where gifts are given on Christmas day). The gifts are said to come from the Three Wise Men, hence the connection with the Kings (Reyes). Therefore, there is a great deal of excitement involved for all and especially for the children, who wait eagerly for the Kings to come to bring them gifts.

The tradition of placing a little trinket (often a figure of the Christ child) in the cake is very old. The baby Jesus, when hidden in the bread, represents the flight of Jesus from King Herod's massacre of the innocents. Tradition says that whoever finds the baby Jesus figurine is blessed. That person must bring the figurine to the nearest church on February 2, Candlemas Day (Día de la Candelaria). Another tradition includes hiding a dry bean in the Roscón as well as the figurine of the baby Jesus. In this tradition, whoever finds the figurine is crowned "king" or "queen" of the banquet. Whoever finds the bean unfortunately has to pay for next year's Roscón!

The history of this dish is, however, much older than Christianity. The traditional Roscón de Reyes dates back to ancient Rome and its Saturnalia festivities that took place between 21st and 23rd December to celebrate the winter solstice. Tradition has it that Roman patricians shared round bread containing honey, figs and dates with the slaves and freedmen of their cities. This was a sign that they would live together in harmony in the New Year and mutually celebrate the rebirth of the year after the short winter days leading to the solstice.

Over the years, the Roscón has had some powerful enthusiasts. They say the biggest promoter of the cake was Louis XV of France. Apparently, Louis' cook was of Slavic origin, and entertained the monarch at Epiphany with a traditional Roscón from his own country with a surprise baked inside the cake: a medallion of diamonds purchased with the collaboration of other members of the royal court!

While the tradition was lost in Eastern Europe, Louis XV was so delighted with the invention that he decided to propagate the recipe, with a coin inside as a surprise, when entertaining French and other European aristocracy. So it was that during the eighteenth century, the Roscón came to Spain, where it rapidly became a welcome traditional treat at noble tables. Soon the customs of the Roscón spread to the tables of the common people in Spain and then gradually throughout the Spanish colonies.

It is best served with a cup of hot chocolate whilst awaiting the arrival of the three Kings and their sacks of presents!

Ingredients:

> 650 g flour
> 250 ml warm milk
> 25-30 g fresh yeast
> 120 g sugar
> 120 g butter, melted
> 2 eggs and 1 egg yolk
> 10 g salt
> 2.5 tablespoons of orange blossom water
> Grated peel of 1 large lemon and 1 orange

To decorate:

> Candied fruits to taste
> Sugar
> 1 egg, beaten
> An orange
> Bakeable figurines (not too small!)

Preparation:

1. Starter yeast: Mix some of the warm milk with 2 or 3 tablespoons of the flour. Add 25-30 g of crumbled fresh yeast and mix well. Cover the mixture and let it ferment for about 15 to 20 minutes in a warm place.

2. Once the starter mixture has begun to ferment, make the dough. Put the remaining flour into a large mixing bowl and gradually mix in all

the other ingredients: sugar, grated lemon and orange peel, salt, milk, eggs, sugar, the fermenting starter yeast, orange blossom water and finally the melted butter. Stir well until it becomes a smooth mix.

3. Place the dough on a floured work surface and knead it for a few minutes by hand. If necessary, add a little more flour to work the dough.

4. When it is well mixed, shape the dough into a round cake and place it in a large airtight container or in a bowl covered with a damp cloth. Leave it to rise for a couple of hours in a warm place.

5. After this time, the dough should have risen to about twice its size.

6. Take the dough from the container and on a floured work surface, knead it again and slowly shape it into a ring. With these quantities, we can also make two medium-sized roscones.

7. When shaping the roscones, remember that the hole in the middle will become smaller during baking, so it is best to make the hole in the middle quite big.

8. When they are shaped, leave them again to rest for about an hour, covered and in a warm place. A useful tip is to heat the oven to 50°C, switch it off and put the roscones in the oven to keep them warm and get them to rise.

9. Finally, coat the roscones with egg, and decorate the top to your liking, for example, with all kinds of candied fruit, candied oranges, sliced almonds, sugar, etc. If you want to hide a figurine in the Roscón, this is the time to do it!

10. Once the roscones are decorated, put them into a preheated oven at 180°C for about 20 minutes.

11. When baked, take them out and leave to cool.

12. Some people like to cut them in half and fill them with cream, chocolate mousse, baker's cream or some other favourite filling.

ROSCOS DE ANÍS

Anís Doughnuts

Anís doughnuts are found in many parts of Spain but especially in the South. They are very popular in Murcia and the region has several variants of them. A very similar rosco is also made in the province of Almeria.

Ingredients:

>120 ml olive oil for frying
>50 g ground almonds (without skin)
>1 tablespoon of cinnamon powder
>1 tablespoon of aniseed
>500 g pastry flour
>100 g sugar
>1 glass of sweet Moscatel wine
>120 ml olive oil
>Sweet anís liquor (to taste)
>Icing sugar (to coat the doughnuts)

Preparation:

1. Pour a little olive oil into a frying pan and roast 50 g of ground almonds (without the skin), taking care not to burn them.

2. Take a large bowl and put in the almonds, ground cinnamon, aniseed, the pastry flour, the sugar, olive oil, Moscatel wine and a little sweet anís liquor (according to your taste).

3. Knead all the ingredients together until the dough is smooth and compact.

4. Coat your hands with flour and start to make the doughnut rings by rolling and shaping the dough.

5. Fry the doughnuts in hot oil, taking care not to burn them.

6. When the roscos have turned a golden brown, remove them from the oil, drain them on kitchen roll and coat them with icing sugar.

ROSCOS CARREROS DE MÁLAGA

Doughnut "volcanoes" of Málaga

This doughnut is a favourite in many rural areas of the province of Málaga. These roscos are made in the shape of a volcano with a hole in the middle. This recipe comes from Alfarnate, a small mountain village north of Málaga. With their spicy flavour of cloves and cinnamon, these roscos evoke the tastes of the Nasrid past of this remote Arabic village which lies on the ancient Arab route between Málaga and Granada.

Ingredients:

> 12 eggs
> 1 kg of lard (or butter) at room temperature
> 1.5 kg flour
> 250 g sugar
> Half a glass of brandy
> 5 ground cloves
> Cinnamon powder (to taste)

Preparation:

1. Separate the egg yolks and whites.

2. Beat the egg whites.

3. Mix all the ingredients (except the egg yolks) in a large bowl and work the mixture together into a consistent dough.

4. Tear off small portions of the dough. Roll them out on a work surface and shape the strips of dough into little conical "volcanoes". Place them on a baking tray and baste with the beaten egg yolks.

5. Bake at 180°C for 10 minutes.

ROSCOS DUROS DE NAVIDAD

Crispy Christmas Doughnuts

This is a traditional Asturian recipe for small crispy Christmas doughnuts. They smell and taste delicious. The dough is very easy to make and very manageable to work when making the doughnuts.

Ingredients:

> 550 g flour
> 220 g sugar
> 200 ml olive oil
> 115 ml white wine
> 15 g of sesame seeds
> 15 g of aniseed

Preparation:

1. Put the sugar, oil, wine, aniseed and sesame seeds in a bowl. Mix them all very well and then add the flour. Knead thoroughly into a smooth dough.

2. Let the dough rest for 15 minutes while the oven is preheated to 220ºC.

3. Make the doughnuts and place them on a greased oven tray or line the tray with baking paper. Put the tray into the oven.

4. The baking time will depend on the size of the doughnut. A smallish doughnut takes about15 minutes, until they start to colour.

5. Take the roscos out of the oven and put them on a rack until cooled.

ROSCOS DE MINUTO DE ALFARNATE

One-Minute Doughnuts from Alfarnate

For when you have an unexpected Christmas visitor, here is a rustic recipe from Alfarnate in Málaga province to rustle up some festive doughnuts in a hurry.

Ingredients:

For one egg:

> 8 tablespoons of milk
> 8 tablespoons of sugar
> 6 tablespoons of olive oil
> 1 teaspoon of ground cinnamon
> 1 pinch of aniseed
> 1 glass of brandy
> 8 g baking powder
> Flour as required to make a dough

Preparation:

1. Beat the egg white until stiff, and then add the yolk, sugar, milk, cinnamon, aniseed, oil and brandy.

2. Add the flour and baking powder and knead well until it becomes a consistent dough - but not very sticky.

3. Make doughnuts with a diameter of about 8 cm. Fry them in plenty of oil. When they are fried, place them on some kitchen paper to drain and coat them with icing sugar.

ROSCOS DE NARANJA

Orange Doughnuts

The Rosco de Naranja (Orange Doughnut) is a traditional Christmas dish in Eastern Málaga. Locally, the recipe is known as the "recipe of ten", because for every kilo of flour, it takes ten oranges, ten tablespoons of oil and ten tablespoons of sugar.

These doughnuts are delicious! A similar lemon doughnut is made with much the same recipe but substituting the oranges with a similar weight of lemons (also known as "Rosquillas de Limón").

Ingredients:

> 1 kg flour
> 10 medium oranges
> 10 tablespoons of olive oil
> 10 tablespoons of sugar
> 1 teaspoon of cinnamon
> 1 teaspoon of aniseed
> 1 teaspoon of baking powder
> 1 pinch of salt
> Sunflower oil for frying
> Cinnamon mixed with sugar for coating the doughnuts

Preparation:

1. Heat the olive oil. When the oil starts to smoke, add the aniseed and remove the pan from the heat.

2. Mix the flour, sugar, salt, cinnamon, baking powder and the grated peel of one orange in a bowl.

3. Gradually stir in the olive oil with aniseed, and the orange juice and mix the dough until it becomes smooth. Leave to stand for 30 minutes.

4. Take small pieces of dough, roll them into little balls, flatten them slightly and make a hole in the middle with your finger.

5. Fry them in plenty of hot sunflower oil over a moderate heat. Dry on absorbent kitchen paper and coat them with the sugar and cinnamon mixture.

ROSCOS DE NARANJA DE PERIANA

Orange Doughnuts of Periana

Here is another recipe for Roscos de Naranja (Orange doughnuts), this time from Periana in Andalucía.

Ingredients:

> 2 eggs
> 10 tablespoons of oil
> 10 tablespoons of orange juice
> 10 tablespoons of sugar
> 500 g flour
> 16 g baking powder
> 1 tablespoon of ground cinnamon
> Grated lemon peel
> Olive oil

Preparation:

1. Beat the eggs in a bowl.

2. Add the sugar, oil, orange juice, cinnamon, grated lemon peel, flour and baking powder.

3. Beat the ingredients together into a smooth mix.

4. When the dough thickens, oil your hands and manually knead the dough for about 10 minutes.

5. Make the fritters either round, like a doughnut, or straight.

6. In the meantime, warm up a pan of olive oil on a medium heat for frying.

7. Fry the doughnuts until they are golden brown, making sure not to let the oil get too hot.

8. When the roscos are fried, place them on some kitchen roll to drain and sprinkle each doughnut with sugar.

ROSCAS DE SAN BLAS DE VALENCIA

Lemon Rings of San Blas, Valencia

This traditional Valencian sweet is prepared on the feast day of San Blas on the 3rd February. In the past, these rings were taken to the local church and blessed. They were eaten as a traditional cure for colds - San Blas being a doctor!

There are many local variations: Some are glazed and others use dough with a lot of olive oil added which makes them very crumbly. You can also use grated orange peel and orange juice and / or a dash of anís spirit.

Ingredients:

> 2 Eggs
> 250 g sugar
> 160 ml olive oil
> 1 small spoonful of cinnamon powder
> Grated peel of 1 lemon
> 600 g flour (approximately)
> 34 g Baking powder

Preparation:

1. Preheat the oven to 180°C.

2. Mix the eggs and sugar well in a bowl.

3. Add the grated lemon peel and the oil. Continue to beat until it is thoroughly mixed.

4. Add about 250 g of flour, the cinnamon powder and the baking powder. Mix well.

5. Start kneading by hand and add enough flour until the dough is no longer sticking to your hands.

6. Cut small quantities of dough with a knife and roll it out to create a sausage shape. Form a ring like a doughnut (the size is up to you but they are usually about 10 to 15 cm in diameter). Place them on baking paper on a baking tray.

6. When you have used all the dough to form the rings, they are ready for the oven.

7. Bake in the preheated oven for 15 to 18 minutes at 180°C until they are lightly browned.

8. Remove the roscas from the oven and allow them to cool and harden. Serve.

ROSCOS DE VINO DE MÁLAGA

Wine Doughnuts of Málaga

This is a traditional Christmas sweet originating in Málaga. It has its origins in traditional spicy Moorish dishes but is also now associated with Christian religious events. Several convents make their own versions of this sweet, often wrapped in delightful, old-fashioned packaging with obvious strong Christian images. This is one such old convent recipe made on a catering scale! Reduce the quantities for family consumption.

Ingredients:

> 1 kg butter or lard (at room temperature)
> 150 olive oil (this should heated and cooled in advance)
> 1 glass of white wine
> 400 g icing sugar
> 15 g ground cinnamon (according to taste)
> 20 ground cloves
> 2 glasses of dry brandy
> 3 kg flour
> Icing sugar (to coat the doughnuts)

Preparation:

1. Beat the butter. Gradually add the olive oil and the wine, stirring constantly.

2. Add the sugar, cinnamon, ground cloves, brandy and flour, whilst mixing continuously to form a consistent dough.

3. Take small pieces of the dough, roll them and form into doughnuts. Place them on an oven tray lined with baking paper.

4. Put the tray in the preheated oven and bake at 180°C for 15 minutes or until golden brown.

4. Remove the doughnuts from the oven and allow them to cool. Once cold, sprinkle them with some water and coat with icing sugar.

5. Finally, let them stand for a few minutes for the sugar to set, and then wrap them in kitchen paper to keep them moist until they are to be served.

ROSQUILLAS DE YEMA DE ALCALÁ

Egg Doughnuts of Alcalá

These coated doughnuts are sold in many parts of Madrid City and province and are renowned for their characteristic yellow colouring. Traditionally, they are believed to originate in Alcalá de Henares, which is a town close to the capital. However, there are so many types of "Rosco" and "Rosquilla" in Spain it is quite likely that they have a Moorish origin. They are made with several layers of puff pastry and when baked are dipped in a coating of egg yolk and sugar.

They are generally eaten at breakfast or merienda.

Ingredients:

> 2 sheets of puff pastry
> 70 ml water
> 3 tablespoons of water
> 200 g granulated sugar
> 5 egg yolks
> 100 g icing sugar

Preparation:

1. Preheat the oven to 200°C.

2. Spread the puff pastry sheets and place one on top of the other.

3. Gently roll the sheets together with a rolling pin, but without putting too much pressure on them.

4. Use a pastry cutter of about 5 cm in diameter to cut out the doughnuts and use a small cutter for the central hole in each. (There are doughnut pastry cutters available that make the central hole at the same time.)

5. Place the doughnuts on a baking tray lined with baking paper. Spray them with a little water.

6. Bake the doughnuts at 200°C for about 15 to 18 minutes. Remove the tray from the oven and allow the doughnuts to cool.

7. Make the coating by mixing the 70 ml of water with the granulated sugar and boil for 4 or 5 minutes until the sugar mix starts to form fine strands. Allow to cool until luke warm.

8. Beat the egg yolks with a whisk and add the syrup, whisking continuously.

9. Warm the mix on a low heat, stirring continuously, until it thickens. It should not boil.

10. Whilst the syrup is still hot, immerse the rosquillitas in it and place them aside to dry and cool for about an hour.

11. Whisk the icing sugar with the 3 tablespoons of water until it becomes white.

12. Immerse the doughnuts in this glaze mix and place them aside to dry again before serving.

SOPLILLOS DE LA ALPUJARRA, GRANADA

Meringues of the Alpujarras, Granada

The Alpujarras are a remote mountainous area south of Granada. During the expulsions of the Jews and Muslims from Spain, the area became a temporary safe haven for those fleeing the brutality of the Christian invaders.

The Alpujarras have many unusual culinary traditions, This meringue is one of the most delicious and is considered to have originated in the Moorish period. The villages of Murtas, Cádiar and Ugíjar are especially well known for this particular sweet. After the Christian conquest, as with many other traditional Moorish sweet dishes, the monastic orders took control of the production of these highly tempting sweets. Thus, in many villages, soplillos have become traditional sweets during Easter and Christmas.

The Alpujarras is rich in both almonds and honey and it is believed that the original meringue recipes were made with honey rather than sugar. Sugar was introduced by the Arabs but was grown mostly in coastal areas far from remote, mountainous regions such as the Alpujarras.

Soplillos are taken as a sweet or with coffee during merienda.

Ingredients:

> 6 eggs
> 300 g sugar
> 150 g raw almonds (or equivalent in roasted almonds)
> 1 lemon

Preparation:

1. Roast the raw whole almonds in a hot, non-stick frying pan without oil. Keep moving and turning the almonds until they begin to brown, but avoid burning. Take the almonds out of the pan and put them aside.

2. Separate the egg whites from the egg yolks. Store the yolks in an airtight container in the fridge.

3. Grate the lemon peel and squeeze the lemon juice.

4. Whisk the egg whites until stiff. Whilst whisking, gradually add the lemon juice and the grated lemon peel. You know the egg whites are ready when the egg white is firm and holds its shape. Next, add the sugar very gradually so as not to cause the egg whites to soften.

5. Coarsely chop the roasted almonds with a knife. Preheat the oven to 100°C.

6. Carefully add the roasted almonds to the bowl of meringue with a spatula making folding movements from bottom to top. This needs to be done slowly in order not to lose the foaminess of the egg whites.

7. When the meringue mixture is made, then place baking paper on a baking tray and use a spoon to create small mounts of meringue of between 4 and 6 cm in diameter. Leave plenty of space in between because they will expand.

8. Place the tray in the preheated oven for between 1.5 and 2 hours. They are ready when they begin to crack on the outside and brown very slightly (they should remain soft on the inside).

9. Remove the soplillos from the oven and allow them to cool. If you wish, you can sprinkle some icing sugar on top. When cool, they are ready to eat.

TARTA CAPUCHINA DE YEMAS

Capuchina Egg Cake

As the name implies, this recipe originates with the Capuchin nuns of St. Clare, also known as the "Poor Clares". This order of nuns was founded in the 13th century and today they divide their time between contemplation and work. They maintain their community's economy in various ways but are famous for their sweet bakery skills.

Traditionally, in wine producing parts of Spain, the bodegas would use the egg whites for clarifying their wine and donate the egg yolks to the "Poor Clares". The nuns quickly realised that they could use these egg yolks to create a whole range of rich pastries and sweets. The tarta capuchina is one such cake.

Ingredients (for a 25cm round baking tin):

15 egg yolks
2 whole eggs
40 g corn starch
For the syrup:
150 g sugar
Enough water to cover the sugar in a saucepan

Preparation:

1. Preheat the oven to 180°C.

2. Grease a round baking tin with butter and sprinkle with flour.

3. Separate the egg whites from the yolks and put all the yolks together with the two whole eggs in a mixing bowl.

4. Beat the mixture vigorously for about 5 minutes until the yolks triple their volume, whiten and form a spongy mixture.

5. Sift the corn starch onto the mixture and fold into the eggs until well mixed.

6. Pour the mixture into the mould and place this in the oven until it is golden. Test that it is baked by pricking with a toothpick. If it comes out clean, then it is baked.

7. Remove the mould from the oven and place it on a rack to cool.

8. Whilst the cake is cooling, prepare the syrup by mixing the sugar and water in a saucepan and boil for a few minutes until the mix becomes a soft syrup.

9. Use a pastry basting brush to coat the whole cake thoroughly and then leave the cake to absorb the syrup.

10. To serve, sprinkle the entire surface of the cake with icing sugar and use a knife to cut diagonal lines in the sugar to create the characteristic diamond motif on the top of the cake.

TARTA DE MONDOÑEDO DE GALICIA

Almond, Fig and Cherry Tart of Mondoñedo, Galicia

The tarta de Mondoñedo is a famous and traditional sweet tart of Galicia, based on similar fruit tart recipes originating in the middle ages. The tart is reputedly depicted on a 12th century lintel in Compostela and the tart has won many awards and accolades down the years.

It has a slightly flaky pastry, is based on angel hair, a layer of sponge and then a layer of almond. It is often decorated with cherries and figs but there are several versions with different fruits. Fresh or preserved fruit may be used, such as figs in syrup or candied cherries. This makes this cake a year-round favourite. It is eaten as a dessert or with merienda.

Ingredients:

For the Filling and Decoration:

> 200 g angel hair
> 250 g puff pastry dough
> Candied cherries
> Figs in syrup

For the Sponge Cake:

> 4 medium eggs
> 4 tablespoons of flour
> 4 tablespoons of sugar

For the Almond Layer:

> 200 g raw chopped almonds
> 250 ml of water with a dash of lemon juice
> 300 g sugar

Preparation:

1. Firstly, make an ordinary sponge cake with the eggs, flour and sugar. This should be made in the same or a slightly smaller mould than the one to be used for the tart. Bake at 180 °C for about 20 minutes.

2. When baked, remove the cake from the mould and place it on a grid to cool. Soak with some syrup (see the next step, where the syrup is prepared).

3. Put the water and lemon juice in a saucepan and add the 300 g of sugar. Put it on a gentle heat and let the sugar dissolve. When it is dissolved, increase the temperature to bring it to the boil. As it becomes syrup, add the chopped almonds and cook for 5 minutes. Drain the syrup into a bowl and let the almonds cool. Use the syrup to soak the sponge cake.

4. Preheat the oven to 180 °C - 200°C.

5. Roll out the puff pastry on a floured work surface until it has a thickness of about 5 mm. Place it in the bottom of the baking tin (lined with baking paper) and trim it to shape. Perforate the bottom of the dough with a fork so that it does not rise.

6. Crumble the soaked sponge cake on top of the puff pastry. Coat this with angel hair and then cover with the almonds and syrup mix.

7. Finish off the tart with remaining strips of puff pastry to form a lattice pattern on top.

8. Bake the tart for 20-25 minutes in the oven at 180 °C - 200°C until the puff pastry is golden brown.

9. Take the tart out of the oven and remove it from the mould. Decorate it with candied cherries and figs and finish off by glazing it with some of the remaining syrup.

TARTA DE QUESO AFUEGA'L PITU

Afuega'l pitu Cheesecake of Asturias

Asturias, with its high rainfall, is dairy country and has some wonderful cheeses. The cheese Afuega'l Pitu is famous and popular in the region and throughout Spain. Afuega'l Pitu cheese is made from Friesian cow's milk in the area around the Sierra del Aramo. It is a dense and fatty cheese and is believed to be one of the oldest cheeses produced in Spain. The cheesecake made with this cheese is firmer than most cheesecakes and is always served with a sweet topping, usually honey. It is eaten as a dessert or with breakfast or merienda.

Ingredients:

> 250 g Afuega'l Pitu cheese
> 30 g flour
> 65 g granulated sugar
> Half a teaspoon of salt
> Half a teaspoon of lemon extract or finely grated lemon peel
> 28 g unsalted butter (softened)
> 150 g whipping cream
> 1 large egg

Preparation:

1. All ingredients except the cream should be at room temperature.

2. Break the cheese into small pieces with a fork in a mixing bowl.

3. Add the sugar, cream and butter and mix by hand or with an electric mixer.

4. Add the salt and lemon and continue to mix.

5. Slowly add the flour while mixing gently or stirring by hand.

6. Preheat the oven to 160°C.

7. Grease the bottom and sides of a cake tin (a springform tin is best) with margarine and pour in the cheese filling. Spread the cheese with a wooden spoon.

8. Place the cake tin in the oven on a centre rack and bake for approximately 35-40 minutes, checking often.

9 The cheese should set, but be careful not to overcook it.

10. Remove the cheesecake from the oven and allow it to cool for 15 minutes.

11. When it is still warm, run a thin knife around between the cake and the tin, and carefully remove the sides of the tin.

12. Serve the cheesecake warm, with a little honey over the top of each serving.

13. Any leftover cheesecake can be covered tightly with shrink-wrap, and stored in the fridge for 2 to 3 days.

TARTA DE SAN MARCOS DE CASTILLA Y LEON

St. Marks Cake of Castilla y Leon

This is a cake based on cream and egg yolk topping which is very attractive and delicious. It is circular and about 20 cm in diameter and usually made about 5-6 cm high. It is soft and spongy and in some versions, it is coated with a layer of ground almond around its whole outer edge.

It is a traditional rich cake of Leon, where several local confectioners make it, but it is also found in the Monastery of La Santa Cruz de Sahagún.

Generally the cake is made to be around 1 kg but one version of this cake is a smaller version which are known as "Pastel de San Marcos". It is eaten as both a dessert and a sweet cake for merienda.

Ingredients:

Sponge cake:

>   3 eggs
>   180 g sugar
>   120 g flour
>   100 g butter (very soft)
>   Butter to grease baking tin
>   2 tablespoons of flour to dust the baking tin
>   A pinch of salt

Filling:

>   3 eggs
>   180 g sugar
>   Cream

Preparation:

Sponge cake:

1. Separate the egg yolks from the egg whites.

2. Put the egg whites in a bowl with a pinch of salt and beat until stiff.

3. Add the egg yolks and then the sugar. Continue mixing without stopping for about 10 minutes.

4. Gradually stir in the flour, a spoonful at a time, and finally add the softened butter and mix until you have a consistent sponge mix.

5. Pour the sponge mix into a round baking tin, greased and dusted with flour.

6. Bake the cake for 45 minutes in a moderately hot oven (about 180°C).

7. Allow it to cool.

Filling:

8. Cut the sponge in half as follows: Make a very shallow cut (about 1 cm deep) all around the side of the sponge about halfway up the sponge. Put a strong thin cotton thread around this cut, cross the ends of the threads and gently pull to split the sponge in two.

9. Separate the two halves. Fill with cream and place the two halves together again.

10. Lightly spread the rest of the cake with the remaining cream.

The Syrup:

11. Put the sugar and a few spoonfuls of water in a saucepan.

12. Bring to a boil over a medium heat. When the mix starts to boil, add half a glass of water.

13. Whilst the syrup is warm but not hot, add the egg yolks slowly, one by one, stirring continuously until it has a smooth consistency.

14. Remove the syrup mix from the heat and allow it to cool slightly. Then use a brush to coat the top of the cake with the syrup. Finally decorate the outer edge of the top of the cake with little spirals of cream.

15. An alternative variation: coat the sides of the cake with cream and then coat the cream with chopped almonds.

TARTA DE SANTIAGO

St. James' Cake of Santiago, Galicia

This famous and delicious almond cake is named in honour of Santiago (St. James), the patron saint of Spain. It is said that his remains are buried in the city of Santiago de Compostela, Galicia. During the Middle Ages, the pilgrimage to Santiago was the most important religious journey of the Christian world. Today, many people still make the trip to Santiago, not just for religious reasons, but also as a cultural, historical experience.

The cake's origin is not certain, but it may have been brought to Galicia by an early pilgrim. Today, the cake is sold all over Santiago de Compostela and it is popular with tourists and pilgrims alike. It is also a very popular sweet throughout Spain, particularly at Christmas.

Tarta de Santiago is made of almond, eggs, sugar and butter. The cross of Santiago is made on the top of the cake with icing sugar, using a stencil, thus giving the cake its distinctive appearance. This is an old recipe and we decided to leave the original measures but modernise the preparation.

Ingredients :

2.6 cups of ground almonds
0.75 cup of flour
1.25 cup of sugar
4 eggs
8 tablespoons of butter at room temperature
Half a teaspoonof baking powder
Half a cup of water
Grated zest of 1 lemon
Icing sugar to decorate

Preparation:

1. Blanch the almonds and then, using a grinder or a food processor, grind them until fine and set aside.

2. Heat the oven to 180°C. Grease a round baking tin of 20 cm.

3. In a large mixing bowl, beat the eggs and sugar together. Add the butter, flour, baking powder and water and mix well.

4. Stir the almonds into the dough. Add the grated lemon peel and stir until thoroughly mixed.

5. Pour the cake mix into the baking tin. Bake in the oven on the middle shelf at 180°C for approximately 45-50 minutes. Check after 45 minutes. It is done if a toothpick inserted into the centre of the cake comes out clean.

6. The traditional way to decorate the cake is to sprinkle icing sugar on the top, with a cut-out of the sword of St. James or a cross in the middle. Place the template of the cross in the centre of the cake and dust the top with the sugar. A small flour sifter works well for this.

TARTA DE SIDRA DE ASTURIAS

Cider Tart of Asturias

Asturias is famous for its apples and cider. This is a traditional apple tart from the region made with both apples and cider.

Ingredients:

Sponge cake:

> 200 g sugar
> 200 g flour
> 70 g butter
> 6 eggs
> 1 teaspoon grated lemon peel

Compote:

> 4 apples
> 50 g sugar (depending how sweet the apples are)

Tart:

> 750 ml sparkling cider
> 400 ml whipping cream
> 10 leaves of gelatine
> 150 g icing sugar

Preparation:

Sponge cake:

1. Preheat the oven to 180°C. Line the bottom of a cake tin (springform) of about 24 cm with baking paper and coat the sides with butter.

2. Beat the eggs with the sugar until it becomes frothy. Add the lemon peel and sift in the flour. Stir well until it becomes a consistent mix. Add the soft butter and blend together well. Pour the mix into the mould and bake for about 30/40 minutes.

3. Remove the tin from the oven and allow the cake to cool. When it has cooled, remove the mould and cut the cake horizontally in half to obtain two bases. Put aside.

Compote and Coating:

4. To make the compote, peel, core and chop the apples. Cook them with the sugar and a glass of water on a low heat. When soft, mash the apples into a puré.

5. Warm the cider and dissolve 6 leaves of gelatine in it (the gelatine should be pre-hydrated). When the cider is warm, whisk the cream with the sugar and fold it carefully into the cider so that the cream does not collapse.

Cake:

6. To assemble the cake use the ring from the baking tin and put it on a large plate. Place a base of the sponge cake in the bottom of the ring. Cover it with the compote and place the other sponge base on top. Then pour on the cream mix and leave it in the refrigerator to set, ideally overnight.

7. The following day, remove the cake from the fridge. Heat the remaining half bottle of cider and dissolve in it the remaining 4 leaves of gelatine (previously hydrated). When it is almost set, pour it over the cake.

8. You can decorate the top of the cake with slices of boiled apple before the last layer of gelatine and cider. Alternatively, you can decorate the finished cake with fresh soft fruits.

TARTA DE TURRÓN DE CANTABRIA

Nougat Tart of Cantabria

This is a delicious simple dessert to enjoy at family gatherings during Christmas. It comes from Cantabria and Asturias and is typical of the many different tarts made with soft nougat. It is also taken with merienda.

Ingredients:

300 g of soft nougat
100 g of icing sugar
1 litre of cream
3 egg yolks and 3 egg whites
Melting chocolate for the sauce

Preparation:

1. Whip the cream and add the egg yolks and the beaten egg whites, the sugar, and the melted nougat, so that the mixture takes on the consistency of a paste.

2. Fill some round pudding moulds with this paste and put them in the freezer for 6 hours.

3. When frozen, remove the tarts from the moulds and serve them with a hot chocolate sauce.

TERESICAS DE ARAGÓN

Sweet Empanadillas of Aragón

Teresicas are a traditional carnival sweet, and another of the fried doughs of Moorish - Sephardic origin. This one is filled with a sweet paste.

Ingredients:

> 250 g flour
> 50 ml white wine
> 25 g lard (can be substituted with butter or margarine)
> 100 g butter (at room temperature)
> 100 ml of water
> 5 g of fresh yeast
> 1 teaspoon of sugar
> 1 pinch of salt
> Pastry cream (there are many recipes for this elsewhere in this book)
> Sugar for basting
> Olive oil to fry

Preparation:

1. Put the water, wine, salt, sugar and lard in a saucepan and bring it to the boil. Remove the pan from the heat and allow the mix to cool until luke warm. Stir in the yeast and let the mixture cool completely.

2. When completely cold, add the sifted flour to the mixture. Blend and knead well until obtaining a consistent dough.

3. Use a rolling pin to roll out the dough and then use the warm butter to coat the dough.

4. Fold the dough into four (as you would to make puff pastry) and repeat the process of rolling, buttering and folding the dough at least three more times.

5. Roll out the dough as finely as possible and cut it into squares. Take each square and place a tablespoon of the pastry cream in the centre. Fold the squares in the same way as an "empanadilla", like a little envelope.

6. Fry each empanadilla in plenty of olive oil.

7. When the teresicas are golden brown, remove them from the oil, drain on absorbent kitchen roll and coat them with sugar. They are ready to eat!

TORTA DE ACEITE Y ALMENDRAS DE LA AXARQUÍA

Almond and Olive Oil Cake of the Axarquía

This is a traditional recipe for almond cake that is found in several villages in the Axarquía, Málaga. We have left the measures as in the original, rural recipe.

Ingredients:

> 3 cups of flour
> 1 cup of olive oil
> 1 cup of whole milk
> 1 cup of sugar
> 16 g baking powder
> 1 pinch of cinnamon
> 150 g almonds
> 2 teaspoons of aniseed

Preparation:

1. Brown some almonds in a frying pan with a little oil and put them aside.

2. Put the flour, milk, sugar and baking powder into a large bowl and knead all the ingredients together.

3. Heat up some of the olive oil. When it just begins to smoke, remove it from the heat and put the aniseed into the hot oil to toast. Do not let it burn.

4. Mix in the remaining olive oil and add it to the flour mix. Stir well.

5. Preheat the oven to 180°C. Grind most of the almonds (keeping a few whole ones for decoration) and add them to the mix.

6. Continue to knead the dough until smooth. When it has the required consistency, put the dough in a baking tray and spread it evenly with a spatula. Garnish the top with the remaining whole almonds.

7. Bake the cake in the middle of a preheated oven at 180°C for 30 minutes. Check regularly to prevent burning.

8. Allow the cake to cool and serve.

TORTA DE HORNAZO DE PUERTO SERRANO

Almond and Anís Cake of Puerto Serrano

This cake was traditionally baked for the Easter celebrations. It originates in the area around Puerto Serrano and Olvera in the province of Cádiz. It is now available all year round and is a typical sweet of the area, taken with breakfast or merienda. It is also eaten as a sweet after dinner. The Easter version is sometimes baked with a whole egg in the centre.

Ingredients:

> 500 g flour
> 50 g fresh yeast
> 2 tablespoons of toasted sesame seeds
> 2 tablespoons of toasted aniseed
> Grated peel of 1 lemon
> 200 ml olive oil
> 200 ml warm milk
> 200 g sugar
> 1 egg yolk
> Almonds and candied fruits to decorate

Preparation:

1. Crumble the yeast into the warm milk and mix thoroughly.

2. Heat the olive oil and just before it begins to smoke, take the pan off the heat and add the aniseed. Put aside and leave to cool.

3. Pour the flour into a bowl in a heap. Make a hole in the middle and add the yeast and milk. Then add the oil and aniseed, lemon peel and sugar. Mix thoroughly until you have a consistent dough and knead well.

4. Grease a baking tin. Put the dough into the tin and smooth it by hand. Let the dough rest for 1 hour to rise.

5. Preheat the oven to 200°C (bottom heat only).

6. Paint the surface of the dough with beaten egg yolk and decorate with sesame seeds, almonds, walnuts and candied fruits. Scatter 2 tablespoons of sugar on top of this.

7. Bake at 200ºC for 15 minutes, reduce the heat to180ºC and bake for a further 30 minutes or until baked through. Remove the cake from the oven and allow it to cool before serving.

TORTAS DE MOSTO DE MURCIA

Anís and Mosto Wine Cakes of Murcia

Mosto is a very young wine made throughout Spain in rural areas. Traditionally, every rural family will make their own mosto as soon as the grapes are ripe. It is very easy to make and provides a warming, cheerful wine in the late autumn and during the winter. It is made with a very basic process involving picking and macerating the ripe grapes around September (traditionally by stamping them with your bare feet - a family affair generally!) Then the juice is pressed from the mash, put into earthenware containers (nowadays plastic or steel), and allowed to ferment with the natural yeast and sugar of the grapes. After some weeks, it is roughly filtered and again allowed to stand and ferment until the sugars are converted to alcohol. It may be filtered again to separate it from the sediment but in any case, it is a rather cloudy, fruity, very young wine. It can be quite potent!

There are no standards for mosto - every village and farm produces its own particular version. It may be dry or sweet, depending on the level of fermentation and type of grape. It may be quite strong or fruitier depending on the amount of time it has fermented.

Mosto can be made from many types of grape. It can vary in colour from light yellow, golden brown to dark purple. Generally, it is fermented for no less than 60 days. Mosto ("must" in English) of one kind or another has existed in all parts of the Mediterranean since ancient Greece. It was/is often used in cooking and bakery. Sometimes mosto is used in a reduced form by gently boiling off excess water. In the event that the reader cannot find mosto, the best alternative is to use any sweet young white wine.

Here we have a popular small cake made with anís and mosto that is traditionally made in the late autumn in Murcia using the plentiful supplies of partially fermented mosto. There are several variants of the basic recipe. For instance, one recipe uses mashed sweet potato as a base instead of a flour dough. This rural recipe is for a large batch of tortas. You can easily reduce the quantities to suit your household.

Ingredients:

> 1 litre of must (mosto)
> 500 ml olive oil
> 750 g sugar

3 kg flour
Aniseed or Anís liquor to your taste
Ground cinnamon to your taste
50 g dried yeast

Preparation:

1. Firstly, reduce the mosto by leaving it to simmer for a few minutes in a saucepan.

2. When the mosto is reduced, add all the other ingredients except the yeast. Then mix and knead into a dough.

3. Dissolve the yeast in a little warm water and add this to the dough. The dough should be quite firm and not stick to your hands.

4. Leave the dough to rise.

5. When the dough has risen, the tortas are made with pieces of dough formed into flattened balls. Place them on an oven tray lined with baking paper and allow them to rise again.

6. Preheat the oven to 175°C.

7. When the tortas have risen, paint them with a little beaten egg and sprinkle the tops with sugar.

8. Bake them for between 15 and 20 minutes until golden brown.

9. Remove the tray from the oven and allow the tortas to cool. They can then be served immediately.

TORTAS DE NUEZ DE MORATALLA DE MURCIA

Walnut Cakes of Moratalla, Murcia

Murcia has a strong tradition of sweet bakery, which is distinguished by the use of many local products. Many of the traditional recipes have an ancient background and much of this sweet bakery is directly related to Arab recipes using dried fruits, nuts and sugar. This is one such recipe

Moratalla is the highest and coldest municipality in the region of Murcia. It is a small mountain town dominated by an impressive castle. Much of the municipality is protected for its important biodiversity. The area around the town is important for its production of almonds, apricots, peaches, plums and olives. Its Roman and Arab history is well known and still has an influence on the local cuisine.

One of the best-known and popular pastries of the town is the "torta de nuez", the walnut cake.

Ingredients:

> 1 kg peeled walnuts
> 600 g sugar
> 200 ml milk
> 6 eggs
> Grated lemon peel

Preparation:

1. Crush the walnuts in a grinder / blender or by hand and put them in a large mixing bowl.

2. Add the remaining ingredients. Mix and knead gradually until you have a soft dough.

3. Preheat the oven to about 180° C.

4. Use small rectangular baking tins lined with oven paper and place portions of the dough in each. Sprinkle with cinnamon. You can also use paper moulds as used for magdalenas.

5. Bake until the cakes are well browned and toasted on top. Leave them to cool, and serve.

TORTA DE NUECES Y PASAS DE VALENCIA

Easter Walnut and Raisin Cake of Valencia

This is very traditional sweet bread found in Valencia. It is particularly popular during Easter but is now eaten at all times of the year. It is very often accompanied by a cup of hot chocolate as a delicious merienda.

This sweetbread is also called "Panquemao", which means "burned bread" because it is usually baked until it is quite dark. Traditionally, it was baked for Easter Sunday when families celebrated the resurrection by having picnics in the countryside. In Valencia, this sweet bread was an essential component of the Easter picnic basket.

This traditional recipe calls for the use of "mistela". Mistela is made by adding strong liquor to fermenting young wine (mosto). The strong liquor stops the wine fermenting and preserves the fresh, fruity taste of the mosto. Here it is used to macerate raisins.

Ingredients:

Starter dough:

> 80 g bread flour
> 40 ml warm water
> 15 g fresh yeast

Main Dough

> 250 g bread flour
> 40 g sunflower oil
> 15 g fresh yeast
> 2 eggs (keep a little aside to coat the top of the torta)
> Grated peel of 1 orange
> 40 ml milk
> Half a teaspoon of salt
> 75 g sugar (plus a little to decorate)
> 50 g raisins (plus a few to decorate)
> 50 g of walnuts (plus a few to decorate)
> Anís liquor or mistela to soak the raisins

Preparation:

Starter dough

1. Crumble the yeast into a bowl with the warm water and sift in the flour. Mix well and then roll up into a small ball.

2. Let the starter dough sit overnight, covered with a cloth.

Main Dough

3. The next day, soak the raisins and walnuts in a glass with some mistela or anís liquor.

4. Put the starter dough in a bowl and add the sunflower oil. Crumble in the yeast and add the eggs, milk, salt, grated orange and sugar. Stir well and then gradually sift in the flour, little by little and mix thoroughly.

5. Rub some oil onto the work surface and your hands and knead the dough for several minutes until it becomes elastic but not sticky.

6. Add the raisins and walnuts to the dough. Fold in and continue kneading.

7. Make the dough into a ball and flatten slightly. Put it aside in a bowl covered with a cloth and let the dough rise somewhere warm for a couple of hours.

8. Preheat the oven to 180°C top and bottom.

9. When the dough has risen, paint the top with some beaten egg. Decorate with some of the liquor-soaked raisins and walnuts. Use the same liquor to moisten some sugar and add this to the top of the torta.

10. Bake at 180°C for approximately 25 minutes. If it looks as if the top is getting too brown, put some aluminium foil over the torta to avoid burning.

11. Remove the cake from the oven and allow it to cool. Serve.

TORTO PASIEGO DE CANTABRIA

Butter and Rum Sponge Cake of Cantabria

Cantabria is a region of milk and butter production and has been for centuries. It is also remote and very rural in many areas. Arising from this abundance of butter, local villages have been making this simple but rich buttery sponge dessert for many generations, not only for themselves but also to sell in the town markets to make a little extra cash.

These sponge cakes are also known in some areas as "sobaos". Today they are so emblematic of the area that, in 2004, commercially produced sobaos were awarded European Geographic Indication protection to denote their origins and unique method of production.

Originally, sobaos were made with left over bread dough to which eggs, sugar and butter were added and given its distinctive flavour with the addition of grated orange peel and/or a shot of rum or anís liquor, but these are optional. They have a reputation as being highly nutritional. For this reason, they were often given to patients recovering from illness to help them recover their strength. These days they are baked specially for weddings and fiestas but also eaten as a dessert or with breakfast.

The name of the sponge cake stems from the remote valley areas in which the cake originated, known as Pasieguería. The people of the area are sometimes called "pasiegos".

This is a simple cake to make. The only complication is that it is baked in square shallow paper moulds that you traditionally make from thick baking paper. However, you can use small, square shallow baking tins lined with baking paper instead and a bigger version can be made in a larger shallow lined baking tin.

Ingredients:

>   250 g butter
>   250 g flour
>   250 g sugar
>   15 g baking powder
>   3 eggs
>   1 tablespoon of honey
>   Little rum or anís (optional)
>   Grated peel of a lemon (optional)

Preparation:

1. The butter should be allowed to warm to soften. Place it in a bowl, add the eggs, and mix well. Next, add the honey, sugar, flour and baking powder. (The lemon peel and/or rum or anís liquor can be added at this stage). Mix very well until you have consistent, smooth dough.

2. Put this mixture into a pastry bag.

3. Preheat the oven to 180°C

4. Prepare some small, shallow square baking tins by lining with baking paper. You can also try to create shallow paper trays. These are traditionally made by folding thick baking paper.

5. Bake for 15 minutes until golden brown - do not over bake them or they will be too dry.

6. Remove from the oven and allow the cakes to cool before serving.

TORTAS DE RECAO DE MURCIA

Anís and Almond Christmas Tarts of Murcia

This is one of Murcia's most traditional Christmas tarts and has a long history. Given their ingredients, they are almost certainly of Arab origin. The "modern" version is also called "tortas de conde" (tarts of the count) because they were a great favourite of the Condes de Heredia Spínola, who were important property owners in Murcia in the 17th century. The name "recao" is used because these tarts were "made to order" by local bakers for these same aristocrats.

Ingredients:

>   1 kg flour
>   340 g raw ground almonds
>   340 ml olive oil
>   250 ml anís liquor
>   150 ml freshly squeezed orange juice
>   340 g sugar
>   Grated peel of 1 lemon
>   2 teaspoons of baking soda
>   Honey
>   Chopped almonds

Preparation:

1. Heat the oil in a pan. Preheat the oven to 200°C (top and bottom, with fan).

2. Pour the flour into a heat-resistant bowl. When the oil begins to boil, pour it over the flour. Mix the oil and flour with a wooden spoon.

3. Add the sugar, grated lemon and ground almonds. Stir well.

4. Add the orange juice and anís liquor and mix thoroughly until you have a consistent pastry dough.

5. Line an oven tray with oiled baking paper. Take balls of dough and place them on the oven tray.

6. Shape the tarts by pressing the dough flat in the centre and leaving the sides a little raised. They should be about 8 cm in diameter.

7. Sprinkle the tops with chopped almonds.

8. Bake until the tarts begin to turn golden brown.

9. Remove the tray from the oven and, whilst the tarts are still hot, pour a trickle of honey over them and then let them cool down before serving.

TORTAS DE LA VIRGEN DE LAS ANGUSTIAS, GRANADA

Angel hair, Cinnamon and Almond Tart of Granada

The last Sunday of September is "the Day of the Virgin" in Granada. It is an important festival in the city as the Virgen de las Angustias is the patron saint of Granada. There is a major procession through the streets attended by the people of the city and province.

As with many religious celebrations in Spain, food plays an important part in the fiesta and there is a large autumn fruit market in Granada. The market has many cake and pastry stalls and one of the most popular sweets sold is the torta de la Virgen de las Angustias. This popular cake is eaten for both breakfast and merienda. It is a large cake and can be round, rectangular or oval. There are many variants of the cake (some people add raisins to the filling, for example) but the one we give here is fairly typical and traditional in Granada.

Ingredients:

> 700 g bread flour
> 300 g pastry flour
> 350 ml water
> 50 g fresh yeast
> 2 eggs
> 20 g salt
> 75 g lard
> 75 ml olive oil
> 100 g sugar
> Grated peel of 1 orange
> Cinnamon powder
> Almonds (chopped)
> Angel hair
> Sugar for decoration

Preparation:

1. Roast the almonds in a frying pan with a little olive oil and cinnamon. Put aside.

2. Mix the two types of flour in a large bowl.

3. Warm the water a little, add the crumbled yeast and mix well. Let it sit for 5 minutes.

338

4. Make a hole in the centre of the flour and add the grated orange peel, the sugar, salt, eggs, olive oil, lard, and the mixed water and yeast.

5. Mix the ingredients together and then knead until you have a smooth, consistent dough.

6. Cover the dough with a cloth and let it rise - depending on the temperature, this could take between one and two hours. You can also put it in an oven preheated to 45°C and it will rise more rapidly.

7. Flour the work surface and place the dough on it. Divide the dough into two equal parts. Roll out one piece of dough and place it in a shallow baking tin of the correct diameter (a standard oven tray could be used).

8. Spread the dough with angel hair and the chopped, roasted almonds.

9. Roll out the second half of the dough to the same size and cover the angel hair. Seal the edges with a fork or with your fingers.

10. Sprinkle the surface with plenty of sugar.

11. Put the tart in the oven at 50°C and let it rise for 10 or 15 minutes more and then remove it from the oven.

12. Preheat the oven to 200°C and then put the baking tray back in the oven again for about 12 to 15 minutes with heat from top and bottom.

13. When baked, remove the tray from the oven and place the tart on a grid to cool before serving.

TRONCO DE NAVIDAD

Christmas Trunk

The Christmas Trunk is not originally Spanish at all, but French, and still known as the "Buche de Noel". It is thought to have been originated by an innovative French pastry chef (in the late 1800s) who came up with the idea of replacing the real 'Yule' log (an ancient tradition of celebrating Christmas and the winter solstice by burning a large wooden log in the hearth) with a cake that was log shaped. It resembles a large Swiss roll with a rich filling, completely coated in chocolate and made to look like a log.

There are now many recipes for this throughout Europe, but Spain still manages to produce some of the richest and most sinful versions of this delicious rolled and filled cake. This recipe uses chestnut jam, which is a particular favourite in southern Spain, but many other fillings can be substituted.

Ingredients:

> 75 g flour
> 75 g sugar
> 3 eggs
> 1 jar of sweet chestnut jam
> 1 tablet of chocolate fondant (250 g)
> 100 ml cream
> 50 g butter
> Icing sugar

Preparation:

1. Whisk the eggs with the sugar until the mix has doubled in volume. Add the flour through a sieve and mix gently.

2. Pour the mixture into a shallow baking tin lined with baking paper, greased and floured. Bake at 180°C for 8-10 minutes.

3. Turn the warm cake out onto a clean, smooth, lightly floured kitchen towel, remove and discard the baking paper and then roll up the cake with the towel. Leave to cool for 30 minutes before filling.

4. Fill the roll with chestnut jam and re-roll it.

5. Coat the "log" with a chocolate fondant, which is melted in a microwave or "au bain- Marie" in a double boiler together with the cream and butter.

6. Use a fork to create the appearance of a trunk in the melted chocolate, sprinkle icing sugar on it and decorate the log with a Christmas theme of your choice (holly, stars etc.).

TRUCHAS DE NAVIDAD DE LAS ISLAS CANARIAS

Almond and Sweet Potato Fritters of the Canary Islands

This is a delicious traditional Christmas recipe influenced by the strong connections between the Canary Islands and Spain's American colonies, using a mixture of ingredients from both "worlds" - almonds from the old world and sweet potato from the new world.

They are called "truchas" because of their shape, which somehow resembles that of a trout.

A variation of this recipe uses raisins (150 g soaked in orange blossom water) blended into the filling mixture. The "truchas" were traditionally deep-fried in olive oil until browned, but they can also be baked, which makes them a little lighter.

Ingredients (makes 24 truchas):

Crust:

>700 g puff pastry (ready-made)
>
>or
>
>500 g white flour
>2 heaped teaspoons of sugar
>Pinch of salt
>Approximately 250 ml cold water
>225 g butter

Filling:

>1 kg white or orange sweet potato
>2 star anise
>100 g sugar
>1 egg yolk
>100 g whole peeled almonds
>Half a teaspoon of cinnamon
>1 tablespoon of anís liquor (to your taste)
>Grated peel from 1 lemon
>Icing sugar for dusting

Preparation:

1. To make the pastry from scratch, place the flour, sugar and salt in a large mixing bowl. Cut the butter into tablespoon-size pieces and add to the flour, mashing with a fork to mix. Sprinkle in a few tablespoons of

the cold water and continue to mix with a fork. Add some more water and gently knead the mixture just enough so that it becomes a smooth dough, no longer sticking to your hands. If the dough is kneaded for too long, it will become tough. Cover the dough in the bowl and place in the refrigerator whilst the filling is prepared.

2. Clean the sweet potatoes and place them whole and unpeeled in a pot. Cover them with water. Add one or two star anise to flavour the potatoes. Bring to the boil and cook them for approximately 20-30 minutes until soft. The potatoes are cooked when you can easily insert a fork into the thickest part of the potato. Drain and place them on a plate, allowing them to cool completely.

3. Grate the lemon peel onto a plate. Grind the almonds in a mortar or blender. Put the yolk of one egg into a small bowl for later.

4. When the potatoes are cool enough to handle, remove their skin. It should rub off easily. Cut the potatoes into large chunks, place them in a mixing bowl and mash the pieces with a potato masher. Add the lemon peel, ground almonds, cinnamon and anís liquor. Stir together, add in the sugar and mix thoroughly.

5. Preheat the oven to 200°C whilst making the "truchas".

6. Lightly flour a work surface. Roll out the dough thinly and cut out circles of approximately 7 or 8 cm in diameter.

7. Place a portion of sweet potato filling on each circle of dough. Then fold the circles in half to form a semi-circle. Press the edges together with a fork to seal. Place each trucha on a baking tray lined with baking paper (just like an empanadilla).

8. Whisk the egg yolk and brush the top of each trucha with it. Bake them for approximately 15 minutes or until they turn golden brown. Remove the tray from the oven and let the truchas cool for about 10 minutes.

9. Dust them with icing sugar and serve warm. They can also be reheated later.

TRENZA DE ALMUDÉVAR, ARAGÓN

Raisin and Walnut Sweetbread of Almudévar, Aragón

The Trenza de Almudévar is a braided sweetbread with walnuts and raisins from the small village of Almudévar in the region of Aragón. It is a traditional pastry which is made today by the baking family Tolosana. It is an extremely popular pastry and is often taken with breakfast or more usually with coffee at merienda.

There is a modern version which uses pre-prepared puff pastry and is quite quick to make but the traditional recipe we give you here takes longer and is quite convoluted - but delicious!

The preparation of the traditional version takes place over three days: day 1 to prepare the starter dough, day 2 to prepare the main dough and filling, and day 3 to bake the final cake.

Ingredients (2 loaves):

Starter Dough:

> 150 g flour
> 120 ml lukewarm water
> 3 g dried yeast

Dough:

> 400 g flour
> 120 ml warm milk
> 55 g softened butter
> 3 eggs
> 80 g granulated sugar
> 5 g salt
> 4 g dried yeast
> 200 g softened butter

Egg Filling:

> 150 g sugar
> 50 ml water
> 4 egg yolks
> 1 tablespoon of corn starch
> 50 g shelled walnuts, coarsely chopped
> 60 g raisins
> Glazing:

100 g icing sugar
50 g water

Preparation:

The Starter Dough:

1. Dissolve the yeast in the lukewarm water, mixing with a fork until the yeast is completely dissolved.

2. Put the flour into a mixing bowl and add the yeast mixture. Stir until a solid dough forms.

3. Shape into a ball and cover with a towel. Leave the dough to rise in a warm place away from drafts, and allow it to double in volume. This may take several hours, usually overnight.

The Dough:

1. Mix the flour with the yeast.

2. Cut up and mix in the 55 g of softened butter. Use your hands to mix until it is thoroughly blended.

3. Add the sugar and salt, and mix.

4. In a separate bowl, beat the eggs and add the milk. Blend this into the flour mixture.

5. Add in the starter dough and knead until the dough becomes consistent and elastic. Form the dough into a ball.

6. Make a cross cut in the top of the dough, and wrap it in plastic film. Refrigerate for at least 6 hours, or better still overnight.

To form the dough into a puff pastry:

7. Take the dough out of the refrigerator and roll it out with a rolling pin.

8. Cut the 200 g softened butter into 0.5 cm slices, but keep the slices of butter together in the centre of the rolled out dough.

9. Fold each of the four corners of the dough over the butter in the centre, sealing each side by gently pressing down on the edges with your fingers, creating an "envelope".

10. Cover and chill the dough in the refrigerator for 1 hour.

11. Remove the dough from the refrigerator and roll it out with a rolling pin in one direction. Then, turn the dough a quarter turn and roll

out again. Fold the dough again, this time in thirds. Cover with plastic shrink wrap, and refrigerate for 1 hour.

12. Remove the dough from the fridge. Repeat the rollout and refrigerate process 5 more times, chilling for an hour each time.

13. After the last refrigeration, cut the dough in half. Each piece will make a single loaf.

Egg Filling:

14. Make syrup with the water and the sugar by bringing to the boil and stirring until the sugar is completely dissolved.

15. In a small saucepan, beat the four egg yolks with the corn starch. Place on a low heat.

16. Add the syrup very slowly whilst whisking. Continue to stir until the mixture thickens. Remove immediately from the heat and allow to cool.

17. Roll out one piece of the dough into a long rectangle. Thinner is better but remember that the thinner the dough, the harder it is to work with.

18. After rolling out the dough, cut it in half lengthwise, separating the two sides slightly, and leaving a few centimetres at one end uncut. This will form the top of the braided loaf.

19. Spread the egg filling down the middle of each of the two halves. Sprinkle raisins and the chopped walnuts on top. Do not fill too much. Fold the dough lengthways over the filling.

20. Take the two ends of the dough, and carefully braid them. Repeat the filling and braiding process with the other half of the dough for the second loaf.

21. Allow the two braided loaves to rise until they double in size. Remember to keep the dough in a warm place, away from drafts.

22. Heat the oven to 175 °C.

23. Beat the remaining egg white, and brush the top of the dough.

24. Bake the loaves on an ungreased baking paper in the middle rack of the oven for about 45 minutes, or until the loaves have become a deep golden brown.

25. While the cake is baking, make a sugar glaze with icing sugar and water. Mix the sugar and water together in a small sauce pan. Heat the mixture, stirring often.

26. When the bread is baked, use a spoon to pour the glaze over the top of the loaves.

27. Allow to cool and serve.

VIROLOS DE BAEZA, JAÉN

Angel Hair Pastry of Baeza, Jaén

This pastry is quite famous in Jaén and particularly in the old town of Baeza. Several bakeries there have produced them for over 150 years. It is a very light puff pastry filled with angel hair. It is eaten for breakfast, as a dessert (usually with a liqueur like oruga) or with merienda. One interesting combination may sound a little strange but is apparently very tasty is a virolo stuffed with ham (jamón serrano).

Virolos are very easy to make.

Ingredients (10 to 18 virolos):

> 1 sheet of puff pastry
> Icing sugar
> Angel hair

Preparation:

1. Spread the puff pastry out on the work surface and cut it into rectangles, depending on the size of the virolos you want. Cut the pastry so that it is not deformed by the blade.

2. Spoon a little angel hair onto each rectangle of pastry (do not let it spill over the sides) and then fold the long sides over it so that it is closed. Do not seal the sides otherwise the pastry will not rise correctly. Place the pastries on an oven tray lined with baking paper.

3. Preheat the oven to 180°C.

4. Bake the virolos for 10 to 15 minutes until golden brown. When baked remove them from the oven and sprinkle the tops with plenty of icing sugar. Serve cool.

XUXO (XUIXO) DE GIRONA

Cream Filled Pastry of Girona

Pronounced "chucho", the xuixo is a famous, very popular, traditional Catalan breakfast and merienda pastry, said to have originated in the city of Girona in 1920. It is usually a cylindrical pastry filled with a pastry cream known as "crema catalana". It is then deep-fried and coated with sugar. It is listed as a traditional product of the area "Producte de la Terra" by the Ministry of Agriculture of Cataluña. A version of the pastry is also found in Valencia, Castellón de la Plana and. Tarragona. Some modern versions are coated with chocolate.

The pastry and its legendary origins are so emblematic in Girona that the local government organises an annual family procession around the city culminating in everyone enjoying some xuixos prepared by the officially recognised pastry chefs of the city. The procession celebrates the legend of Tarlà the acrobat who entertained the people of Girona during a disease epidemic. He is credited with passing the recipe to a local baker.

The recipe we give here is the traditional version, but there are many versions that are much faster to make using pre-made puff pastry with pre-made baker's cream (pastry cream).

Ingredients:

For the cream filling:

> 65 g sugar
> 185 ml milk
> 1 vanilla stick
> 1 small slice of orange peel (without the white)
> 1 small slice of lemon peel (without the white)
> 20 g corn starch
> 65 g liquid cream
> 2 egg yolks
> 30 g butter

For the dough:

> 90 ml milk
> 1 egg
> A pinch of salt
> 10 g fresh yeast

45 g sugar
250 g bread flour
1 teaspoon of vanilla essence
Sugar for decoration
15 g of butter
Olive oil (mild) or sunflower oil for frying
Cinnamon powder

Preparation:

For the cream filling:

1. Prepare the cream in advance so that it has time to cool before the pastry is ready.

2. Place the milk, cream, and 35 g of sugar, a vanilla stick cut lengthwise, the orange skin and the lemon skin in a saucepan. Bring it to the boil on a low heat. When the milk starts to boil, turn off the heat.

3. Allow the milk to stand for 5 minutes, and then strain it, removing the fruit peels and vanilla.

4. Whisk the egg yolks with 30 g of sugar, until they turn white and increase in volume. Add the corn starch and mix until it is fully blended. Place the milk on the heat again. When it is warm, add the egg yolk mix while stirring, until the mix becomes a little thicker.

5. Cut the butter into small pieces and add those to the mix, stirring until they melt.

6. Remove from the heat and place aside to cool. Cover with cling film until the xuixos are ready to fill.

For the dough:

7. Sieve the flour into a bowl with the salt and sugar.

8. Slightly warm a little milk and crumble the yeast into the milk. Mix it until it is dissolved.

9. Take the bowl of flour, salt and sugar and make a hole in the centre. Start to pour in a beaten egg. Mix very slowly using a wooden spoon and add the milk, little by little, continuously stirring.

10. Add the butter, which should be at room temperature, mixing it all with your hands until the dough is smooth and consistent.

11. Cover the bowl with a cloth and let it rest until the dough doubles in size. This can take 1 to 2 hours.

12. When the dough has risen, place it on the work surface dusted with flour. Roll out the dough with a rolling pin, until it is 8-10 mm thick and then cut the dough into elongated triangles as you would for croissants.

13. Fill a pastry bag with the cream filling and place some cream on each triangle. Then roll the dough as you would a croissant.

14. Cover a baking tray with baking paper. Place the xuixos on the tray and cover them with a cloth, allowing the dough to rise again for between 30 and 60 minutes.

15. Prepare a frying pan with olive or sunflower oil and fry the xuixos until golden brown. Turn them frequently. Do not fry them at too high a temperature! They need to be cooked a little on the inside.

16. Place them on kitchen paper to absorb the excess oil and allow to cool a little.

17. Finally roll the xuixos in a mixture of sugar and cinnamon powder and they are ready to be served.

YEMAS DE BATATA

Sweet Potato Balls

This is another sweet that is originally Arabic. However, like many Moorish recipes, it was adopted by the Christian religious orders after the Christian conquest of Spain.

Today it is still made in the 15th century Dominican convent of Madre de Dios de Piedad in the Bartolomé district in Sevilla. This convent specialises in Arabic sweets and this is one of their most popular. Despite the name of the sweet including "yemas" - egg yolks, the sweet contains no eggs or flour and is therefore suitable for both vegans and celiacs. Over the centuries, the nuns have substituted sweet potato as the base of the original Arabic recipe. Yemas are simple to make, delicious and very filling.

Ingredients (30 yemas):

> 500 g roasted sweet potatoes
> 180 g sugar
> 150 g ground almonds
> 1 teaspoon of cinnamon powder
> White sugar mixed with cinnamon to coat

Preparation:

1. First, wrap the sweet potatoes in aluminium foil and roast them in the oven for 30 minutes or longer at 180°C until tender. When they are tender, carefully remove the skin and weigh out 500 g approximately. (You can also boil them in water, but they need to be thoroughly drained).

2. Whist still hot, put the sweet potato in a bowl and mash with a fork, add the sugar and mix well.

3. Add the ground almonds and the cinnamon, and mix again. The dough should be sticky but easy to work. If it is not, then add some more ground almonds.

4. Prepare a mixture of sugar and cinnamon (to your taste). Use a teaspoon to take out portions of the dough and roll them into balls. Coat these with the sugar/cinnamon mixture. Set aside on a rack to let them cool. When cool, place in cake cups and they are ready to serve.

---oOo---

2.4 Savoury Pastries, Empanadas and Pies

Savoury baking is well developed in Spain. It very often involves meat or fish fillings, although there are also many vegetarian and vegan savoury baking recipes using cheese, eggs and / or vegetables fillings.

Savoury baking can be roughly divided into empanadas (pasties) and hornazos (pies) although the terms are often interchanged. Generally, though, empanadas are traditional Spanish pasties. They come in all shapes and sizes from bite-sized "wraps" (empanadillas), traditional pasties right up to large covered pies. Usually empanadillas are served whole, whereas empanadas may be sliced if they are large. Hornazos are normally covered pies, which are cut into portions to serve. Northern Spain, especially Galicia, is famous for its hornazos.

The terms empanada and hornazo are normally reserved for savoury baking but both terms are also used in sweet bakery. Here we have collected a range of savoury empanadas and hornazos with some popular fillings, but the possibilities for combinations of filling are limitless. For the vegetarian or vegan, these savoury pastries also provide a delicious way of presenting meatless dishes in a traditional way.

A third savoury pastry type is the "Coca" which originates in Eastern Spain and the Balearic islands (Islas Baleares). This is an open pastry with the "filling" on top, very much like a pizza. Indeed, pizzas are believed to have originated in Spain during its occupation of the Kingdom of Naples and probably had their origins in the coca.

COCA DE TREMPÓ DE MALLORCA

Vegetable Tart of Mallorca

Cocas are typical of and very popular in Eastern Spain. Many claim that they are the inspiration for the Italian pizza. For many years, large parts of Italy were ruled by Spain. This included the kingdom of Naples, the modern home of pizza. In Mallorca, there are many varieties of coca. This vegetable coca is one of the classics using seasonal vegetables as a topping.

In the past, cocas were made with dough that the local baker had to spare. People would buy and mix this dough again with oil and lard. Thus, the dough was made with fresh yeast. However, it can be made with baking powder or dried yeast just as well.

Originally, cocas were eaten as a starter (as pizza is in real Italian restaurants today). However, over time they have become a dish in their own right. They are now served alone with a salad as a complete meal or simply as a snack with a beer or wine, and sometimes as a substantial tapa.

This original recipe uses lard but this can be substituted with margarine.

Ingredients:

> 50 g olive oil
> 100 ml water
> 1 teaspoon of icing sugar
> 20 g lard (or margarine)
> 30 g butter
> 20 g fresh yeast
> 300 g bread flour
> 1 pinch of sugar
> 3 medium-sized tomatoes
> 3 Italian peppers
> 2 medium-sized onions

Preparation:

1. Preheat the oven to 225°C.

2. Mix the water, olive oil, salt, lard (or margarine) and butter in a bowl. The lard and butter should be at room temperature so that they can be easily worked.

3. Crumble in the yeast, add the sugar and finally the flour.

4. Mix everything with your hands until you get consistent elastic dough. It should be a little sticky but not stick to the bowl. If necessary, add a little bit more flour until you achieve the right consistency.

5. Let the dough stand for a few minutes.

6. Meanwhile, cut the tomatoes, peppers and onions into small cubes. Put them in a bowl and dress with olive oil and salt. Mix and put aside.

7. Rub olive oil on your hands. Take the dough and put it in an oven tray on a sheet of baking paper. Extend the dough uniformly over the baking paper by hand until it is about 1 cm thick.

8. Spread the vegetables evenly over the top of the dough.

9. Bake it for between 25-30 minutes at 190°C to 200°C.

10. Remove the tray from the oven and allow the coca to cool. Cut the coca into small squares and serve.

EMPANADA DE ESPINACAS CON CHAMPIÑONES

Mushroom, Goat's Cheese and Spinach Empanada

This empanada is actually a pie rather than a pasty and, cut into slices, is served as a main course. There are many traditional fillings but the combination of spinach, cream, mushrooms and goat's cheese is a popular one, especially in areas where goat's cheese is readily available. It makes for a rich, tasty and healthy filling.

Ingredients:

For the dough:

   250 g flour
   6-8 g fresh yeast
   125 ml water
   3 tablespoons of olive oil
   1 teaspoon of salt
   1 teaspoon of sugar

For the filling:

   150 g onion
   2 cloves of garlic
   300 g fresh spinach
   200 g mushrooms
   150 g goat's cheese
   150 ml cream
   1 teaspoon of corn starch
   Raisins and pine kernels (optional)

Preparation:

1. The dough is similar to that used for pizzas. Put all the dough ingredients in a bowl and mix them together well.

2. When thoroughly mixed, place the dough on a lightly floured surface and knead for about 10 minutes until the dough becomes smooth and elastic. Put it in a covered, lightly greased bowl and let it rest in a warm place until it has doubled in volume. This will take about an hour.

3. Chop the onion. Clean and slice the mushrooms. Wash the spinach and remove the stems, drain and chop a little.

4. Fry the onion in a pan with some olive oil until tender but not browned. Add the mushrooms with the chopped garlic and a little salt.

Fry until cooked and the moisture released from the mushrooms has evaporated. Then stir in the spinach and allow it to lose its volume and surplus moisture.

5. Add the goat's cheese, stirring well to incorporate.

6. Sprinkle in the corn starch, sauté and then add in the cream. Season and cook everything for 5-10 minutes, until all is well mixed and slightly thickened. Allow the mix to cool. Preheat the oven to 200°C.

7. Re-fold the dough on a lightly floured work surface. Divide into two unequal parts (one part for the pie base and one part for the pie top).

8. Roll out the larger portion to the desired size and shape it into the pie mould.

9. Pour the filling of spinach, cheese and mushrooms onto the pastry base without letting it reach the edges. Cover this with the remaining piece of dough. Perforate the top with a fork.

10. Seal the edges of the dough with a fork and bake at 200°C for 25-30 minutes.

11. Remove the pie from the oven when it is golden brown and let it cool on a rack.

12. Portions of the empanada can be served hot or cold.

EMPANADA GALLEGA DE VERDURAS

Galician Vegetable Pie

Galicia is famous for its empanadas and they come in all kinds of shapes, sizes and fillings. This simple and traditional vegetable empanada is actually a pie.

In Spain, it is quite easy to buy ready-made doughs and most supermarkets will keep chilled or frozen empanada dough. For busy urbanites, this allows them to save a lot of time whilst still baking at home. However, we have also given a generic recipe for empanada dough if you prefer to make it yourself (see the index).

Ingredients:

    2 sheets of empanada dough
    2 onions
    2 tomatoes
    1 red pepper
    1 green pepper
    1 carrot
    Salt

Preparation:

1. Preheat the oven to 200°C.

2. Peel and chop the onions and carrot into small pieces. Cut the peppers into short, fine strips.

3. Chop the tomatoes into segments and blend into a sauce.

4. Put all the vegetables, except the tomato sauce, into a frying pan with a little oil and fry until brown.

5. Coat a pie tin with a little olive oil and line it with a sheet of dough.

6. When the vegetables are golden brown, stir in the tomato sauce and let the mix simmer for another 5 minutes.

7. Pour the vegetable mixture onto the dough in the pie tin, and spread it out. Next, cover the filling with the second sheet of dough and seal the edges. Decorate the top of the pie with strips of dough.

8. Bake for 30 to 45 minutes until golden brown.

EMPANADA MASA

Empanada Dough

In Spain and many Latin American countries, the closed semi-circular empanadas are so popular that it is quite normal to go to any supermarket and buy ready-made empanada dough, already cut into circles and ready to fill and bake. The same dough is also sold in larger square sheets, ready-made for larger pie empanadas. This pastry dough for the sealed empanadas is simple to make and can be used in any of the closed empanada recipes, large or small. There are quite a few recipes for empanada dough. Some use a little yeast or baking powder whilst other recipes add egg. This is the most simple and basic version.

Ingredients:

> 500 g flour
> Half a tablespoon of sugar
> Half a tablespoon of salt
> 40 g butter
> 235 ml water

Preparation:

1. Melt the butter in a saucepan. Warm the water.

2. Put the flour in a bowl and add the salt and sugar, then mix thoroughly. Make a hole in the centre of the flour mix.

3. Pour the melted butter and warm water into the flour, and start mixing and gently kneading the dough for between 5 and 8 minutes.

4. When the dough is thoroughly kneaded put a cloth over the bowl and let it rest for 30 minutes.

5. After 30 minutes, the dough is ready to use. Roll it out quite thinly on a floured surface and cut out circles to form the individual empanadas.

6. The size of the empanada is up to you but they are generally between 10 to 15 centimetres in diameter. It all depends on the type and amount of filling to be used.

7. The dough can be stored for a maximum of two days in the refrigerator and can be deep-frozen as discs or sheets with greaseproof kitchen paper to separate each one.

EMPANADA DE ESPINACAS Y QUESO DE CABRA

Empanada with Spinach and Goats Cheese

The Arabs introduced spinach into Spain in the 12th century and it quickly became popular, it being a tasty and easy to grow vegetable. All social classes, from peasant to lord, ate it. Indeed, it was the favourite vegetable of Catherine de' Medici! Meanwhile, Moorish cuisine had many ways of using spinach and one of these was in a "fatayer", a folded pastry filled with spinach, which is still popular today in many Arab countries. Another popular fatayer is filled with goat's cheese.

This empanada is a delicious combination of goat's cheese and spinach and certainly the descendant of the original Moorish fatayer. A popular variant of the closed empanada comes in the form of a larger pie (also called an empanada) which is made in much the same way and cut into portions.

The empanadas here can also be fried instead of baked. In this case, they should not be coated with egg and the empanada should be fried in abundant olive oil.

A variety of different goat's cheeses can be used; the most popular being the "rulo de queso de cabra", (goat's cheese in a roll), which can be bought in any Spanish supermarket.

Ingredients (10-16 empanadas depending on diameter):

> 16 empanada disks (see recipe for empanada dough)
> 200 g fresh spinach
> 30 g walnuts (or pine nuts)
> 50 g goat's cheese ("rulo de queso")
> 1 egg to coat the empanadillas
> Olive oil
> Salt

Preparation:

1. Fry the nuts in a frying pan for a couple of minutes at a high temperature in a little oil until browned. Put them aside.

2. Lower the temperature under the frying pan and add the spinach and a pinch of salt. Sauté the spinach for five minutes to reduce. When reduced, stir the nuts into the spinach and remove the pan from the heat.

3. Preheat the oven to 180°C.

4. Lay out the empanada discs. Place a teaspoonful of the spinach filling on each disc (not too much) and put a few pieces of goat's cheese on top.

5. Fold each empanada disc in half and lightly press the edges a little with your fingers. Seal the empanada by flattening the edge with a fork.

6. Put the empanadas on baking paper on a baking tray.

7. Beat the egg and paint the tops of the empanadillas with a brush.

8. Bake for about 10 minutes until the empanadas are golden brown. Take care - they burn easily.

9. Remove from the oven and allow them to cool a little before serving.

10. These empanadas can also be eaten cold, but when served hot the melted cheese is delicious.

EMPANADA DE HOJALDRE CON ESPINACAS Y REQUESÓN

Empanada with Puff Pastry, Spinach and Cottage Cheese

This is a pie made with spinach and a type of cottage cheese found in Spain called "requesón". You can also use ricotta or cottage cheese. It uses a puff pastry casing rather than empanada dough.

Ingredients:

A sheet of puff pastry dough
200 g of requesón or ricotta cheese (or cottage cheese)
200 g of spinach

Preparation:

1. Blanch the spinach, drain very well and chop it finely.

2. Mix the cheese with the spinach, once it has cooled.

3. Cover a baking tray with oven paper and line with a thin layer of puff pastry. Spread the spinach-cheese mix onto the pastry, place another sheet of puff pastry on top of the filing and seal the edges very well with a fork.

4. Place the pie in a preheated oven and bake it for around 30 minutes at 175°C.

5. Take the pie out of the oven, cut it into small slices and serve.

EMPANADILLA DE VERDURAS

Vegetable Empanadilla

This vegetable empanada is very similar to its ancestor - the samosa. Samosas are traditionally made with a savoury filling, often just a mixture of fried vegetables. Samosas are popular from the Far East, throughout the Middle East and many parts of the Mediterranean. They can be fried or baked. This version is baked and is usually served with a sauce.

Ingredients:

For the pastry:

>Dough for 12 small empanadas (circular 10-15 cm in diameter) - see recipe
>Flour
>Olive oil

For the filling:

>1 chopped onion
>2 cloves of garlic, finely chopped
>Salt to taste
>Pepper to taste
>Oregano to taste
>50 ml olive oil
>200 g broccoli, cooked
>200 g cauliflower, cooked
>200 g diced carrots, cooked
>2 tablespoons of flour
>380 ml hot milk

Preparation:

1. Sauté the onion and garlic in olive oil with a pinch of salt. Add the broccoli, cauliflower and carrots. Mix well and sprinkle with flour.

2. Gradually add the hot milk, stirring gently until the filling becomes creamy. Season the mix with salt, pepper and oregano. Allow it to cool.

3. Roll out the pastry and cut out small circles of 10-15 cm in diameter. Place a spoonful of filling mixture in the centre of each circle. Fold them over and brush the edges with water, close them and seal them with a fork.

4. Arrange the empanadas on a lined, floured oven tray and sprinkle them with olive oil.

5. Bake them in a preheated oven at about 200°C until golden brown (about 15 minutes).

6. Remove the empanadas from the oven and serve them immediately.

HOJALDRE DE MEMBRILLO Y QUESO DE CABRA

Quince Jam and Goat's Cheese in Puff Pastry

There is a long-standing Spanish love affair with the combination of cheese and quince jam and it is not confined to any particular region. The combination of sweet and savoury flavours has its roots in Moorish cuisine - for instance, the combination of cheese and honey or fried aubergine and molasses. The tradition of combining sweet and savoury is still very much alive and well in modern Spanish cooking and baking.

Here we have a recipe that combines goat's cheese with quince jam in a puff pastry envelope. Variants of this recipe use the same ingredients but make it as an elongated flat or a braided pastry and one local Murcian recipe adds caramelized onions to the filling. This recipe uses tomato chutney: a sweet tomato jam (mermelada de tomate). The recipe also suggests "rulo de queso de cabra" which is young goat's cheese in a roll, available from any Spanish supermarket.

Ingredients:

> 1 sheet of puff pastry
> 1 "rulo de queso de cabra" (goat's cheese roll)
> Sweet quince jelly
> Tomato chutney
> 1 egg
> Brown sugar

Preparation:

1. Lay out the puff pastry and cut into equal triangles. You should make them large enough to make a portion for one person, so about 5-8 cm wide.

2. In each triangle lay a strip of quince jelly from the top to the bottom of the triangle and a piece of goat's cheese in the middle

3. Put a teaspoon of tomato chutney on top of the cheese.

4. Fold the corners of the triangle towards the centre of the dough to form a pocket. Seal the joints with a little water so that they do not open.

5. Coat each pastry with beaten egg and sprinkle with a little brown sugar.

6. Preheat the oven to 200°C.

7. Put the pastries on a baking tray lined with baking paper and place them in the oven for 15 or 20 minutes or until they are browned.

8. When well browned, remove them from the oven and let them cool on a rack.

9. Serve warm or cold.

PANADONS DE ESPINACAS DE SEMANA SANTA DE CATALUÑA

Easter Spinach Pasties of Cataluña

This is really a large form of empanada using bread dough and combines savoury and sweet flavours. It is a traditional meatless dish prepared during Lent and Easter and originates in the old city of Lleida (aka Lérida) in Cataluña.

The pasty can be made with a variety of vegetables or dried fruits and nuts. This version uses spinach with currants and pine nuts. They can also use chopped roasted almonds instead of pine nuts.

Ingredients:

Dough:

> 250 g bread flour
> 5 g fresh yeast
> 5 g salt
> 150 ml water
> 50 ml olive oil

Filling:

> Fresh or frozen spinach
> Soaked currants (according to your taste)
> Pine nuts (according to your taste)
> 1 clove of garlic
> Olive oil
> Salt

Preparation:

Dough:

1. Mix the yeast with a little warm water.

2. Mix the flour with the water, olive oil and yeast in a bowl. Add the salt.

3. On a work surface, knead the dough for about 15 minutes until it is elastic and does not stick to your hands. Form the dough into a ball and place it in a bowl. Cover the bowl with well-oiled kitchen film and let the dough rise for about 90 minutes in a warm place.

4. Lightly oil the work surface and knead the dough gently to expel the fermentation gases. Divide the dough into two equal portions.

5. Roll out the portions into circles of about 20 cm diameter and about half a cm thick.

Filling:

6. Boil or steam the chopped spinach and then drain it thoroughly by squeezing or pressing it.

7. Heat some olive oil in a pan and briefly toast the pine nuts, chopped garlic and raisins.

8. Add the spinach to the pan, then season, stir and put aside.

9. Preheat the oven to 180°C.

10. Spoon a little of the spinach mix onto each circle of dough, add plenty of olive oil and close the pastry over the filling by folding the dough over. Seal the joint and ends of the pasty with a fork as you do with empanadillas. Place on a baking tray lined with baking paper and sprinkle with some more olive oil.

11. Bake at 180°C for 15-20 minutes until they are browned. Then remove from the oven and allow to cool.

12. Serve panadons when cool or reheat and serve warm.

PANIZAS GADITANAS DE GARBANZOS

Chickpea Flour Pancakes

The paniza is a kind of pancake made from chickpea flour. Chickpea flour has been used for centuries in India, throughout the Levant, and often in Mediterranean cuisine too. In Spanish cuisine, this flour is an important ingredient for the famous "tortillitas", which are a type of fritter from Cádiz: vegetables fried in a chickpea batter. Here we have a simplified chickpea pancake. Strictly speaking, this is not a baked dish but it is a popular and delicious pancake.

Ingredients:

> 280 ml chickpea flour
> 500 ml water
> Salt
> Pepper
> Olive oil for frying

Preparation:

1. Mix all ingredients and let the mix stand for a couple of hours.

2. Boil the mixture in a saucepan, stirring constantly for about 5 minutes, until it forms a thick creamy batter. Remove from the heat.

3. Put the mixture in a bowl and allow it to stand until it solidifies. This is best done the day before the batter is needed, or put it in the fridge for a few hours.

4. Cut the dough into thick slices and fry these in plenty of olive oil until golden brown.

5. Serve the panizas on a small plate with a little salad.

PASTEL DE CIERVA DE MURCIA

Chicken Tart of Murcia

This is a popular chicken pie from the small coastal town of San Javier in Murcia. It is an interesting combination of sweet and savoury flavours.

The recipe appeared in the late 19th century. It was reputedly given to a pastry chef in San Javier by the chef of a Russian ship anchored off the coast. It was prepared for the famous Murcian and Spanish politician, Juan de la Cierva y Peñafiel. He was so delighted by the tart that the chef named the pie after him.

It is served in slices, warm or cold, frequently as a starter.

Ingredients:

250 g lard (or butter / margarine)
250 g sugar
1 egg (to coat the pastry)
Grated lemon peel
500 g - 700 g flour
2 hard-boiled eggs
150 g - 250 g cooked chicken meat
Salt to taste

Preparation:

1. The chicken is first cooked in water, oil, salt with laurel until tender. Remove any bone and skin. Use a blender to roughly mince the meat. Put the meat and 100 ml of the broth aside in the fridge.

2. Hard-boil the two eggs and put aside in the fridge.

3. Thoroughly mix the lard (or butter) with the sugar and salt until you have a consistent, smooth paste. Add the egg and lemon peel and continue to mix.

4. Add the flour, little by little, until you have dough that is dense and not too dry. Knead thoroughly.

5. Let the dough rest in the fridge for 30 minutes.

6. Mix the chicken meat with the chopped hard-boiled eggs.

7. Divide the dough in two parts and roll it out to cover a round baking tin. Generally, these pies are around 25 cm in diameter.

8. Preheat the oven to 150°C - 160°C.

9. Line the baking tin with the first sheet of dough and fill with the chicken and boiled egg. Add the broth to maintain the humidity of the pie.

10. Close the pie with the second sheet of dough and seal the edges.

11. Coat the top with beaten egg.

12. Bake at between 150°C -160°C until the piecrust is golden brown.

13. Remove the tin from the oven, allow the pie to cool or serve warm.

TARTALETAS DE ALCACHOFA, QUESO Y CEBOLLINO
Artichoke, Cheese and Onion Tarts

This is really a Spanish version of quiche in a miniature form using artichokes, one of the most popular vegetables in Spain, and goat's cheese. It is just an example of a number of similar tarts that probably originated in France. They can be made any size but this recipe is for small, single serving tarts with a diameter of about 10-12 cm. It is served as a starter.

Ingredients:

> Puff pastry or shortcrust pastry
> 3 eggs
> 200 ml light cream (around 18% fat)
> 140 g of natural yogurt
> A pinch of salt
> A pinch of black pepper
> Half a teaspoon of tarragon
> Half a teaspoon of onion powder
> Goat's cheese ("Rulo de Queso de Cabra")
> Artichoke hearts (frozen or from a jar)
> Fresh chives

Preparation:

1. Prepare the topping by mixing the eggs, the cream and yogurt together with a pinch of salt and pepper, the tarragon and the onion powder in a blender. Put aside.

2. Roll out the pastry with a rolling pin and cut circles slightly larger than the base of the tarts, using the tart moulds themselves as a guide (the moulds are about 10-12 cm in diameter with corrugated edges.)

3. Grease the moulds with oil or butter. Place a piece of pastry into each mould and trim the edges.

4. Pierce the bottom of the pastry base with a fork and then fill the moulds with the topping.

5. Break up the goat's cheese by hand and add a generous spoonful to each tart. Cut the artichoke hearts into thin slices and place these on top of the tarts. Sprinkle each tart with chopped fresh chives and a pinch of black pepper.

6. Put the tarts in the oven, preheated to 225°C, for about 10 minutes. Then reduce the temperature to 200°C until the cream is curdled and the pastry begins to brown.

7. Remove the tarts from the oven. Serve them hot or cold, garnished with some chopped fresh chives.

---o0o---

2.5 Confectionary and Sweets

What we have loosely classified as "confectionary and sweets" are products that may be consumed in an informal way, such as street food, rather than only with a meal. However, it does not mean that these products are *always* eaten on the street. Some of these recipes are for dishes served with breakfast, merienda and after a formal lunch or dinner as a dessert.

What's more, some of the products in this chapter are not baked at all. However, most of them are very old and can certainly be found in typical bakers' shops or "baking convents" somewhere in Spain. For this reason, we bent the rules and included some non-baked products.

ALMENDRAS GARRAPIÑADAS

Sugared Roasted Almonds

This is a delicious and simple way to turn raw almonds into an instant, exotic delicacy by caramelising them in hot sugar. This sweet turns up in many regions of Spain, but is particularly popular in Murcia and often prepared in large copper pans and sold on the street at Christmas time and during other festivals. They can be preserved in airtight containers or jars for several months. These sweets are also produced and sold in several convents and a popular variation uses hazelnuts in much the same way as almonds.

Ingredients:

> 150 g almonds (with skin)
> 200 g sugar
> 240 ml water

Preparation:

1. Rinse the almonds and put in a bowl with the sugar and water. Stir to mix and leave to stand for 24 hours.

2. The next day, put the almonds in a heavy-bottomed saucepan and put it on a medium heat.

3. Stir the almonds occasionally with a wooden spoon. When they start absorbing the water and the foam begins to turn white, stir them continuously, scraping the sides of the pan with the spoon, until the almonds start to dry.

4. When the almonds are almost dry, remove them from the heat but keep stirring them until they are loose.

5. Empty the pan into an earthenware bowl or on a cold surface (like marble). Separate the almonds from each other and let them cool. Serve or preserve in an airtight container (a kilner jar or similar).

ARROP I TALLAETES DE VALENCIA

Pumpkin Arrop of Valencia

Arrop is a very old and traditional sweet of Valencia. The word "Arrop" comes from the Arabic word "arrúbb" or classical Arabic word "rubb" which is a thick syrup made by reducing grape juice ("mosto" or grape must) over heat to caramelise the sugars. The result is a thick, almost black syrup.

The Moors in Spain grew grapes but did not drink wine so they used the young fermented wine to produce sweet syrup - considered by many to be the first manufactured sweet that was not based on honey. Arrop was popular in the middle ages and was frequently sold at markets by hawkers. It was also popular in the Sephardic Jewish society of the time. It was later adopted as a moneymaking sideline by various Christian monastic orders after the Christian conquest of Moorish Spain.

In Valencia, this syrup is combined with cubes (tallaetes) of pumpkin to make a sweet. Sometimes plums, melons or peaches are used instead. It has an unusual sweet-acid taste. Because of the high acid content in pumpkins, it is best to use some lime in the cooking of the pumpkin. Using lime in this way is an old method of reducing acidity although it is not much used in modern cookery and you may have some difficulty finding cooking lime.

Although still sold in street markets, pumpkin arrop is sometimes served as a dessert in restaurants. Some recipes add cinnamon to taste. Other variants make the syrup from figs rather than reduced mosto. A further variant serves the arrop and pumpkin wrapped in a pancake.

Ingredients:

    Cooking lime
    2 litres of grape must (Mosto)
    2 litres of water
    500 g pumpkin

Preparation:

1. The first step is to prepare the pumpkin. The proportion of lime used is about three parts of pumpkin to one part lime.

2. Put 2 litres of water and 200 g of cooking lime in a large saucepan. Bring it to the boil, then switch off the heat and let the lime settle. The

water needs to be completely transparent. When the water is clear, transfer it to a bowl.

3. Peel and cut the pumpkin into wedges and blocks of different sizes. Put the pumpkin into the limewater and leave it to soak for at least 8 hours (some say 24 hours is better). After soaking, remove the pumpkin and rinse it thoroughly.

4. Put the grape must (mosto) in a saucepan and reduce it by half over a moderate heat until you have a dark syrup.

5. Finally, put the syrup and pumpkin together in a container. Store it until the pumpkin has soaked up the syrup before serving.

ARROPÍA DE FRIGILIANA

Arropía of Frigiliana

Arropía is the quintessential sweet of the Axarquía area of Málaga province, based as it is on the molasses still produced from the last remaining sugar cane plantations of eastern Axarquía. It is traditionally made on the street, prepared on demand on a marble slab to the delight of the waiting children. In Torrox and Nerja, as well as in Frigiliana, they traditionally have this sweet during the celebrations of the "Cruces de Mayo", when the village streets are decorated with copious flowers and floral crosses.

The stretching and shaping of the molten arropía is something of an art. It is akin to working with a very long piece of soft plasticine that you are trying to twist into a spiral. It does not break that easily but it is hot and you have to be careful not to stretch it too thinly. Practice is definitely required for this one!

Ingredients:

> 300 g molasses
> A few tablespoons of water
> Olive oil
> Chopped almonds or hazelnuts

Preparation:

1. Put the molasses with a few tablespoons of water in a copper or stainless steel pan. Warm over a medium heat. When the mixture starts to smoke, use a spoon and poor some drops into a glass of cold water to test if it is ready to be used.

2. If the test drops form a soft ball when they contact the water, it is time to remove the molasses from the heat.

3. Spread the hot molasses on a marble surface greased with olive oil, let cool a little, and then start shaping it by stretching and twisting the mix with well-oiled hands and being careful not to be burned…. it stays hot for a while!

4. As the arropía starts to cool, stretch and form it into a long stick and shape it as desired. Usually it is twisted into a long twirl before being allowed to cool further. It is important to keep working the arropía until it begins to cool.

5. It is common to add in chopped almonds or hazelnuts to the molasses as it is being worked.

6. Finally cut the stick of Arropía into small pieces and place them on a plate to cool completely before serving. It is also served slightly warm if the customers cannot wait!

BESITOS DE MONJA

Little Kisses of the Nun

There are many examples of sweets and pastries in Spain which have religious names because the monastic orders in Spain adopted them as artisan products to generate income for their community after the expulsion of the Moors and Jews. Here is another rich and delicious example, which is thought to have originated in Portugal and which is a particular Christmas favourite made with almonds and egg yolks.

The nuns of the ancient Convent do Carmo in Guimarães, Portugal, knew exactly how delicious these sweets were. According to tradition, they would store their "besitos" in a cupboard with a notice on the front that read, "In honour of St. Benedict, don't let the ants come in here!"

Ingredients:

> 110 g blanched almonds
> 80 ml water
> 250 g sugar
> 10 egg yolks
> Sugar to coat

Preparation:

1. Grind the almonds with a mincer or blender (or use ground almonds) and put aside

2. Heat the water and sugar in a saucepan to create a syrup.

3. Sieve the egg yolks through a fine colander to remove the membrane and put aside.

4. Add the chopped almonds and egg yolks to the syrup and cook for about 15 minutes or until the mixture turns into a consistent dough.

5. Place this dough in the refrigerator for 12 hours.

6. Take the dough from the fridge and (with wet hands) make small balls. Roll each one in sugar.

7. Place each besito in a paper baking cup and they are ready to serve.

BORRACHUELOS DE NAVIDAD DE MÁLAGA

Sweet Christmas Fritters of Málaga

Here is a Christmas sweet recipe typical of Málaga province. It is another of those sweet fried dough recipes so beloved of the Moors and Sephardic Jews and now adopted as a Christmas treat.

It is a slightly complicated and time-consuming dish, but it is definitely worth the effort. Borrachuelos are a very typical breakfast treat taken together with a glass of anís liquor on Christmas morning. This recipe assumes you have a large family coming to visit you on Christmas day!

Ingredients:

> 2 kg flour (1kg bread flour and 1 kg plain flour)
> 600 g sugar
> 4.5 glasses of sweet (Málaga) wine
> 2 litres olive oil (half to make the dough and half to fry the fritters)
> Juice of 2 oranges and the peel of 1 orange
> 30 g aniseed
> 75 g sesame seed
> 5 g cinnamon powder
> 1 dash of sweet anís liquor
> Honey
> Water
> Sugar to coat the fritters

Preparation:

1. Heat the 2 litres of olive oil. When it is hot add the orange peel and leave to fry until it is browned, then remove the peel. This gives the oil an aroma of orange.

2. Use a fine steel sieve and fry the seeds in the hot oil. When toasted, put them aside.

3. Form a heap with the two types of flour on a work surface. Add the orange juice and the cinnamon and mix.

4. Begin to incorporate the wine and oil (1 litre) alternately and add the fried sesame seeds and aniseed, whilst working the dough until it is smooth and easy to manipulate.

5. When it is completely workable, roll out the dough, cut out the fritters in little circles or ovals and fold them over. It is best to seal the edges of each fritter with a little water. The size is up to you but they should ideally be bite-sized. They are now ready for frying.

6. Fry in plenty of oil (not too hot) until the fritters are golden brown.

7. Whilst still hot, sprinkle the fritters with sugar. Alternatively, you can coat them in honey, for which the fritters should be cold. In this case, put the honey in a small saucepan together with a little water, warm gently and then baste the fritters with the mix.

8. Serve the fritters cold with a glass of sweet anís liquor. Feliz Navidad!

CHURROS

Churros

On New Year's morning when the festivities of the night are ending, the tradition is to adjourn to a café for breakfast and take churros with coffee or chocolate. It is one of the time-honoured breakfasts for this occasion.

Churros are a simple form of fritters, popular in all of Spain but especially in Andalucía. They are eaten for breakfast or merienda with milky coffee or thick hot chocolate. If you feel up to making them on New Year's Day, here is a recipe!

Ingredients (for approx. 32 churros):

> 275 g flour
> 2.5 g salt
> 550 ml water
> Olive Oil

Preparation:

1. Sift the flour and salt together.

2. Bring the water to the boil and add the flour. Stir briskly over the heat until the flour has been incorporated into a stiff, sticky dough. Leave it to cool a little.

3. While still warm, use a strong piping bag with a narrow, fluted nozzle. Squeeze out the dough into 10 cm to 15 cm lengths straight into the hot frying oil.

4. Deep-fry in batches in very hot oil until brown and crisp.

5. Drain on kitchen paper and eat warm (they can also be slightly sugared).

COQUITOS

Coconut Macaroons

Coquitos are sometimes called cocadas and are small coconut, sugar and egg macaroons. They are a favourite breakfast sweet. They come in various shapes but are generally ball or conical shaped.

Ingredients (for approx. 16 coquitos):

> 150 g grated coconut
> 100 g sugar
> 1 egg
> Grated peel of 1 small lemon

Preparation:

1. Place the grated coconut, sugar and grated lemon peel in a bowl. Stir together until well mixed.

2. Beat the egg and add it to the mixture. Mix well. The dough will not be compact but crumbly.

3. Divide the dough into 16 equal pieces and roll these into balls. Line a baking tray with baking paper and place the macaroons on the tray.

4. Finally, bake in a preheated oven at 180°C for about fifteen minutes until lightly browned. Remove the tray from the oven and allow the coquitos to cool.

5. Serve cool or store in an airtight container.

CRESPILLOS DE BARBASTRO

Borage Fritters of Barbastro

Crespillos are fritters based on borage leaves. This version comes from the old Celtiberian town of Barbastro in Aragón. The origin of the crespillo lies in the traditional rural practice of using the best leaves of the borage, chard or spinach for a main course and using the normally discarded parts for a sweet dessert. The women of Aragón developed this delicious fritter in order to make use of the entire plant rather than just cooking the tender heart of the plant. Every house in this area has its own recipe but the recipe below is typical.

The eating of crespillos has become linked with a well-known local Aragonese fertility festival held every year in late March, celebrating the fertilisation of the flowers of the olive trees in the area. For this reason, we included crespillos as a sweet, often eaten on the street. During this famous festival, crespillos are made and consumed by the thousands in Barbastro!

Crespillos are similar to the dish of "paparajotes" in Murcia where lemon leaves are used. Crespillos can be taken as an appetizer or dessert. If eaten as a dessert, add sugar and/or honey.

Despite the association with spring, crespillos are also a popular dish at Christmas time, to celebrate the end of the old year and the start of the new one.

Ingredients:

> 2 bunches of borage
> 1 glass of brandy or (more traditionally) anís liquor
> 2 eggs
> 3 tablespoons of flour
> 1 small glass of milk
> Sugar
> Honey (optional)
> Olive oil

Preparation:

1. Clean and separate the borage leaves, selecting only the smaller and tender inside leaves. Wash these thoroughly with water and dry them.

2. Cover the leaves with the brandy and leave them to stand for a couple of hours.

3. When the leaves are marinated, make a soft batter with beaten egg white, salt, flour and milk (optionally add a tablespoon of honey). Prepare a frying pan with enough olive oil to fry the fritters.

4. Dip the borage leaves into the batter. They need to be well coated.

5. Fry them in the hot oil until golden brown.

6. Serve sprinkled with sugar if eaten as a sweet. Leave them as they are if eaten as a starter.

GUIRLACHE DE ARAGÓN

Nougat of Aragón

This nougat is made with almonds and solid caramelised sugar. This recipe is very typical of many areas of the former Kingdom of Aragón (Aragón, Cataluña and Valencia). However, similar recipes can be found in many parts of Spain since it has clear Arabic origins.

This particular nougat was popularized by the French in Aragón during the nineteenth century and its name Guirlache is derived from the French word "grillage" (toasted).

Nougat is popular as a Christmas sweet by itself, but it is also used as an ingredient for cakes or desserts. This recipe for Aragonese nougat is quite basic and it is relatively easy to make. Some regional recipe variations add a little honey or substitute the sugar for honey.

Ingredients:

0.5 kg sugar
0.5 kg raw whole almonds (unskinned)
1 small lemon
Aniseed (to taste)
Olive oil

Preparation:

1. Put the sugar in a frying pan with the juice of just under half of the lemon.

2. Over a medium heat, continuously stir the sugar and lemon juice with a wooden spoon to prevent burning. The caramel is formed when the sugar has melted (at 160°C) and turns into a slightly thick, light coloured liquid. It should not be dark. Manage the caramelisation by taking the pan from the heat if necessary and gently swirling the melting sugar around.

3. When the sugar has started to caramelise, add the almonds to the pan, continuously stirring the mixture. Keep stirring until the mixture changes colour and starts to brown. It is very important at this point to prevent the caramel from burning.

4. When you see that the mixture has acquired this nougat's typical brown colour, remove the pan from the heat and pour everything on a

sheet of baking paper, previously rubbed with a little olive oil to avoid the nougat sticking.

5. Spread out the hot nougat, and shake a small amount of aniseed over the surface, according to your taste.

6. Let the nougat cool for 15 minutes before cutting it up to serve.

MAZAPÁN, TRADICIONAL DULCE DE NAVIDAD

Marzipan, the Traditional Christmas Sweet

Marzipan is the archetypal Christmas confection, beloved throughout Europe. However, let us remember that European marzipan actually came from Moorish Spain. It arrived in "Al-Andalus", which was an area covering much of Spain, at the time of the Arab Kingdoms. Some believe marzipan originated in China, from where the recipe moved on to the Middle East and then to Europe via the Caliphate of Córdoba and the Kingdom of Granada when almond cultivation was introduced into Spain.

Marzipan is used to make decorations and as fillings for cakes. Because it is so malleable, many towns and villages in Spain have a tradition of using marzipan to make religious and other figures as well as animals and fruits to provide a decorative and delicious sweet treat at Christmas time. Some of these figures and decorations are truly works of art and it may be hard to bring yourself to eat them!

Here is one basic recipe for the making of marzipan.

Ingredients:

> 280 g skinned, ground almonds
> 400 g sugar
> 240 ml water
> 2 egg whites
> 4 tablespoons icing sugar
> 1 teaspoon vanilla essence

Preparation:

1. Heat the water in a pan with the sugar until the sugar dissolves and the mixture begins to boil.

2. Leave to boil without stirring until it has a temperature of 110°C (use a food thermometer to check).

3. Remove from the heat and stir the mixture very carefully. Add the almonds, beaten egg whites and vanilla. Mix everything thoroughly.

4. Place the saucepan over a moderate heat for a few minutes, just until the mixture starts to pull away from the sides of the saucepan.

5. Put some icing sugar on a smooth surface and add the mixture from the saucepan. Knead well, then make shapes as required or form into a cylinder or cake for later use.

6. Wrap in cling film and put in an airtight container for storage.

FIGURITAS DE MAZAPÁN

Marzipan Figures

Marzipan descends from a centuries' old tradition of combining almonds with sugar. The resulting 'dough' is quite pliable, and confectioners use this fact to create whimsical figures before toasting them in an oven. The result is marzipan 'figuritas', little figures.

During the battle of Navas de Tolosa in the year 1212, it is said that the nuns of the San Clemente convent took care of the wounded soldiers. According to tradition, they ground up their stores of almonds in mortars and pestles, and then kneaded them together with sugar to create emergency rations. This type of bread (pan) produced with a pestle (maza) is supposed to have given rise to the name mazapán in Spanish, marzipan in English. It is a nice story, but the reality is that marzipan was probably introduced into Spain by the Arabs as a super-charged way of preserving high protein foods for their armies when they were on the march, and as a source of protein and sugar during long winters in remote areas.

In later times, marzipan was used to create artistic shapes to celebrate Christmas by making figures and "carving" other religious or domestic objects. This tradition is still alive and well and not just in Spain. The only limit to what can be made in marzipan is your own imagination!

Ingredients:

> 300 g ground almonds
> 300 g icing sugar
> 2 tablespoons of water
> 1 egg white
> Grated peel of half a lemon (optional)
> Cinnamon powder (optional)

Preparation:

1. Put the almonds, sugar and water into a deep bowl. If you like, you can add the grated peel of half a lemon and some cinnamon powder.

2. Knead the mixture with your hands until the marzipan is a uniform smooth paste. Leave it to rest in a cool place for at least two hours.

3. Now comes the creative part: making the figurines. This is definitely a task for the children to enjoy and there are no limits to what you can make. You can buy kits of shaped biscuit cutters to make the cutting

out simpler and more professional but it is not necessary. The most important thing is to make some funny and interesting shapes.

4. When your figures are all finished, paint them with beaten egg white and place them on an oven tray lined with baking paper.

5. Preheat the oven to 200°C. Put the tray in the oven for just 2 minutes. As soon as the marzipan begins to brown, remove it from the oven.

6. Allow to cool, and serve.

PALILLOS DE PERIANA

Sweet Fritters of Periana

This is a rural recipe from the village of Periana in Málaga province and is another of the many sweet fried dough recipes with its origins in Moorish confectionary. These days, palillos are a speciality in the area during the time of the Easter processions (Semana Santa).

Ingredients:

> Eggs
> Olive oil
> Flour
> Sugar
> 1 tablespoon of olive oil for each egg

Preparation:

1. Beat some egg whites until stiff. Mix in the yolks and the olive oil, whisking vigorously.

2. Add some flour until you have dough that can be kneaded. Leave it to stand for 2 hours.

3. After that, shape the dough into short thick sticks or rings.

4. Fry the sticks or doughnuts in plenty of hot olive oil over a low heat.

5. Once fried, leave to drain and cool for a while. Then moisten each fritter quickly with water and sprinkle with sugar to serve.

PAN DE CÁDIZ

Fruit Marzipan of Cádiz

The "Pan de Cádiz" (also called Turrón de Cádiz) has no relationship with bread, except that it is baked in an oven and is often shaped and made to look like a loaf of bread.

It is made using layers of marzipan with fillings of candied fruit and jam in between and then shaped into a loaf. It is the most famous and typical sweet of the city of Cádiz, but it is a relatively recent invention. In its present form, its creation is attributed to the baker Antonio Valls Garrido, who created the Vienna patisserie in Cádiz in the early 1950s.

However, although the shape of the sweet itself was created at this time, the delicacy itself is thought to be based on much older marzipan and fruit balls that were first documented in Cádiz in the 18th century, but may have been made there for much longer.

Pan de Cádiz is now a very popular sweet on Christmas tables throughout Andalucía and indeed, the whole of Spain.

Ingredients:

>   250 g icing sugar
>   250 g of ground raw almonds (preferably Marcona variety)
>   1 egg
>   1 egg yolk to paint the top of the loaf
>   Mixture of candied fruit

Preparation:

1. Make the marzipan as follows: Mix the sugar with the ground almonds and add the beaten egg. Knead the mixture by hand until smooth and consistent.

2. Weigh the whole mix and then divide it into three equal portions (some recipes use four layers).

3. Preheat the oven (grill only) to 250°C.

4. Knead each of the portions of marzipan a little more, and roll them out into an oval shape.

5. Line a baking tray with baking paper and place one of the marzipan ovals on the paper. Cover this with candied fruit, chopped or cut into

strips, and then place another marzipan oval on top. Some recipes use a thick fruit jam for the first or second layer.

6. Repeat the process adding more candied fruit. Finally, cover this with the last oval layer of marzipan, using your thumbs to press down the sides and smooth over the point where the three layers meet. Shape carefully into a "loaf".

7. Carefully make a diamond pattern on the top of the "loaf" with a sharp knife, and brush the top with egg yolk. Place the tray into the oven to brown.

8. There is no need to bake the "loaf"; just to brown the top until it is slightly golden, which does not take very long. As soon as it starts to light brown, remove the loaf from the oven and place it on a rack to cool.

9. Serve when it is cool. To store the loaf wrap it in cling film and put in an airtight container so that it does not dry out.

PAN DE HIGO

Fig Loaf

Fig "bread" (also known as "Dulce de higos") is a typical Christmas dessert in Spain. Together with the famous mantecados, these are the richest and most popular Christmas sweets in Spain. Accompanied by a glass of Moscatel wine, fig bread is a delight for the palate. It is also a very complete and nutritious food containing dried fruits and nuts; very welcome in the cold days of winter! It is often served with cheese.

It is common in Spain to eat nuts and dried fruits, especially during the most important religious festivals, such as Christmas. Historically, the Catholic Church encouraged religious celebrations to be accompanied with plenty of food, it being supposed that the faithful would associate their faith with lots of good food.

Similar recipes for this pan de higo are found in Extremadura, Andalucía and Murcia where figs and almonds grow side by side. They are harvested at about the same time in September and the combination is a natural one.

Ingredients:

> 1 kg dried figs
> 500 g skinned roasted almonds
> 1 tablespoon of ground cinnamon
> 1 glass of rum
> 3 tablespoons of honey
> Half a teaspoon of ground aniseed
> A pinch of ground cloves

Preparation:

1. Remove the tops from the figs and chop them up finely.

2. Roast the almonds and chop them (leave a few large slices for decoration).

3. Mix the figs and almonds, add the ground cloves, cinnamon powder, ground aniseed, the rum and the honey and mix it all thoroughly until you have a consistent, firm dough.

4. Shake flour in a round or square cake tin and fill it with the mix. Place a heavy weight on top of the mixture, using greaseproof paper to cover the "loaf". Let it set for a day or two. You can also make rolls of

fig "bread", coating them with a little flour and let them dry for a couple of days.

5. To serve, cut the loaf into very thin slices.

PAN DE OREJONES Y ALMENDRAS

Apricot and Almond Bread

This is actually not bread at all but rather another sweet based on a dried fruit, in this case dried apricots. As with many dried fruit based sweets this has its origins in Moorish kitchens (note the use of cloves, aniseed and sesame) but was adapted somewhat to Christian tastes with the addition of strong liquor!

Ingredients:

Main mixture:

> 500 g dried apricots
> 100 g of ground almonds (can be slightly roasted before grinding)
> Half a teaspoon of cinnamon powder
> Grated peel of 1 orange
> Dash of anís liquor
> Pinch of ground cloves, to taste
> 1 teaspoon of sesame seed
> 1 teaspoon of aniseed

To decorate:

> 50 g whole almond (raw or slightly roasted)
> Icing sugar

Preparation:

1. Soak the dried apricots in warm water for half an hour and then chop them up. You can chop them finely or coarsely according to the texture you prefer. Put them in a mixing bowl.

2. Add the rest of the ingredients, stirring well. Allow to cool in the fridge until the mixture thickens.

3. For the next step, it is advisable to wear latex gloves because the mixture is very sticky. Form the mixture into balls or squares and flatten by hand to around 2 cm thick. Insert some whole almonds and then cover with a little more of the mixture.

4. Place them on a tray lined with baking paper and coat with icing sugar.

5. Wrap in kitchen film and store in the fridge with a weight on top for 2 or 3 days before serving.

PANELLETS DE CATALUÑA DE TODOS LOS SANTOS

Catalan Almond Sweets for All Saints'

Panellets are a traditional almond sweet of Cataluña and nowadays they are eaten on All Saints' day, 1st November. The "modern" version dates back to the 18th century when they were prepared and eaten on saints' days such as the Holy Cross procession and St Mark's day. They are also something of a Christmas speciality as well. The original version, made on an almond base not unlike marzipan, is almost certainly an Arabic invention.

The panellet is also traditional and important in Valencia. In fact it is so important there that it is now registered as an "ETG" by the European Union, meaning "Traditional Speciality Guaranteed" and that its name is guaranteed to refer only to the original traditional recipe. Another version of the panellet uses candied orange that is finely ground and incorporated into the dough. Sometimes the base of the panellets is made using some potato with almond instead of just almond alone.

There are many modernised versions with various coatings including chocolate and coffee. In Sevilla there is a strikingly similar sweet known as Empiñonados, often made in some of the city's convents.

In Cataluña, panellets are served with a Moscatel wine or glass of cava. Here we have a traditional recipe with several alternative coatings.

Ingredients (for 24 panellets):

Dough:

> 200 g blanched almonds
> 140 g sugar
> 60 ml water
> 1 egg white

Coatings:

The following coatings can be used:

> Pine nuts (whole)
> Pistachios (chopped)
> Almonds (chopped)
> Egg yolk

Preparation:

1. Grind the almonds very finely in a blender. Set aside

2. Heat the water and sugar in a large saucepan and mix. When it begins to boil, add the ground almond and continue to stir until a dough forms and it no longer sticks to the walls of the pan (about 4 or 5 minutes).

3. Remove the pan from the heat and allow it to cool for a while. When it is just warm, add the egg white. Stir until it is completely mixed into the dough.

4. Put the dough in the fridge for at least two hours.

5. When the dough has cooled and stiffened, the panellets can be made by forming small balls of the dough. Do not make them too large.

6. Preheat the oven to 200°C.

7. Roll the dough balls in the different coatings (pine nuts, pistachios, and almonds) and place on a baking tray lined with baking paper.

8. Glaze the panellets with egg yolk mixed with a few drops of water.

9. Bake the panellets for 6 minutes in the upper part of the oven, but be careful not to bake any longer otherwise they will become very dry.

10. Remove the panellets and allow them to cool to room temperature before serving.

LAS PELADILLAS DE CASINOS

Sugared Almonds of Valencia

This is a typical candied sweet, made from almonds coated with sugar. It originates in Valencia and is often present on the Christmas table throughout Spain, accompanying other almond sweets like nougats, polvorones, marzipans, mantecados, etc. It has been widely exported to other countries in the past as a traditional festive sweet.

The major producers of sugared almonds in Spain are found in the towns of Casinos in Valencia and Alcoy in Alicante, where sugared almonds have been manufactured and exported for at least two centuries, based on a traditional manufacturing process.

Besides the traditional sugared almonds, other variants are made with different types of chocolates. In the town of Casinos, every year on the last weekend of November you can visit the annual Feria of handcrafted sweets and try all of these traditional coated almonds and the famous D.O. nougat of Casinos.

This is not a product that can be easily produced in a domestic kitchen, so we make no attempt to provide a recipe. However, it is such a traditional and well-known Christmas sweet that we thought it deserved a mention. The best option for the reader is to buy some from any of the excellent manufacturers in Casinos.

MIEL SOBRE HOJUELAS DE CASTILLA-LA MANCHA

Honey Pancake of Castilla-La Mancha

These honey-coated pancakes are popular in Castilla-La Mancha. They are fried in a plentiful quantity of oil and are generally served cold. They are traditionally eaten during Carnival, Lent and at Easter, although they are believed to have their origin in Moorish cuisine.

Ingredients (for eight people):

6 eggs
1 glass of brandy or anís liquor
Pinch of salt
Water as required
500 g flour
Olive oil for frying
200 g honey to coat pancakes

Preparation:

1. Place the flour in a bowl and make a hole in the centre.

2. Add the eggs, brandy, and salt. Add enough water to make the mixture into a thick batter.

3. Heat a frying pan with the olive oil. When the oil is hot, pour a spoonful of the batter into the pan - enough to cover the bottom.

4. Fry until the pancake is golden brown on one side, then turn it to brown the other side.

5. When browned on both sides remove the pancake and drain on kitchen roll.

6. Cover with a thin layer of honey or shake with sugar and serve cold.

PESTIÑOS

Sweet Fritters

A pestiño is a Christmas or Holy Week fritter that is popular in Andalucía and Murcia in Southern Spain. Several convents are famous for their production of traditional pestiños.

It is essentially a piece of dough, deep-fried in olive oil and glazed with honey or sugar. Pestiños are very easy to make. They can have a lot of different flavours using, for example, white wine, anise, cinnamon or cloves as optional ingredients. Here we give two variations of this recipe just to whet your appetite!

Ingredients:

> 1 kg of flour
> Olive oil
> 1 glass of white wine
> 2 eggs
> Peel of half a lemon
> Peel of half an orange
> Icing sugar or honey to taste

Optional flavourings:

> 30 g aniseed and 60 ml anís liquor
> or
> 2 tsp of cinnamon powder and 6 cloves

Preparation:

1. Fry the lemon and orange peels (and optionally the aniseed) in hot olive oil.

2. In a bowl, whisk the flour, eggs and other ingredients together (optionally adding the anís liquor). Add the oil infused with orange and lemon flavour and stir with a wooden spoon until it becomes a smooth dough.

3. Roll out the dough evenly into a thin layer on a work surface. Cut into rectangular pieces. Fold the 2 opposite corners together and then fry the pestiños in plenty of hot oil.

4. Once fried, coat the pestiños with sugar, icing sugar or honey. Optionally add a little anís liquor.

PESTIÑOS DE MÁLAGA

Pestiños ("Angel Wings") of Málaga

This is the Málaga variant on the previous pestiño recipe. In Málaga, it is also a typical Christmas and Easter week dish - along with sweet doughnuts, cod dishes and rice puddings!

Such dishes are especially favoured during religious feasts, because they are sweet and they contain no lard. Lard was, of course, forbidden during the "holy days of abstinence" including Lent and Christmas eve. Thus, it was possible to enjoy some really rich and delicious delicacies without breaking the rules on fasting!

Ingredients:

> 1 cup of olive oil
> Orange peel
> Lemon peel
> A small glass of white wine
> 1 tablespoon of sesame seed
> 1 small glass of brandy
> 1 pinch of baking powder
> 850 g bread flour
> Sugar
> Cinnamon powder

Preparation:

1. Heat olive oil in a frying pan and fry the orange and lemon peels until brown.

2. Remove the pan from the heat, remove the peel and add a tablespoon of sesame seeds to the oil (be careful not to burn the seed). Pour the oil and sesame seed into a bowl.

3. To this oil and sesame seed, add the white wine (at room temperature), the glass of brandy, a pinch of baking powder, half a teaspoon of ground cinnamon and the flour. Start to knead the mixture until it becomes a smooth, consistent dough. Leave it to stand for an hour.

4. Roll out the dough and cut out small squares Fold these squares over diagonally. Fry each of the pestiños in hot olive oil (not too hot - avoid burning).

5. When browned, remove them from the oil, drain, sprinkle with sugar and cinnamon and serve.

PICARDÍAS DE MURCIA

Caramelized Hazelnuts of Murcia

This is a traditional hazelnuts sweet made in Murcia, in particular in the old towns of Lorca, Cieza, Bullas and Abarán. It is especially popular around carnival and you can buy picardías in any sweet shop in Lorca - but they are simple to make.

Ingredients:

> 0.5 kg sugar
> 0.5 kg hazelnuts
> Cinnamon to taste

Preparation:

1. Shell, peel and toast the hazelnuts.

2. Put the sugar in a saucepan with 2 teaspoons of water and put on the heat until you have a golden caramel. (You can add a little cinnamon to taste). Remove from the heat.

3. Pour the caramel onto a marble surface and place the hazelnuts one by one into the hot caramel, top each with a drop of the caramel.

4. Before the caramel cools completely, cut it into circles or squares around each nut and let it cool.

5. When cooled, remove from the surface and they are ready to eat.

PRESTINES DE EXTREMADURA

Anís and Honey fritters of Extremadura

This is a sweet fritter, typical of Extremadura. This very basic recipe is from the municipality of Villafranca de los Barros in the province of Badajoz. It is traditional and easy to make. You need to use your judgement when adding olive oil. The dough should be malleable and not sticky.

Ingredients:

>4 cups flour
>1 cup sugar
>1 cup red wine with aniseed (to taste)
>Olive oil
>Orange peel
>Honey

Preparation:

1. Boil the wine together with the aniseed.

2. Put the olive oil in a frying pan on a medium heat and add a few pieces of orange peel to give the oil an orange flavour. Take them out when they are fried.

3. Strain the wine (removing the aniseed) and mix the boiled wine and the warm oil with the flour.

4. Mix well and then knead it thoroughly until you have consistent dough. Form about 45 prestines (little balls).

5. Deep-fry the prestines.

6. When the prestines are fried, coat them with honey and serve.

ROQUITAS DE ALMENDRAS

Little Almond and Chocolate Rocks

This recipe combines ingredients of the old and the new world. It was not so long ago that we could see chocolate-coated almonds being made on the streets of Spain's towns and cities. Here is a slightly modernised version that is now very popular around Christmas.

Ingredients:

> 100 g raw skinned almonds (or buy ready toasted almonds)
> 25 g candied orange
> 150 g chocolate fondant
> Half a tablespoon of grated orange peel
> A pinch of ginger powder

Preparation:

1. Toast the raw almonds in a frying pan without oil, stirring constantly to prevent burning. Let them cool. Meanwhile, chop the candied orange into small pieces.

2. Chop up the chocolate and melt it in a double boiler ("au bain Marie"), over a low heat, stirring as needed. Remove the chocolate from the heat and add the orange peel and ginger. Add the almonds, candied orange, and mix well. Keep mixing!

3. Cover a shallow oven tray with baking paper and, with the help of two spoons, form small blobs of the chocolate mix and drop them onto the paper.

4. Put the tray into the fridge until the chocolate is solid and the "little rocks" are easily peeled off the paper.

SUSPIROS DE MONJA

Nun's Sighs

These are a kind of sweet fried doughnut. They continue to have a traditional link with convent bakeries, especially around Salamanca. They certainly have an old tradition as a sweet fried dough, but their association with nuns and their monastic bakeries has generated many theories about the name of the sweet. Some suggest that the lightness of the dough is the reason for the name. There are others that say (somewhat tongue in cheek) that the name refers to various gastrointestinal problems which nuns were reputed to suffer and which this little, light doughnut could solve.

Ingredients (for several dozen):

> 200 g butter
> 400 g granulated sugar
> Whole peel of one lemon
> 500 ml water
> 500 g white flour
> 5 eggs
> 500 ml olive oil for frying
> Dried and candied fruit, such as cherries, for decoration
> Icing sugar for dusting

Preparation:

1. Put the sugar, butter, lemon peel and water in a large saucepan. Heat on medium-high and stir constantly with a wooden spoon until the sugar dissolves. As soon as the water boils, remove and discard the lemon peel.

2. Continue to stir and add the flour a little at a time. Reduce the heat and continue to cook until the batter starts to come away easily from the sides of the pan.

3. Remove the pan from the heat and allow the batter to cool for 15 minutes.

4. In the meantime, beat the eggs. When the batter is cool, gradually stir in the beaten eggs.

5. Continue to stir until the batter is thoroughly mixed. It should be thick and sticky.

6. Pour 2.5 cm of olive oil in a large frying pan and put it on a medium heat.

7. Wait until the oil is hot and then, using a large spoon, drop rounded portions of the batter into the oil. Make sure the portions are not too large or they will not cook fully in the centre. Fry on both sides until golden but ensure that the batter does not burn.

8. Remove the suspiros and drain them on a paper towel. Continue in this way until all the dough is fried.

9. Sprinkle the suspiros with icing sugar. You can also decorate them with dried and candied fruit.

TURRÓN BLANDO O DE JIJONA

Soft Nougat in the Style of Turrón de Jijona

Turrón or nougat is another example of how the production of almonds dominates Spanish and other European confectionary at Christmas time. Turrón has its roots in the Moorish period of Spain. It appears to have originated in the Andalucian Arab kingdoms prior to the Christian conquest of Spain. The Arab culinary tradition of the time included a similar dessert named "turun", so it seems that nougat or turrón production was introduced into the Arab Kingdoms of Al-Andalus after they started cultivating almonds in the Caliphate of Córdoba some time after the 10th century AD.

There is also evidence of a similar confection, named cupedia or cupeto, produced in Ancient Rome and probably adopted by the Arabs as they colonised the remnants of the Roman Empire in the Levant. At any rate, Turrón or Torró has been known at least since the 15th century in the city of Jijona / Xixona in Alicante.

Spanish turrón may be roughly classified as:

- Hard (the Alicante variety): A compact block of almonds in a brittle mass of eggs, honey and sugar. It has 60% almonds.

- Soft (the Jijona variety): Similar to the hard variety, but the almonds are reduced to a paste. The addition of oil makes the mix more chewy and sticky. It has 64% almonds.

What follows is a recipe for the soft nougat or Turrón de Jijona, a very popular traditional Christmas sweet. This type of nougat, manufactured in Jijona in the Valencia region, is highly prized. It carries a D.O. (designation of origin). It consists of a ground mixture of honey, sugar and almonds. In this case, the recipe uses some hazelnuts, pine kernels and cinnamon to add to the taste.

Ingredients:

300 g toasted almonds
200 g honey
200 g sugar
50 g toasted hazelnuts
50 g pine kernels
1 teaspoon of cinnamon

Preparation:

1. Peel and very finely chop the almonds, hazelnuts and pine kernels.

2. Put the honey with the sugar in a saucepan. Heat the mixture for a few minutes, stirring all the time.

3. When the sugar has completely dissolved, pour the mix over the nuts and incorporate them thoroughly.

4. Pour the mixture into a wooden or aluminium mould. (The mould should be shallow and rectangular).

5. Place a weight on top and let the mould stand for 4-5 days in the fridge, to allow the turrón to take the shape and allow the mix to harden, after which the turrón is ready to eat.

Tip: The variety of almond most popular for this particular nougat is the Marcona almond, which is a small round sweet almond.

TURRÓN DE ALICANTE

Hard Nougat of Alicante

The nougat of Alicante is often referred to as "hard nougat". The recipe is very old, and it is still made in pretty much the same way as it always was. It has been in production for centuries and is believed to originate from original Arabic recipes.

There are several theories about the exact origins of nougat. The theory that seems most likely, according to food historians, suggests that nougat was created by the Arabs to provide a portable high-energy source of nutrients. The idea was that the nougat would remain in good condition for long periods and was easy to transport by their armies, without the risk of degradation causing food poisoning.

Whatever the exact origin, the Turrón of Alicante today is considered to be a product of exceptional quality. It enjoys a D.O. (denomination of origin) status.

What follows is a basic recipe. It requires the use of some shallow wooden moulds to form the nougat, but you can improvise with metal cake tins.

Ingredients:

> 350 g honey
> 200 g sugar
> 2 egg whites
> 650 g toasted almonds (roughly chopped)
> 3 tablespoons of water
> 4 drops of anís liquor
> 1 pack of baking wafers

Preparation:

1. Whisk the egg whites until stiff.

2. Mix the water with the sugar in a saucepan on a low heat until you have a syrup.

3. In another saucepan, heat the honey. Once it is liquefied, add it to the syrup. Remove from the heat and mix well with a wooden spoon.

4.. Put the mix on the heat again until it becomes like caramel.

5. Add the chopped almonds, the anís liquor and the egg whites.

6. Stir with a spatula or wooden spoon until you have a consistent mixture.

7. Line the moulds with baking paper and wafers. Pour in the mix.

8. Smooth the top of the mix with a spatula.

9. Put a wooden board on top of the mould with a weight. Leave the nougat to set for a few days somewhere cool before serving.

TURRÓN DE GOFIO CANARIO

Almond and Honey Turron of the Canaries

This sweet is only produced in Gran Canaria and is made with sugar, "gofio" (flour made from roasted grains), almonds, honey, anise and lemon. In many ways, it resembles nougat.

Ingredients:

>   1 kg gofio (preferably mixed wheat & millet)
>   1 kg honey
>   410 ml condensed milk
>   250 g unsalted butter softened to room temperature
>   Grated peel of 1 lemon (or more, according to taste)
>   300 g crushed toasted almonds

Preparation:

1. Put the gofio in a bowl and add the honey, the condensed milk and the soft butter.

2. Finely grate the lemon peel and add it to the other ingredients in the bowl.

3. Crush the almonds with a mortar and add these to the mixture.

4. Mix until you have a dough. It can be quite time-consuming and hard work to get a thoroughly consistent mixture.

5. After mixing, shape the dough into cylindrical "loaves", wrap them separately in foil or kitchen film and put them into the fridge to set. The turrón will last for up to 6 months in the fridge.

6. When ready to serve, remove a "loaf" from the fridge, slice what you need and return it to the fridge. It is important to store it cool because when it gets warm, it will soften.

7. Serve in small quantities - it is very rich.

YEMAS DE SANTA TERESA DE ÁVILA

Egg Sweets of Saint Theresa of Ávila

Yemas de Santa Teresa (Egg yolks of Saint Theresa of Ávila) originate in the province of Ávila in Castilla y León. These little sweets are well known across Spain and very popular at Christmas time.

They have a long history. Some food historians believe them to have originated in Andalucía in the Middle Ages and to be of Arab origin. Meanwhile, others say that they came from the nuns of a monastery in Ávila, and became popular during the life of Saint Theresa of Ávila.

The truth is probably closer to the latter story, because mediaeval winemakers often used egg whites to help purify wine. They did not have any use for the yolks and so gave their egg yolks to the nuns, who traditionally prepared pastries and sweets to sell. The nuns used the yolks to create the "yemas". They have been commercialised in Ávila since 1860, but are still made in many domestic kitchens to celebrate the feast day of St. Theresa, but also around other feast days, such as Christmas.

Two versions of the "Yemas de Santa Teresa" are mentioned in the famous monastic cookery book known as "La Cocina de los Conventos" (The kitchen of the convents). Both versions are similar but one uses a little cinnamon.

An entirely similar sweet is made in Murcia and is known as "Las Yemas de Caravaca".

Ingredients (6-8 balls):

> 75 ml water
> 100 g sugar
> Peel from half a lemon
> 6 egg yolks
> 1 cup of icing sugar

Preparation:

1. Bring the water with the sugar to a boil and make a syrup by dissolving the sugar. Add the lemon peel. Continue to simmer until the mixture is a thick syrup, stirring frequently to prevent burning. Remove from the heat, and remove the lemon peel from the syrup.

2. Lightly whisk the egg yolks. Pour them into the sauce pan with the syrup and then put the pan on a very low heat and stir the mixture slowly and continuously for 3-4 minutes with a whisk, until the yolks begin to solidify. The mixture will start to pull away from the sides and bottom of the pan as it cooks. Remove from heat and spoon onto a plate. Allow to cool.

3. When the mixture is cool, sprinkle icing sugar onto a work surface. Form the "yemas" by making little balls about the size of a walnut and coat them with icing sugar.

4. Place the "yemas" on a plate and chill them in the refrigerator. Serve on a plate, or in small individual paper cake cups.

---oOo---

2.6 Baked Desserts and Puddings

Our simple definition of a baked dessert or pudding is something that is served as a formal part of a meal as a final or almost final course. The laxness of definitions for sweet bakery in Spain means that the recipes we give here are *often* served as a dessert...... but may also be found at breakfast or merienda.

ALAJÚ DE CUENCA

Almond and Bread Pudding of Cuenca

Alajú is a very old sweet dish that originates in Castilla-La Mancha in the province of Cuenca, particularly in the villages of Ademuz and the area of Utiel-Requena. It is a sweet cake made with honey and almonds mixed into a paste with breadcrumbs. Some local varieties add cinnamon and other spices. The paste is sandwiched between two round wafers. Its name comes from the language of their original inventors, the Arabs, "al-Hasu" which means 'filling'.

Alajú is an early precursor of nougat and turron, another Arab introduction into Spain. The use of breadcrumbs is interesting and typical of the "waste nothing" policy of the rural Spanish kitchen. Bread that had become too hard to eat was and is routinely turned into breadcrumbs and used as an ingredient in another dish.

In this recipe, the almonds are sometimes substituted with walnuts.

Ingredients:

> 2 kg breadcrumbs
> 3 kg honey
> 1 kg of blanched almonds
> 1 grated lemon or orange peel
> Baking wafers to sandwich the mixture (size at your own discretion)

Preparation:

1. Heat the honey and before it starts to caramelise add the breadcrumbs and grated lemon or orange peel.

2. Next, add the almonds and mix into a consistent paste.

3. Place the mixture 1-1.5 cm thick on a thin round wafer and add a second wafer on top to make a sandwich of the filling. Let it cool and serve.

ALFAJOR DE LOS VÉLEZ

Almond and Honey Tart of Los Vélez, Almería

In the region of Los Vélez in Almería, this traditional Christmas sweet is made with an equal mixture of sugar and honey. In other areas, only honey is used. Both versions of this tart are very, very rich. The sweet is still made in the traditional way although versions of it are available commercially. The combination of almonds and honey is of typically Moorish origin but the recipe now has a connotation with Christmas celebrations.

Ingredients:

> 250 g toasted and ground almonds
> 125 g sugar
> 125 g honey
> 125 ml water
> Grated peel of 1 lemon
> 1 glass of anís liquor
> 1 teaspoon of cinnamon powder
> Baking wafers

Preparation:

1. Put all the ingredients (except the wafers) into a saucepan and heat them on a moderate heat.

2. Constantly stir the ingredients with a wooden spoon until the mixture stops sticking to the sides of the saucepan. The dough should be thick but fluid at the same time.

3. Lay half of the wafers out on a work surface and coat them evenly with the mixture.

4. Place the other half of the wafers on top of the coating and put the alfajores aside to set a little.

5. Cut into smaller portions and serve

BESOS DE NOVIA DE MURCIA

Carrot and Cinnamon Fritters of Murcia

Besos de novia (translated as "Bride's kisses") are a traditional wedding dessert made in Murcia. They can be made with carrot or pumpkin, depending on the time of year. They are normally served as a dessert.

Ingredients:

>500 g carrots
>2 eggs
>250 g flour
>16 g baking powder
>150 g sugar
>Sugar to coat
>Cinnamon powder to coat

Preparation:

1. Peel the carrots and cook them in boiling water until tender.

2. Blend the cooked carrots until smooth.

3. Beat the eggs and add them to the blended carrot. Next, add the flour and baking powder and mix all the ingredients thoroughly.

4. Use a deep frying pan with plenty of oil. When the oil is hot, take out small portions of dough with a tablespoon and push it into the hot oil with a second spoon.

5. Fry for approximately 1 minute and then place them on a plate covered in sheets of kitchen roll in order to dry the excess oil.

6. Coat the besos with a mixture of granulated sugar and cinnamon (to your own taste) and serve them hot.

BIZCOCHADA DE CASTILLA -LA MANCHA

Cinnamon Milk Pudding of Castilla-La Mancha

This is a very popular and traditional dessert in Castilla-La Mancha. It is made using another traditional biscuit known as Tortas de Alcázar de San Juan as an ingredient. These are a local biscuit from the old Arabic town of Alcázar de San Juan in the same region. You can find the recipe for these biscuits in the "Sweet Biscuit" chapter of this book. In Spain, it is quite common to use surplus bread or biscuits to make another dish - especially in rural areas where past poverty has made wasting food anathema. There are many such examples.

Ingredients (6 persons):

6 Tortas de Alcázar de San Juan
800 ml whole milk
200 ml whipping cream (35% fat)
1 cinnamon stick
1 lemon peel
1 orange peel
80 g sugar
Cinnamon powder for dusting

Preparation:

1. Heat the milk and cream in a saucepan. Add the cinnamon stick and the lemon and orange peel. (Avoid the orange and lemon pith - this is bitter).

2. When the temperature of the milk has reached about 40°C, add the sugar and bring it slowly close to boiling.

3. Remove the pan from the heat, cover it and let the milk absorb the citrus and cinnamon flavours for some minutes (the longer the better). When the flavours have infused the milk, remove the cinnamon and the orange and lemon peels. Strain the milk if necessary.

4. Place each Torta de Alcázar on a plate and very gradually pour the flavoured milk onto each biscuit. There should not be too much milk but just enough to moisten the biscuit.

5. Finish off the sweet with a sprinkling of cinnamon powder.

BIZCOCHO BORRACHO DE CASTILLA-LA MANCHA

"Drunken Sponge Cake" of Castilla-La Mancha

As the name implies this is a light sponge cake with a very alcoholic sauce made from brandy or rum (or sometimes with sherry or sweet dessert wines). It is often served as a sweet after lunch or dinner but is also taken on winter mornings with hot chocolate or as a merienda. There are many regional variations but this one is popular in Castilla-La Mancha. Another similar sweet is to be found in Zamora in Castilla y Leon.

The sponge cake may be simply coated with the alcoholic sauce or the sponge may be soaked in the sauce for up to an hour, which makes for a very heavy but rich and delicious sweet. In addition, the format varies considerably. The cake may be simply a slice from a larger sponge cake but some regional versions are baked in small portions for one person.

This dish is quite emblematic of various traditional customs in several parts of Spain. For instance, during the week-long carnival celebrations of Guadalajara, the opening ceremony involves a large cavalcade of children in carnival masks who then proceed to enjoy this dessert on the streets of the town (possibly a non-alcoholic version!). Despite its alcoholic base, this cake is made and sold by several convents in Spain.

Ingredients (for 1 cake of 20 cm):

For the cake:

> 4 eggs
> 130 g sugar
> 200 g flour
> 1 tablespoon baking powder
> 1 tablespoon cinnamon powder for garnish

For the sauce:

> 80 g sugar
> 230 ml water
> 1.5 tablespoon of honey
> 14 ml brandy or rum
> Cinnamon powder
> The peel of half a lemon

Preparation:

1. Grease a cake tin with butter or vegetable oil and powder with flour.

2. Separate the egg yolks and egg whites. Whisk the egg yolks in a bowl with the sugar until you have a creamy consistent mixture.

3. In a separate bowl, beat the egg whites until stiff. Carefully add the egg yolk and sugar mix to the egg whites with a spatula.

4. Add in the baking powder and flour gradually, making sure that they are well mixed. Preheat the oven to 180°C.

5. Pour the mix into the baking tin and bake for about 20 minutes or until lightly browned. Check if the sponge is ready by inserting a fork into the centre of the sponge. If it is clean when it comes out, the sponge is ready.

6. Whilst the sponge cake is baking, we can prepare the sauce.

7. Mix the water, sugar, cinnamon, honey and lemon peel in a small saucepan. Boil the mixture and simmer for a minute, stirring occasionally. Remove the pan from the heat and add the brandy or rum. Then let the syrup cool.

8. When the sponge cake is ready, remove from the oven and let it cool.

9. Once cool enough cut the cake into pieces and place them on a plate.

10. Sprinkle each piece of sponge cake with the brandy syrup and decorate it by sprinkling the top with cinnamon powder.

BORRACHINOS DE ASTURIAS

Bread Dumplings in Syrup of Asturias

This dish is also known as "Miñuelos" in Asturias. This ancient fritter originated in the villages of Asturias and was made by farm workers to bring with them to be eaten when working on the land far from home. It has a high-energy value and it was a good way to use up old bread. Today it has become somewhat refined and is now a typical Christmas dessert dish in Asturias.

Ingredients:

For the dough:

> 200 g dry bread
> 100 g sugar
> 3 eggs

For the syrup:

> 250 g sugar
> 250 ml water
> 500 ml white wine (young Moscatel works well)
> 1 stick of cinnamon

To fry:

> 250 ml olive oil

Preparation:

1. Trim off the bread's crust and crumble the bread very finely.

2. Beat the egg whites until stiff, mix them with the bread crumbs in a bowl, adding in the egg yolks and the sugar until obtaining a consistent mixture. If the dough is too soft, add more bread crumbs.

3. Heat the olive oil in a frying pan.

4. Put a spoonful of dough into the hot oil and let it fry slowly until brown. Continue in the same way with the rest of the dough.

5. In the meantime, make the syrup by boiling the wine, water, sugar and cinnamon together for 10 minutes. Then add the fried borrachinos, leaving them to cook for 15 minutes.

6. The borrachinos can be served hot, although it is more common to serve them cold.

BUÑUELOS DE VIENTO

Cream Fritters

This is one of many traditional fritters eaten in Spain around the time of All Saints' Day (November 1st). They are generally filled with whipped cream or baker's cream (pastry cream). The recipes for this dough are quite ancient and original versions use honey rather than sugar. The dough is a cross between dough and batter.

Sephardic Jews are thought to have introduced this and similar fritter recipes to Spain around the 10th century to celebrate Hanukah. Their recipe was later Christianised - hence the addition of lard. The use of lard is not essential and the dish can be made with butter or margarine.

Buñuelos can be eaten as a dessert but are also eaten as a merienda.

Ingredients (approx 20 fritters):

Buñuelos Dough:

> 155 ml water
> 35 g lard (can be substituted with butter or margarine)
> 35 g butter
> 100 g flour
> 5 eggs
> Pinch of salt

Filling (Cream):

> 50 g sugar
> 500 ml cream

Preparation:

1. To make the pastry, boil the water with the salt, butter and lard. When the water starts to boil, add the flour and stir well for about 30 seconds.

2. Allow the dough to cool and then add the eggs one at a time, mixing each one in before adding the next. The result should be a thick and creamy dough.

3. Put plenty of olive oil in a frying pan to heat. When it is hot enough scoop spoonfuls of dough into the hot oil. You can also fill a pastry bag and use this to add the dough to the hot oil.

4. Fry the fritters and turn them several times until they are fully fried and golden brown.

5. When cooked, place the buñuelos on sheets of kitchen roll to drain the excess oil. Allow them to cool.

6. When cool, cut a small gap in each fritter with scissors.

7. Whisk the cream and sugar until stiff and fill each of the buñuelos with a portion of cream.

8. According to your taste, the buñuelos can also be coated with sugar or honey.

COCA DE FRAGA DE CATALUÑA

Quince Tart of Cataluña

A "coca" or "cóc" is a word derived from the Germanic word (modern German "Kuchen") which also was the root for the English word "cake".

"Coca" is a word used in Cataluña to describe a variety of open sweet and savoury tarts with various toppings. These tarts come in different shapes and sizes but usually they are rectangular and have a covering somewhat like a pizza. In this case, it is an open sweet tart topped with quinces - a favourite fruit in Spain.

In many parts of Spain, quinces are a "must-have" fruit tree in rural areas and a family will often have at least one tree to supply the household.

The original recipe for this Coca de Fraga has a kind of bread dough as a base, similar to that used in a pizza, but it can also be made with puff pastry. It is eaten as a sweet after lunch or dinner, or at breakfast or merienda.

In this recipe, the quinces can be substituted with apples: if you cannot find quinces, you can substitute the quantities in the recipe with apple, sliced in the same way, in which case, of course, it becomes "Coca de Manzana" (apple cake).

When the coca is served as a dessert, it is normally eaten warm.

Ingredients (6-8 servings):

Base:

> 500 g puff pastry (or you can make a pizza dough instead)

Topping:

> 2 large, raw quinces
> 100 g brown sugar
> 100 g granulated white sugar
> 65 g chopped walnuts
> Olive oil (mild-fruity)

Preparation:

1. Allow the puff pastry to thaw for approximately 20 minutes.

2. Roll out the pastry thinly and place on a baking tray lined with baking paper. Prick the dough with a fork to allow steam to escape.

3. Preheat the oven to 190°C.

4. Peel, core and slice the quinces. Arrange the slices of quince over the dough. Sprinkle the brown sugar and the white sugar over the top and add the chopped walnuts. Baste with plenty of olive oil.

5. Bake in the middle of the oven for 20-30 minutes, or until quince is cooked, the sugar has melted and the pastry is browned.

6. Remove from the oven and allow to cool for approximately 10 minutes before slicing.

7. Serve warm or cold.

COCA DE ISLA CRISTINA, HUELVA

Sesame, Anís and Wine Tart of Isla Cristina

Coca de Isla Cristina also known as Coca de Lepe is an emblematic dessert in this fishing town on the coast of Huelva in Andalucía. Traditionally it is prepared for the Easter week celebrations and served with a glass of Pedro Ximénez sweet wine, but is also served as a dessert course with lunch or dinner.

Ingredients:

For the dough:

>75 ml olive oil
>75 ml white wine
>275 g flour
>1 tablespoon of sesame seed
>1 tablespoon of aniseed
>1 egg
>Pinch of salt

For the filling:

>4 eggs
>125 ml sunflower oil
>125 g white sugar
>1 tablespoon of cinnamon powder
>Grated peel of 1 lemon
>400 g angel hair
>200 g ground almonds
>Almond flakes (to decorate)

Preparation

Dough:

1. Heat the olive oil in a frying pan and lightly toast the aniseed and sesame seed. Be careful not to burn them. Remove from the heat and allow to cool.

2. Put the flour in a mixing bowl and stir in a pinch of salt. Make a hole in the centre of the flour and pour in the white wine, the olive oil with seeds, and add the egg.

3. Mix thoroughly and then knead by hand until you have smooth dough that does not stick to the bowl.

4. Roll out the dough thinly. Line a rectangular baking tin (with a removable base) with baking paper. Line the bottom and the sides of the tin with the dough. Prick the dough to allow steam to escape.

5. Preheat the oven to 170°C.

Filling:

6. Break the 4 eggs into a mixing bowl. Add the sunflower oil, the sugar, cinnamon, and grated lemon peel. Mix thoroughly and put aside.

7. Spread 200 g of angel hair on the dough in the baking tin, then 100 g of the ground almonds, followed by half of the egg mix.

8. Repeat with another layer using the remainder of the angel hair, the last 100 g of ground almonds and then what is left of the egg mix.

9. Sprinkle with plenty of sugar and almond flakes to decorate.

10. Bake for 60 minutes at 170°C.

11. Remove from the oven when baked and allow to cool before serving.

FILLOAS DE GALICIA

Galician Crêpes

Filloas de Galicia is Galicia's own answer to the crêpe. They have an infinite number of fillings, sweet or savoury, and are always welcome at any table. Traditionally, they were baked on very hot smooth granite rocks. They are believed to have a Celtic origin. They are normally eaten at carnival time but also at other religious festivals such as Christmas. In some areas, they are eaten with ham or cheese or as a plain accompaniment to a stew. One savoury version uses chicken stock instead of milk. However, they are always a popular dessert.

There are many delicious fillings for filloas, including the following: Apple compote with cinnamon, honey, chestnut purée, quince jam or chocolate (there are many more).

Ingredients:

> 6 eggs
> 500 g flour
> 1 litre milk
> 1 piece of lard or butter
> Pinch of salt

Preparation:

1. Beat the eggs with the milk in a large bowl, adding a pinch of salt and gradually adding the flour until it is well mixed. Allow the mixture to rest.

2. Grease a non-stick frying pan with some lard or butter.

3. Put the frying pan on medium heat and pour in some batter to cover the bottom of the pan.

4. When the filloa has solidified and browned a little, turn it over to brown the other side.

5. Repeat until there is no more mixture.

6. Serve with a sweet filling of your choice.

FLAÓ DE IBIZA

Cheese and Peppermint Flan of Ibiza

This cheese flan is very typical of the traditional cuisine of the islands of Ibiza and Formentera and traditionally prepared on Easter Sunday.

The recipe originates in the Middle Ages and it is often associated with the rural traditions of the many goatherds' and shepherds' families of the islands. During the Easter period when there is an abundance of eggs, fresh cheese and wild mint, it was (and is) a traditional seasonal dish.

These days, Flaó is so popular that it can be found at any time of year as a dessert in most restaurants and cafés. The combination of goat's cheese and mint makes for a delicious and refreshing taste.

Ingredients:

For the base:

> 500 g flour
> 1 tablespoon of lard (or margarine)
> 3 eggs
> 200 g sugar
> 1 tablespoon of baking powder
> 2 tablespoons of anís liquor

For the filling:

> 500 g fresh goat's cheese
> 4 eggs
> 375 g of sugar
> 10 mint leaves

Preparation:

For the base:

1. Beat the 3 eggs and sugar together.

2. Add the remaining ingredients and knead together.

3. Let the dough stand for 15 minutes.

For the filling and pie:

4. Beat the 4 eggs and sugar together.

5. Add the finely crumbled cheese. Mix well.

6. Add 6 mint leaves (finely chopped). You can add more mint if you like the taste.

7. Roll out the dough with a rolling pin on a floured work surface.

8. Grease a baking tin and cover it with the dough.

9. Pour the filling mix onto the dough.

10. Bake the flan in a preheated oven at 180ºC for 50 minutes.

11. Allow the flan to cool, sprinkle with sugar and serve

12. As decoration, place 4 mint leaves in the centre.

FRIXUELOS ASTURIANOS

Asturian Anís Crêpes

This recipe is for a very traditional Asturian crêpe. These are anís-flavoured pancakes, usually served dusted with sugar, although there are several variations. In some districts, the crêpes are coated with honey or filled with cream and more traditionally with applesauce. They are often served as a dessert after lunch or dinner but you may also find them served with breakfast.

Ingredients:

> 250 ml milk
> 100 g flour
> 2 eggs
> 1 heaped tablespoon of sugar
> Pinch of salt
> Grated lemon or orange peel
> 1 tablespoon of anís liquor

Preparation:

1. Beat the eggs in a bowl with the milk and sugar and gradually add the flour. Ensure that it is very well mixed and smooth. A good pancake batter is not too thin and not too thick.

2. Add the grated orange or lemon peel and the anís liquor and let the batter rest in a cool place for half an hour.

3. Put a thin layer of mild olive oil in a non-stick frying pan and heat until its hot enough for frying. Pour a thin layer of batter into the pan and fry, turning the crêpe over carefully to fry both sides. When browned, place on a plate in a pile to keep them warm.

4. Serve the crêpes with a filling of your choice or just sprinkled with sugar.

GAÑOTES DE ALJARAFE, SEVILLA

Wine and Anís Fritters of Aljarafe, Sevilla

Gañotes are a traditional fritter of Aljarafe in Sevilla. They are served as a sweet dessert course.

Fried sweet batter has Moorish and Jewish origins and is still very popular in Spain, especially in Andalucía. Look at "pestiños" to see similar recipes from another part of southern Spain, which is a doughier version of the gañote.

Ingredients:

> 2 whole eggs
> 6 tablespoons of mild olive oil
> 3 tablespoons of white wine
> 1.5 tablespoons of anís liquor
> 500 g pastry flour
> Sugar and cinnamon to coat
> Grated peel of 1 lemon or orange
> Olive oil for frying

Preparation:

1. Break the eggs into a bowl, beat well and then add the other ingredients, apart from the flour. Mix thoroughly.

2. Add the flour until you have created a smooth, uniform dough that does not stick to your hands. Let the dough rest for half an hour.

3. Put some olive oil in a frying pan to deep-fry the fritters. Heat the oil until it is ready to fry.

4. Cut off small portions of dough (about the size of a ping-pong ball) and flatten them with a rolling pin until very thin. Roll up the thin pastry circles and then use a fork to fry the pastry in the hot oil. Be careful, they burn easily, being very thin.

5. Put the fried fritters on a plate on some kitchen paper and then coat them with a mixture of sugar and cinnamon powder.

6. Allow to cool before serving.

GREIXONERA DE IBIZA

Cinnamon Bread Pudding of Ibiza

Greixonera is a typical sweet cake of the island of Ibiza. The greixonera is actually the name for the earthenware dish in which the cake is made, although it can be made in a conventional cake tin.

Greixonera is a bread pudding minus fruit and uses the popular ensaimadas cakes (leftovers from the previous day) but any similar sweet bread works fine, such as hot cross buns. Some recipes add a little anís liquor to taste. This is a very simple dish to prepare and is often eaten as a sweet with cream or ice cream or just as it is.

Ingredients:

1 litre of milk
4 ensaimadas from the previous day
8 medium eggs
Peel of 1 lemon
400 g sugar (brown or white, to your taste)
1 cinnamon stick
Cinnamon powder and brown sugar for decoration
Half a shot of sweet anís

Preparation:

1. Boil the milk whilst mixing in 300 g of the sugar, the lemon peel and cinnamon. Once boiled, allow it to cool and then remove the cinnamon stick and lemon peel.

2. In a separate bowl, beat the eggs, break up the ensaimadas (does not need to be in very small pieces) and add the half glass of anís liquor. When these ingredients are mixed, add the cooled milk and mix everything well.

3. Select a baking tin and caramelise 100 g of sugar in it. When done, add the milk and ensaimada mixture to the baking tin.

4. Preheat the oven to 180°C.

5. Bake the pudding for about 45 minutes or until baked. Allow it to cool before removing from the baking tin.

6. Sprinkle a little cinnamon powder and/or brown sugar over the pudding and allow it to cool completely before serving.

HUESOS DE SAN EXPEDITO

The Bones of Saint Expeditus (and others)

Saint Expeditus was a Roman centurion in Armenia who was martyred in what is now Turkey because he converted to Christianity around April 303. The Roman Catholic Church commemorates him on 19 April. The connection with this sweet is not quite clear but these sweet rolls are supposed to represent his bones.

Traditionally, these sweets are eaten in Sevilla during the huge festivities surrounding Semana Santa (Holy Week) but they are also popular throughout Spain at other times of year as a sweet dessert after lunch. Several convents in Andalucía still make and sell this delicious, rich pastry.

In fact, very many "saints' bones" recipes originate in the many convents in Spain. For instance, another dessert known as "Huesos de San Froilán" is, in truth, almost identical to the recipe for the "Huesos de San Expedito" and indeed quite a lot of other "saints' bones" recipes. There are many, many variants, most of which are cylindrical, and contain a rich filling, often made with egg yolk and plenty of sugar. In the case of Saint Froilán, he was a 9th century hermit, monk and later bishop in León in Northern Spain. He was very much revered in his time and considered very holy. León still celebrates a weeklong fiesta in October in honour of San Froilán. His bones are revered in culinary circles!

Ingredients:

> 250 g of flour
> 1 teaspoon of baking powder
> 1 egg
> 1 egg yolk
> 2 tablespoons of sugar
> 5 teaspoons of anís liquor
> Olive oil
> 50 g icing sugar

Preparation:

1. Mix the baking powder and flour in a bowl. Add the egg, the egg yolk, sugar, anís and 2 tablespoons of oil. Mix and knead the ingredients into a consistent dough. Shape into a ball, cover with a cloth and allow the dough to sit for 30 minutes.

2. Take pieces of dough and roll them tightly to form long cylinders about the thickness of a finger, and then cut into 6 cm sections to form the "huesos" (bones) and make a cut along one side.

3. Pour plenty of olive oil in a deep frying pan and warm it up. When the oil is warm (not hot), place the huesos in the oil and fry them well on all sides. When golden brown, take them out of the oil and place them on kitchen paper to drain the excess oil.

4. Coat the huesos in icing sugar or honey.

HUESILLOS DE EXTREMADURA

Little Bone Fritters of Extremadura

This is a very traditional dish from the region of Extremadura. These fritters are traditionally made on All Saints' Day and again during Carnival, Lent and Easter. The slightly sinister name (huesillos = little bones) and bone shape of the fritter is testament to the sometimes dark sense of humour of the Spanish, where few subjects are taboo including death and human bones! When the huesillos are fried, they grow and open slightly to resemble a bone.

There are many fried dough sweets in southern Spain and the origin of sweet, fried doughs is firmly linked to Moorish and Sephardic culinary traditions, still fully alive and flourishing in the Levant.

Huesillos are eaten both as a dessert and as an accompaniment to a coffee.

Ingredients:

> 500 g flour
> 125 g sugar
> 2 medium-sized eggs
> 100 ml mild olive oil
> 100 ml whole milk
> Grated peel of1 lemon
> 1 teaspoonful of ground aniseed
> 8 g baking powder
> 1 lemon peel
> 1 orange peel
> Sunflower or light olive oil for frying
> Sugar to decorate

Preparation:

1. In a frying pan, heat the olive oil with a strip of orange peel and another strip of lemon peel. Let the skins fry for 2 or 3 minutes and then turn off the heat. Allow the oil to cool somewhat.

2. Thoroughly mix the eggs, oil, milk, sugar and aniseed in a bowl.

3. Add the flour, baking powder and grated lemon peel. Mix well using a fork.

4. Place the dough onto a work surface. Knead until the mixture has turned into a consistent dough.

5. Prepare a deep frying pan with plenty of oil on a moderate heat.

6. Oil your hands slightly and then take out portions of dough of about 25 g. Form into rolls of about 15 cm in length.

7. When the oil is hot, place the huesillos into the oil to fry. Take care not to fry at too high a temperature because it is important for the inside to be cooked as well as the outside.

8. When the fritters are golden brown, remove them from the oil and place them on some kitchen paper to absorb the excess oil. Finally, roll them in sugar to coat.

9. Allow to cool before serving.

HUESOS DE SANTO

Saint's Bones - Filled Marzipan of All Saints' Day

There was apparently no limit to the inventiveness of the baking nuns when it came to bones of the church's saints. Here is another "saints' bones" recipe from Northern Spain.

This time, it is a marzipan roll filled with an egg and sugar filling that is a particular favourite for All Saints' Day (1st of November) coinciding with the end of the almond harvest.

This popular dessert and sweet is thought to have originated in the region of Castilla y León in the early 17th century. It gets its name from the fact that the sweet looks like a bone and given that it is eaten on All Saints' Day, it has acquired the name of Saint's Bone. They are now popular throughout Spain and many bakeries make them by hand especially for this religious festival. Some modern versions use angel hair, jam or chocolate.

The filling is traditionally rolled into the marzipan but this is quite fiddly. An easier solution is to first make the tubes of marzipan and then use a pastry bag to fill the marzipan tubes at each end.

Ingredients:

Marzipan:

> 125 g ground almonds, raw, skinned
> 100 g granulated sugar
> 50 ml water

Filling:

> 50 g granulated sugar
> 2 egg yolks
> 25 ml water

Preparation:

1. You can grind your own blanched almonds into fine flour or buy finely ground almond flour.

2. Pour the water and sugar into a medium-sized saucepan. Put on a high heat and bring to the boil while stirring until the sugar has dissolved.

3. Remove the pan from the heat and stir in the ground almonds. Set aside to cool.

4. When cool to the touch, put the mixture into the refrigerator to chill for 30 minutes. This will make the marzipan less sticky and easier to work.

5. Remove the marzipan from the fridge. Dust a work surface generously with caster sugar. Place the marzipan on the surface and dust the top with sugar.

6. Roll out the marzipan to around half a cm in thickness using a rolling pin. Cut into squares of about 6 x 6 cm.

7. Use the handle of a wooden spoon or something similar to create the marzipan tubes by wrapping the marzipan squares around the handle. Press the ends of the marzipan together to seal. Carefully remove each tube from the wooden handle, and place them on a sheet of baking paper.

8. To prepare the filling: pour water and sugar into a small saucepan and bring to the boil to form a syrup.

9. At the same time, break the eggs and place the egg yolks into a heatproof bowl. Whisk thoroughly. Slowly pour the syrup into the beaten eggs while whisking.

10. When mixed, transfer the bowl to a double boiler (Au bain Marie). Continue to stir the filling until it becomes very thick.

11. Spoon the filling into a pastry bag. Squeeze the filling into each marzipan tube, one by one, from each end.

12. Use a fork to score the marzipan to create decorative ridges. Allow to cool before serving.

LECHE FRITA

Fried Milk Pudding

Leche frita (translated as "fried milk") is actually a firm milk pudding that is coated with a warm, crunchy fried shell of flour and egg.

Leche frita is one of Spain's most popular desserts and is found in every region in the country in all grades of restaurants and cafés. It is served hot or cold.

Ingredients:

> 60 g flour (half is used to coat the leche frita before frying)
> 28 g corn starch
> 110 g sugar
> 950 ml whole milk
> 1 cinnamon stick
> 2 eggs
> 60 ml olive oil
> 28 g butter
> Cinnamon powder for decoration

Preparation:

1. Put the sugar, the corn starch and half the flour together in a large bowl. Add one cup of milk and whisk well. Leave to thicken for 10 minutes.

2. Heat the remainder of the milk with the cinnamon stick in a saucepan over medium-low heat.

3. When the milk begins to boil, strain it little by little into the sugar and flour mixture, stirring well.

4. Pour the sugar, flour, and milk mixture back into the saucepan and put it on a low heat, again stirring well, for 10 minutes.

5. Oil a 28 cm x 18 cm glass baking dish with olive oil. You can also use a smaller oven dish to increase the depth of the leche frita to a minimum of 2 cm. If it is too thin, it is more difficult to cut and to fry.

6. Pour in the leche frita mixture to a depth of 2 cm (you can use two baking dishes if you have enough of the mixture).

7. Leave to cool in the fridge, ideally overnight.

8. After cooling, run a knife around the edge of the leche frita to ensure it is not sticking and very quickly turn it out.

9. Cut the leche frita into 6 cm squares.

10. Pour the olive oil in a frying pan to a depth of about 0.5 cm and put on a medium heat. Add the butter.

11. Beat the eggs together. Coat each of the squares of leche frita in the other half of the flour then dip in the beaten egg, and fry in the hot oil for approximately 1 minute on each side, until very lightly golden.

12. When fried, sieve powdered cinnamon over the leche frita and serve immediately, or allow it to cool and serve.

PANECICOS DULCES DE HELLÍN

Cinnamon Fritters of Hellín, Albacete

This is a cinnamon-flavoured fritter from Hellín close to the town of Albacete, Castilla-La Mancha. It is also found in parts of Murcia. Although it is a typical Easter dish, it originated in Arabic times when many fried doughs were popular. The fritters are served marinated in citrus flavoured syrup.

Such rich dishes were a great treat to poor people in earlier times and only afforded during important religious festivals. Nowadays, panecicos are a popular dessert.

Ingredients:

> 2 eggs
> 1 egg white
> 50 g breadcrumbs
> 500 ml water
> 1 cinnamon stick
> 2 cloves
> 250 g sugar
> Peel of 1 lemon (avoid the bitter white pith)
> Peel of 1 orange (avoid the bitter white pith)
> Olive oil for frying

Preparation:

1. Beat the eggs and the egg white until they begin to stiffen.

2. Add the breadcrumbs and mix until you have a soft paste.

3. Allow the mixture to stand for 5 minutes until the egg has been absorbed by the breadcrumbs and becomes a more solid dough.

4. Put a frying pan on the heat with plenty of olive oil.

5. When the oil is hot, place spoonfuls of the dough into the hot oil and fry them until golden brown. Remove the fritters from the pan and put them on absorbent kitchen paper to dry.

6. To prepare the syrup, put the water, sugar, cloves, and the cinnamon stick, orange and lemon peel in a saucepan and let it boil for around 15 minutes until a light syrup forms.

7. Place the fritters into the syrup and heat them over a low heat for about 20 minutes.

8. Allow the fritters to cool and absorb the syrup. Leaving them overnight is even better. They can be kept in the fridge for several days without any problem.

PAN DE CALATRAVA, MURCIA

Murcian Bread Pudding

This simple cold dessert is found in many rural parts of Murcia. It has now established itself as a classical Spanish dessert. It is made with leftover bread, rolls, biscuits or other cake with some added ingredients to turn waste into something delicious. There are many such imaginative recipes to be found in rural Spain, where food is rarely wasted, especially during hard times.

This recipe is popular during Easter week and a version is often served as a dessert in many a Murcian restaurant.

Ingredients:

> 1 litre milk
> 300 g sugar
> 150 g old biscuits, dry bread, sponge or other sweet cake
> 50 g grated or coarsely ground almonds
> 1 glass of brandy
> 1 cinnamon stick
> 1 lemon peel
> 6 eggs

Preparation:

1. Preheat the oven to about 160°C.

2. Line a rectangular cake tin with aluminium foil and a layer of baking paper to keep the pudding dry during its baking in a double boiler (au bain marie).

3. Next, make the caramelised sugar that is used at the bottom of the baking tin. To do this, put half of the sugar (150 g) in a saucepan and heat it until it starts to caramelise, stirring all the time to prevent burning. Coat the bottom of the cake tin evenly with this caramel.

4. Put the milk in another saucepan and heat it together with the cinnamon stick, lemon peel and the rest of the sugar (150 g). Bring to the boil. Meanwhile beat the eggs together.

5. Sieve the milk to remove cinnamon and lemon and then add the milk to the beaten eggs in a bowl. Continue beating until all is well mixed.

6. Chop up and crumble the dried bread, cake, rolls etc. Fill the cake tin with the crumbs. Coat the crumbs with the grated almonds and then pour a glass of brandy over all of this.

7. Evenly pour the mixture of milk and eggs into the cake tin. The entire contents of the tin need to be saturated with this mixture.

8. Cover the top of the cake tin with a sheet of aluminium foil as a lid. Prepare a bain-marie in the oven: In a large deep ovenproof bowl or deep oven tray, put 2 or 3 cm of water to act as a double boiler. Place the cake tin into the bain-marie and leave it in the oven for about 45 minutes.

9. Take the cake tin from the oven and wait for it to cool completely.

10. Remove the pudding from the tin. Decorate it with fresh fruit according to your taste. (You can also add candied fruit to the cake before you put it in the oven).

11. Allow the pudding to cool down further in the fridge overnight before serving.

PANTXINETA / PANCHINETA DE PAÍS VASCO

Cream and Almond Pastry of the Basque Country

The panchineta (or in Basque "Pantxineta") is a typical sweet pastry from the Basque Country. It is generally served as a sweet course and may be served cold or lukewarm. It is based on puff pastry with baker's cream and topped with almond and sugar.

The pantxineta was invented in the early twentieth century in the provincial capital of San Sebastian by the grocers, bakers and confectioners Otaegui. At the time San Sebastian was a royal resort frequented by many wealthy people especially those fleeing to Spain from the First World War in France. Many of these wealthy patrons brought their own chefs with them and the pantxineta has both French and Spanish culinary influences. The House of Otaegui still exists more than one hundred years later and is still famous for its pantxineta.

Ingredients:

For the pastry and topping:

> A sheet of puff pastry
> 50 g flaked almonds
> Icing sugar

For the pastry cream:

> 40 g flour
> 40 g corn starch
> 250 ml milk
> 40 g sugar
> 4 egg yolks
> 1 vanilla pod

Preparation:

For the pastry cream:

1. Mix the flour and the corn starch in a saucepan with the egg yolks and a little milk.

2. Boil the rest of the milk with the vanilla, remove the vanilla pod and pour the milk over the egg mixture. Cook over a low heat, stirring constantly for 4 minutes.

For the pastry:

3. Preheat the oven to between 160°C and 180°C.

4. Line the bottom and side of a round pie tin with a sheet of puff pastry and bake it in the oven until it begins to brown.

5. Remove the pie tin from the oven, coat the pastry with the cream and cover the surface with sliced almonds. Some recipes suggest a second sheet of puff pastry and then the sliced almonds.

6. Put the pie back in the oven and bake until the almonds start to brown.

7. Remove the pie from the oven and sprinkle it with icing sugar.

8. Serve cold or slightly warm.

PAPARAJOTES DE MURCIA

Lemon Leaf Fritters of Murcia

Paparajotes are a typical dessert from the region of Murcia but is hardly known outside Murcia. It is delicious and easy to prepare if you have access to a lemon tree, which many people in southern Spain do, of course. It is economical and nutritious and is thought to have originated in the early Middle Ages in southern Spain during the Moorish period. The lemon leaves themselves are for flavour only and are not eaten. If you cannot find lemon leaves, you can use slices of lemon peel.

Ingredients:

500 ml milk
500 ml water
6 medium eggs
700 g flour
Grated peel of 1 lemon
Cinnamon powder
100 g sugar
Lemon leaves (only use the young, bright green leaves)
Icing sugar
Olive oil

Preparation:

1. Separate the egg whites and yolks. Whisk four egg whites until they begin to stiffen.

2. Mix the milk and water in a bowl. Beat in the egg yolks one at a time.

3. Continue whisking whilst adding the flour in spoonfuls. Add the grated lemon peel, a couple of teaspoons of cinnamon powder and the egg whites. Continue to whisk until you obtain a consistent mix. Leave it to stand for 30 minutes.

4. Heat about 3 cm of olive oil in a deep frying pan. The paparajotes need to be fully immersed in the oil to fry properly.

5. Take clean, fresh lemon leaves. Dip each leaf in the batter so that it is completely coated. Fry in the hot oil for a few seconds until the batter is golden brown. Do the same for each leaf.

6. When fried, place each fritter on absorbent kitchen paper to drain the excess oil.

7. Sprinkle the fritters with icing sugar and cinnamon powder to your taste and serve.

PASTISSETS - TORTAS DE ALMA - RUBIOL

Sweet Pasties of Cataluña

These pasties are sweet empanadillas and are typical of Cataluña, Aragón, Valencia and Mallorca. In Cataluña, they are called Pastissets, Flaons or Casquetes. In Aragón, they are referred to as Tortas de Alma ("Soul Pies"). In Mallorca, they are often called Rubiol.

They are all semi-circular pasty-shaped cakes filled with various sweet mixtures and are then fried or baked. The contents may include angel hair, sweet potato jam, or almond mixtures and they may be flavoured with Moscatel wine or anís liquor. After frying or baking, they are coated with sugar.

Here we give the most basic traditional version of this recipe with angel hair baked in the oven.

Ingredients (for 12 pasties):

> 500 g flour
> 200 ml olive oil
> 50 ml Moscatel
> 50 ml sweet anís liquor
> 300 g angel hair
> 1 teaspoon of cinnamon powder
> Sugar for coating

Preparation:

1. Preheat the oven to 180°C.

2. Put the olive oil, Moscatel, anís and cinnamon powder into a bowl and mix.

3. Sift the flour and add it to the mix. When fully combined, remove the dough and knead on a work surface.

4. Divide the dough into portions of approximately 50 g each. Mould these portions into balls.

5. Place each ball on a sheet of baking paper and place a second sheet of baking paper on top. Roll out the balls of dough into circles.

6. In the centre of each circular piece of dough, place a portion of angel hair. Using the baking paper, fold the dough over the filling into a

semi-circle and then seal the edges of the pasty with your fingers as you would with a pasty or empanadilla.

7. When sealed, place the pasties into a baking tray lined with baking paper.

8. Bake at 180°C with heat from top and bottom for about 20 minutes.

9. When baked, remove them from the oven. Sprinkle with some anís liquor and coat the tops with sugar. Allow to cool before serving.

QUESADA ASTURIANA

Asturian Cheesecake

This Asturian dessert recipe is very similar to the "Quesada Pasiega de Cantabria" (Cantabrian cheesecake). The regions are neighbours and have similar climates and agricultural produce (including many dairy products and some excellent cheeses) so obviously they share many traditional recipes. This recipe is made using fresh goat's cheese but ricotta can be used instead.

The Quesada Asturiana is eaten as a sweet after dinner but also during merienda with coffee.

Ingredients (6-8 servings):

> 300 g granulated sugar
> 115 g butter at room temperature
> 1000 g requeson cheese (ricotta)
> 250 g flour
> Grated peel of 1 lemon
> 2 eggs
> 1 shot of brandy
> Pinch of cinnamon powder
> Icing sugar and / or fresh fruit for decoration

Preparation:

1. Preheat the oven to 190°C

2. Grease the bottom and sides of a round glass baking dish (about 24 cm diameter).

3. Put the requeson together with the sugar in a large bowl and mix thoroughly. Add the eggs and the softened butter and beat together.

4. Add the grated lemon peel, cinnamon and brandy and continue to mix. Whilst beating, gradually add in the flour. Continue mixing until the dough begins to thicken. Pour the mix into the baking tin.

5. Bake for approximately 30 minutes or until the quesada turns a golden colour at the edges.

6. Remove from the oven and allow to cool before serving.

7. Decorate by sprinkling icing sugar and putting some fresh fruit on top.

QUESADA PASIEGA DE CANTABRIA

Cantabrian Cheesecake

Quesada Pasiega is a typical dessert dish of the Pasiegos valleys (Valles Pasiegos) which is a region of Cantabria. In particular, this cheesecake is found in the villages of Vega de Pas, Selaya, Villacarriedo and Alceda-Ontaneda and is probably the most famous and emblematic dessert dish of Cantabria.

It is traditionally made with curdled cow's milk (fresh pasiego cheese). The fresh pasiego cheese is hard to find outside of Cantabria, so this recipe uses yogurt as a substitute.

If you want to make the cake a little more aromatic, you can add some grated lemon peel and/or a pinch of cinnamon to the mixture. The lemon version is known as "Quesada de limón" (lemon cheesecake).

Ingredients (24 cm diameter cake tin):

2 eggs
1 natural yogurt
80 g butter
150 g flour
450 ml milk
150 g sugar

Preparation:

1. Preheat the oven to 180°C. Grease a 24 cm cake tin with butter.

2. Warm the butter until it melts.

3. Use a large bowl and mix the melted butter with the eggs, yogurt, flour, milk and sugar. Mix thoroughly. Pour the mixture into the cake tin.

4. Bake for 50 minutes at 180°C. Check to see if it is baked by piercing with a cocktail stick. If it comes out dry then the cheesecake is baked.

5. Allow the cheesecake to cool and then remove from the mould.

6. It can be served cold or slightly warm.

RUBIOLS DE BALEARES

Sweet Easter Pasties of Mallorca

This is a traditional Easter week pasty (empanadilla) from Mallorca although it is now available at other times of the year. There are quite a few variations. These include fillings with requesón cheese, angel hair or quince jam. The following recipe makes both requesón cheese and angel hair fillings in the same batch.

Ingredients (for 36 rubiols):

For the dough:

> 1 kg pastry flour
> 100 g icing sugar
> 2 egg yolks
> 200 ml olive oil
> 200 ml orange juice
> 150 ml water
> 200 g butter at room temperature
> Grated lemon peel

For the fillings:

> Filling 1: 0.5 kg angel hair
> Filling 2: 0.5 kg cottage cheese (ricotta), mixed with 200 g sugar, grated lemon peel and 1 egg yolk

Preparation:

1. Put all the dough ingredients into a large bowl, mix well and knead until they form a smooth, consistent dough. Wrap the dough in shrink wrap and put in the fridge for at least half an hour.

2. Remove the dough from the fridge. Take portions of dough and roll them out. Use a pastry cutter to cut out round pasty sized pieces of dough. You are aiming to make 36 rubiols, more or less (you can weigh the dough and divide it by weight).

3. In the centre of each piece of cut dough, place one tablespoon of the filling (angel hair or cheese). Fold and seal the edges of the rubiols by lightly pressing the edges with a fork (or with your fingers).

4. Bake in a preheated oven at 180°C for thirty to forty minutes until golden brown. Allow them to cool and sprinkle them with icing sugar. Serve warm or cold.

TORRIJA DE CANTABRIA
Dipped Toast of Cantabria

Torrijas or dipped toast is very similar to so-called "French toast", but the Spanish version has reached a new level of variation. Traditionally, it was a way of using up old bread and it was eaten by the workers as a cheap but tasty, high-protein and high-energy food. The torrija appears to have been mentioned for the first time in the fifteenth century by Juan del Encina with his list of ingredients as "honey and many eggs to make French toast", and it is described as a dish suitable for "recovery in labour". The first recipes date back to the "Book of Cozina" by Domingo Hernandez de Maceras in 1607 and "Art Cozina" by Francisco Martinez Motiño in 1611. In the early twentieth century, torrijas were very common in the taverns of Madrid, served with glasses of wine.

Over the centuries, torrijas became synonymous with Lent and Easter in most of Spain, when they are eaten as part of the tradition of abstinence from meat during Lent and on other fast days. However, torrijas are so popular, that many bakeries make and sell torrijas all year round and even keep stale bread to sell to customers wanting to make their own!

Only in Cantabria have they also become a traditional Christmas sweet. Here we present the Cantabrian torrija, which is really a richer (and sometimes alcoholic) version of the normal torrija. Any kind of stale bread may be used to make torrijas, but in modern Spain, most people use slices of baguette.

One particular version of this dish is called "Torrija del Vino" which uses Moscatel wine instead of milk. Another version adds a shot (or two) of rum to the milk ("Torrija de Ron y Canela").

Ingredients:

> 1 baguette (from yesterday)
> 500 ml of milk
> 250 g sugar (or honey)
> 1 cinnamon stick
> Cinnamon powder and icing sugar
> Peel from half an orange
> 2 eggs
> Olive oil and butter for frying

Preparation:

1. Boil the milk with the cinnamon stick, the sugar (or honey) and the orange peel for a few minutes.

2. Slice the baguette, but not too thinly. Beat a couple of eggs in a bowl.

3. Dip the slices of bread in the milk and sugar mixture, drain them and then coat them in the beaten egg.

4. In a frying pan, heat a little butter and some olive oil.

5. Fry the dipped slices of bread in the hot oil until golden brown.

6. Sometimes a little brandy is dribbled onto the torrijas to prepare them for serving. Coat them lightly with a mixture of cinnamon powder and icing sugar.

TORRIJA DE PASTOR

Dipped Toast of the Convent

Torrija de Pastor is a little known variant of the Torrija. The torrija was first documented in the famous monastic recipe book - "Recetario de Sor María Isabel. Los dulces de las monjas" ("Recipes of Sr. María Isabel - The sweets of the nuns").

This is a popular, cheap and simple recipe, produced in several convents to be sold or given to the poor of the neighbourhood. It is economical to produce because it uses up stale bread. Many supermarkets sell bread specially for making torrijas in the days coming up to Easter Week.

Ingredients: (For about 12 torrijas)

12 slices dry bread
A handful of walnuts
125 g honey
1 glass of water
2 large eggs
Olive oil for frying
Sugar and cinnamon to decorate

Preparation:

1. Peel and chop the walnuts. Push the nuts into the slices of bread. Put aside.

2. Heat the honey with the water in a saucepan until it boils and then let it cool.

3. Soak the slices of bread in the honey syrup on one side only. Place the slices on their dry side on a rack, cover with a clean cloth and leave them overnight.

4. Next day dip the slices in the beaten eggs and then fry in plenty of oil.

5. When they are golden brown, let them cool and drain on absorbent kitchen paper.

6. Coat with sugar and cinnamon and pour on a little honey.

7. Serve cold.

TARTA BORRACHA DE LOS PADRES MINIMOS DE VERA

Drunken Tart of Vera, Almería

Vera is an old coastal town in Almería. The tarta borracha is one of the town's most famous cakes. The name "de los Padres Minimos" refers to the monastic order that was once famous for producing the cake. The religious order, in English, is known as the "Order of Minims". The order spread throughout Europe and was well known for being the brewers of Munich's famous Paulaner beers despite their extremely strict rules on fasting and personal abstinence. As you will see, there is not much abstinence in this cake!

The "Padres Minimos" ran a monastery in Vera until 1823 when it was closed, but the recipe has survived them. It is a bit complicated to make but definitely worth the trouble. It is usually eaten as a (very rich) dessert.

Ingredients:

Sponge:

      8 eggs
      200 g flour
      200 g sugar
      1 dessert spoon of grated lemon peel

Filling and Syrup:

      1 litre milk
      165 g flour
      3 eggs
      1 cinnamon stick
      1 grated lemon peel
      1 grated orange peel
      300 g of angel hair
      500 ml water
      250 ml rum
      100 g of sugar

Chocolate:

      125 g cooking chocolate
      100 g icing sugar
      60 g butter

4 tablespoons of water
1 grated lemon peel
1 cinnamon stick

Preparation:

<u>Sponge:</u>

1. Separate the egg whites from the yolks.

2. Beat the egg whites with half of the sugar until stiff.

3. Beat the egg yolks with the rest of the sugar until it starts to expand.

4. Blend the two egg mixtures together slowly, using a flexible spatula. Then gradually add the sifted flour and the grated lemon peel, continuing to stir gently.

5. When completely mixed, pour the sponge batter into a shallow baking tray that has been greased with butter on which a little flour has been shaken.

6. Bake in a preheated oven at 180°C for 30 minutes.

<u>Filling and Syrup:</u>

7. Heat the milk in a saucepan with the cinnamon stick and the lemon and orange peel until the milk starts to boil Remove from the heat and put aside for a moment.

8. Whisk the eggs with the sugar and flour.

9. Sieve the milk and gradually add it to the mixture. Beat well.

10. Put this mixture on a low heat and keep stirring until it starts to thicken. Remove from the heat. When it is cooled, add the angel hair, mix thoroughly, and put aside.

11. Prepare a traditional syrup by bringing an equal amount of water and sugar to the boil and then put aside to cool.

<u>Chocolate topping:</u>

12. Melt the chocolate in a bain-marie (double boiler). When it has melted, add the icing sugar, whilst stirring continuously, then add and mix in the softened butter.

13. When all the ingredients are well blended remove from the heat and mix in two tablespoons of cold water.

<u>Final preparation:</u>

14. Cut the sponge into three layers. Coat each layer with syrup. In between layers spread the filling and then coat the layers again with syrup and rum.

15. Finally, on top of the sponge pour a coating of the chocolate sauce. You can optionally decorate it with some almond slices. Place the cake in the fridge to cool thoroughly to make it easier to cut. Serve the cake cold.

TARTA DE CÍTRICOS CON MIEL DE ROMERO DE CÚTAR

Citrus Tart with Rosemary Honey of Cútar

This cake contains all the flavours of the Axarquía region in Málaga province. It incorporates many typical sweet Arabic confectionery items like dried fruits and honey.

Cútar is a charming village of Arab origin. During the "Monfí Festival" in October, the town returns to its Moorish roots and the streets are filled with music, souks and traditional Arab foods, including this tart.

Ingredients:

> 300 g flour
> 250 g Muscatel raisins
> 150 g candied cherries
> 150 g prunes
> 200 g dried apricots
> Grated peel of an orange, a lemon and a grapefruit
> 220 g butter
> 150 g rosemary honey of the Axarquía
> 50 ml orange liqueur (cointreau)
> 25 ml orange juice
> 25 ml lemon juice
> 25 ml grapefruit juice
> 4 eggs
> 2 egg yolks
> 200 g sugar

For the topping:

> 250 g white chocolate
> 150 g of rosemary honey
> 50 g of cream

Preparation:

1. Put the raisins, cherries, prunes, apricots, citrus peels, cointreau, and juices into a container. Let them marinate overnight in the fridge.

2. Mix the flour, butter, honey, eggs, egg yolks and sugar, stirring vigorously with a spatula.

3. Add the dried fruits with their marinade, mix and form the dough.

3. Pour a layer of about 2 to 3cm of the dough mix into a rectangular baking tin. Bake at 160°C for about 50 minutes. Leave to cool.

4. To make the topping: Put the cream with the honey in a saucepan and warm the mix without boiling. Remove from the heat and add in the chopped chocolate. Stir to melt the chocolate completely. Place in the refrigerator and stir occasionally until the mixture has the consistency needed to coat the top of the cake.

5. Serve each slice of cake topped with slices of orange, mandarin, grapefruit.

TORTA DE ALMENDRAS Y CHOCOLATE DE TOTALÁN

Almond and Chocolate Tart of Totalán

In the village of Totalán in Málaga province, almonds are an important agricultural product and the main ingredient in many of the local traditional recipes. These can be tasted in the village's baking competition during the village's cultural festival in the first week of October, or during the "Feria de Chanfaina" held on the last Sunday of November. Here is one such almond dish that is typical of the village.

Ingredients:

> 300 g almonds
> 250 g butter (at room temperature)
> 250 g sugar
> 125 g chocolate for coating
> 5 whole eggs
> Vanilla essence
> Icing sugar
> Vanilla ice cream
> Red fruit syrup

Preparation:

1. Very finely chop the almonds - almost to a powder - and put aside. Chop the chocolate into small pieces and put aside

2. Beat the butter with the sugar into a mix with a creamy consistency. Separate the egg yolks from the whites and, one by one, stir the egg yolks into the mix, making sure to blend in each yolk fully before adding the next one.

3. Add the chopped almonds, the chopped chocolate and the vanilla flavouring to the mix.

4. Whisk the egg whites until they are stiff and, with a spatula, gently fold them into the mixture.

5. Grease a cake tin of 25 cm diameter. You can also use several smaller cake tins. Pour in the dough.

6. Bake the tart in a preheated oven at 180°C for 30 to 40 minutes.

7. Sprinkle with icing sugar and serve with a scoop of vanilla ice cream and some red fruit syrup.

TORTILLITAS CON MIEL DE CAÑA DE NERJA

Pancakes with Cane Syrup of Nerja

This is a simple pancake served with the famous molasses of Nerja in Málaga province. The area boasts the first and last remaining sugar cane plantations of Europe and its molasses (known as "Miel de Caña") is famous and delicious.

Ingredients:

> 1 egg
> 250 g wheat flour
> Pinch of salt
> Water
> Saffron
> Olive oil
> Molasses

Preparation:

1. Beat the egg.

2. Put the flour, the beaten egg, a pinch of salt and a little saffron in a large bowl. Mix into a smooth batter with water as required.

3. When the batter has the right consistency, spoon some of the mix into a frying pan with hot olive oil and fry on both sides.

4. Serve with a little molasses poured over the pancakes.

TORTITAS CON MIEL DE ARAGÓN

Honey Pancakes of Aragón

Much older Arab culinary traditions use honey as a sweetener. Honey is plentiful throughout Spain. Another typical Levantine sweet favourite found in both Jewish and Moorish traditions to this day is the use of sweet fried dough. The combination here of a sweet pancake drenched in honey is a popular traditional sweet in the region of Aragón but there are many similar sweet dishes and variants throughout rural Spain and their common Moorish influence is obvious (minus the brandy, of course).

This variation is eaten warm at breakfast, as a dessert or with merienda. They can be prepared in advance and heated in a toaster as required.

Ingredients (for 24 pancakes):

> 3 tablespoons of sugar
> 350 g flour
> 6 tablespoons of olive oil
> 6 eggs
> 2 tablespoons of brandy
> Olive oil for frying
> 250 ml honey

Preparation:

1. Break the eggs into a bowl. Lightly beat the eggs and then add the olive oil, sugar, and brandy. Stir with a wooden spoon.

2. Little by little, add the flour, while continuing to mix until obtaining a consistent dough (you may need to use your hands to finish the mixing).

3. Roll out the dough with a rolling pin on a floured work surface until it is about 3-4 mm thick.

4. Use a dough cutter to cut circular pieces of dough of 7 to 10 cm in diameter. Place these on a piece of greaseproof paper. Cover with a clean cloth and leave for about 10 minutes somewhere away from drafts.

5. Pour 2-3 cm of olive oil into a large frying pan, and heat at medium to high.

6. When the oil is hot, fry the pancakes on both sides, until they are golden brown.

7. When they are cooked, take them out of the pan and allow them to drain on a piece of absorbent kitchen paper and serve at once with warm honey or allow to cool.

8. If the pancakes have cooled, heat some honey in a double boiler (bain-marie). Heat the pancakes slightly in a toaster and pour the honey over them to serve warm.

TORTITAS DE PLÁTANO DE CANARIAS

Banana Pancake of the Canary Islands

Bananas have been grown in the Canary Islands (Islas Canarias) for considerably longer than in the Caribbean. They originated in South East Asia and were introduced into Africa and the Mediterranean in the 7th century. By the 10th century, the bananas of the province of Granada were considered the best bananas in the Arab world!

They arrived in the Canary Islands probably in the 15th or 16th century. There are many sweet dishes using bananas as a base in the Canary Islands. This simple banana pancake or fritter is eaten as a breakfast dish, with merienda or as a dessert after lunch or dinner.

Ingredients:

> 500 g bananas from the Canary Islands
> 1 lemon (grated peel and juice)
> 3 eggs
> Half a shot of anís liquor
> 120 ml of milk
> 1 teaspoon of cinnamon powder
> 3 tablespoons of sugar
> 250 g flour
> 1 pinch of salt
> Sunflower or other neutral vegetable oil for frying

Preparation:

1. Beat the whites of the 3 eggs with a pinch of salt and add the sugar, one tablespoon at a time. When mixed, add the egg yolks. Continue beating whilst adding the cinnamon powder, and the grated lemon peel.

2. Add the anís liquor.

3. Crush the bananas with a fork and add the lemon juice. Add to the egg mixture.

4. Add the milk and mix in the flour little by little to produce a light batter. (You can first try to fry one pancake to see if the batter has the right consistency.)

5. Heat the vegetable oil in a frying pan.

6. Pour portions of batter into the hot oil and immediately lower the temperature so as not to burn them. Turn the pancakes to ensure they are golden brown on both sides.

7. When fried, place the pancakes on some absorbent kitchen paper to remove excess oil.

8. Serve hot with a little honey or molasses.

TURRÓN DE YEMA

Egg Nougat

Egg Nougat is one of the richest and most traditional Christmas sweets in the Catalan cuisine. It was originally created to use the waste egg yolks and pieces of hard and soft nougat left over from other dishes. However, since then, it has developed into a very popular dish in its own right.

Ingredients (2 nougats):

500 g ground almonds
400 g sugar
120 g water
6 egg yolks
A pinch of salt
Grated peel of 1 lemon
2 g cinnamon powder

Preparation:

1. Pour the water into a saucepan, add the sugar and heat slowly until it turns into syrup and takes on a bit of colour. (If you have a thermometer, it should be 121°C.)

2. In a separate bowl, mix the ground almonds, the cinnamon, grated lemon peel, salt and egg yolks. Add to the syrup in the saucepan. Keep stirring, on the heat, until it does not stick and it becomes a consistent thick paste.

3. Prepare one or more wooden nougat moulds (depending on the size of your moulds) with greaseproof paper for the bases.

4. Pour the egg nougat into the mould(s), cover with greaseproof paper and place a smooth weight on top covering the entire surface of the mould to make sure the top of the nougat becomes smooth and the nougat is firm.

5. Let the nougat set somewhere cool for 24 hours and then remove the weight and the mould.

6. Finish off the egg nougat by sprinkling sugar on its surface and then grill it quickly in the oven until it browns.

7. Store the finished egg nougat wrapped in greaseproof paper to prevent it from drying out and hardening too quickly. You can keep it in an airtight container until ready to serve.

YEMAS DE SAN LEANDRO DE SEVILLA

Sweets of Saint Leander of Sevilla

The Yemas de San Leandro are a typical dessert of Sevilla that have been handmade for centuries in the Convent of San Leandro in the historic centre of the city. This rich dish was prepared for the first time in the 18th century by the Augustinian nuns of the convent and the convent is now famous for its yemas.

Ingredients:

> 8 egg yolks
> 5 tablespoons of sugar
> 7 tablespoons of water
> A cinnamon stick
> Lemon peel
> Sugar for coating
> Small paper cake cups

Preparation:

1. Put the sugar together with the water in a saucepan with the cinnamon stick and lemon peel.

2. Heat the mixture until it boils and begins to form strands.

3. Separate the egg yolks and strain with a fine colander.

4. Put the egg yolks in another saucepan.

5. When the syrup is ready, pour it onto the yolks. Stir very well with a wooden spoon and very slowly let the egg yolks solidify on a gentle heat. Remove the cinnamon and lemon peel before the mixture sets.

6. When the paste no longer sticks to the saucepan, transfer it to a bowl and allow it to cool.

7. When the paste has cooled, use your hands to form the paste into small balls. Roll these in icing sugar and place them on paper cake cups. They are ready to serve.

---oOo---

Index of Recipes - Spanish Names

---oOo---

Index of Recipes - English Names

About the Author

Malcolm Coxall, the author, is the proprietor of the family's 110 acre organic farm in Southern Andalucía in Spain. The farm produces olives, almonds and culinary herbs. It incorporates a small factory for the packing of organic herbs, dried fruits and nuts.

Apart from running the farm, Malcolm also provides IT consultancy and business services especially to other organic food producers in the region. He has published several books and many articles on traditional Spanish food, sustainable agriculture, organic food production, forest biodiversity, environmental protection, politics and economics. He is active in the European food and environmental movement, and has taken several successful legal actions in defence of European environmental standards in the European Court of Justice.

Malcolm is passionate about local food production, culinary diversity, agricultural sustainability and traditional gastronomy. He believes that our traditional recipes have much to teach a generation that lives on a largely homogenised processed diet and has forgotten how real food is grown and prepared. He believes that truly *good* food is local, ethical, organic and slow and that how and what we eat defines who we are as a society.

As he says: "Societies that knowingly eat chemically adulterated junk foods, produced in heartless factory farms, reveal an intrinsic social, political and health malaise and a profound lack of empathy for the planet. How can such food be *good* food? It cannot. Such societies reveal their lack of sustainability, an inherent ignorance of the world we share and a disconnection from their natural and social context. Contrast this "care-less" mentality with those societies that treasure their land, their natural environment, their people, their traditional cuisine and the quality of their food.

"Spanish traditional food is one of the last bastions of good food in Europe. The Spanish are fiercely proud of their local agricultural produce and with some justification. Few other culinary traditions in Europe are as vast in range, as imaginative, healthy and delicious as that of Spain. The Spanish love good food and good company, they enjoy life and they love their land and its produce.

"Explain to me again why we need fast food and how 'industrial agriculture' fits in with the larger concepts of human and environmental well-being and sustainability. To be sustainable, we need to start to understand food again - beginning with the basics both on the farm and in the kitchen. To begin, we could do worse than to try to re-discover our own local gastronomic heritage. Not only is this socially worthwhile and important, it is also great fun to make and enjoy real food again!"

Malcolm Coxall, Málaga 2018

---oOo---

Made in the USA
Middletown, DE
15 June 2019